UNHOLY MATRIMONY

"...LLING . . . The simple prose and straightforward
...rting lend *Unholy Matrimony* a miasma of
...or that a more emotional narration could never
...ly."

—*Cosmopolitan*

"COMPELLING . . . From the beginning it's clear
that Dillmann is a policeman who cares. Everything
rings true and has the authenticity of real experience,
closely observed . . . The reader gets a chance
to stand at Dillmann's side as he tries to get
the hard evidence to indict the murderer. We share
his frustrations in knowing someone's guilt but
being unable to prove it in court. It is difficult
not to root for him—and impossible to put the
book aside."

—*Kirkus*

JOHN DILLMANN spent eighteen years with
the New Orleans Police Department and
was involved in over five hundred homicide
investigations. He was five times awarded the
New Orleans Medal of Merit, that city's highest
honor for bravery. He now heads a private
investigating firm.

UNHOLY MATRIMONY

A TRUE STORY OF MURDER AND OBSESSION

JOHN DILLMANN

BERKLEY BOOKS, NEW YORK

*To my grandparents, John P. Dillmann, Sr., and
Germaine Constancy Dillmann*

I want to thank my wife, Diane, and my children, Todd and Amy; John
Dillmann, Jr., and Beverly Dillmann; Judy Hoffman; Jim Drury, "The
Virginian," who first saw the case as a book; Fred Dantagnan; Ralph
Whalen; Harold and Rosemary Walzer; Donald and Linda Guillot; Jim
Gosdin; Charles Ced; Betty Duke; Jack Burleson; Lea, Ethan, and Micah
Lewis; Paul Drouant; James Eaton; Michael Rice; Donald Saucier; Louis
Berard; Robert Lambert; all my friends in the New Orleans Homicide unit;
Harry Connick; Dr. Frank Minyard; Nick Scheib; Ned Chase; Dominick
Anfuso; Lisa Collier; Gary Hoffman; Bill and Jackie Sharp; Mo Reich; Jim
and Donna Cherrier; and especially Stanley and Josephine Albanowski.

This Berkley book contains the complete
text of the original hardcover edition.
It has been completely reset in a typeface
designed for easy reading and was printed
from new film.

UNHOLY MATRIMONY

A Berkley Book / published by arrangement with
Macmillan Publishing Company

PRINTING HISTORY
Macmillan edition published 1986
Berkley edition/April 1988

ISBN: 0-425-10878-3

A BERKLEY BOOK ® TM 757,375
Berkley Books are published by The Berkley Publishing Group,
200 Madison Avenue, New York, NY 10016.
The name "BERKLEY" and the "B" logo
are trademarks belonging to Berkley Publishing Corporation.

PRINTED IN THE UNITED STATES OF AMERICA

10 9 8 7 6 5 4 3 2 1

—1—

AT 10:00 A.M. on January 29, 1974, with no inkling of the fantastic case that awaited, I sat at my small desk, crammed up against other small desks, in the gray, depressing Homicide Unit of the New Orleans Police Department.

Lieutenant Robert Mutz emerged from his somewhat more impressive office and said he wanted to see me.

Commander Mutz—Mother Mutz, detectives called him behind his back, because he was always over their shoulders fussing about details (not a bad habit in a man who every day found himself up to his eyeballs in murder) —told me to sit down and asked what I was doing.

I said I was wrapping up an armed robbery-murder case, had paper to cut on two suicides, and a suspect for the victim to identify in the French Quarter rape investigation. "I'm not very busy," I added, hoping, as I had many times before, that Mutz would assign me a "heater" case, one that challenged, drew the attention of the media, and would be observed closely by fellow homicide detectives. This last point was most important. I wanted to be accepted by my peers, men I admired, most of them made weird in some way by the work they did but nonetheless very good at their jobs.

At twenty-seven years old I was the youngest homicide detective in the city; at twenty-four, when I'd been promoted to the position, I was the youngest in New Orleans history. Needless to say, the toughest cases weren't assigned to me. Indeed, due to my inexperience, that would have been folly, so I worked killings arising out of domestic disputes and barroom fights. But now I yearned for something else, for the chance to prove what I could do, and prayed that's why Mutz had called me into his office.

"Study this," he said, sliding papers toward me, and my heart sank right away. What he handed me was a letter from a New Jersey lawyer and a copy of a New Orleans traffic accident report. At a glance I could tell that this was worse than routine (What did I know? Maybe this was why he hadn't given me tough assignments—what I held would turn out to be the start of one of the hardest and most interesting investigations in the city's history), an instance of make-work, the detective's efforts directed not to solving a crime but to mollifying a few members of the public. Or so I believed. I cursed Mother Mutz under my breath and thought how ridiculous he looked in those purple pants and that electric-green shirt.

The name of the lawyer was Jay G. Destribats, and he had written on behalf of Mr. and Mrs. Stanley Albanowski of Trenton. Their daughter, Patricia Ann Giesick, had been killed in New Orleans on January 16, 1974, in a hit-and-run accident, and the parents suspected that the husband had killed her.

The letter said Patricia married Dr. Claudius James Giesick on January 2, 1974, not, according to the parents, out of great love for him, but because he was so insistent. Shortly thereafter, in a telephone conversation with her mother, Patricia said she was afraid because Giesick had taken a "large" insurance policy on her life.

I read carefully, but nothing Destribats had to say made my pulse race. Just a few hours before her death, Patricia told her mother that the car she and her husband drove was in a repair shop and that they would have to spend another night in New Orleans before continuing their honeymoon trip. However, *after* the death, Dr. Giesick informed the

Albanowskis that he and Patricia had driven the car to a spot near the accident scene, gotten out, and walked a short distance before the hit-and-run occurred.

Destribats' letter was a long one. He said Giesick informed the Albanowskis he could not describe the hit-and-run vehicle because of darkness and fog. But a New Orleans newspaper reported the car was a blue or green Oldsmobile Cutlass or Chevrolet Malibu. How could a newspaper know, the Albanowskis wondered, if the only living witness didn't? Also, Giesick told the Albanowskis he had not seen the driver, yet the same newspaper said the driver had "a dark complexion and light-colored eyes."

Finally, Patricia told her parents that Giesick had been married previously and that his wife and child had been killed in a hit-and-run accident.

When I finished the letter, I wanted to look at Lieutenant Mutz and register my disappointment. The lawyer Destribats himself, presumably being paid for this effort, didn't sound like a man even mildly persuaded that something other than hit-and-run was involved. My job would be to confirm the hit-and-run, then do a public relations job on the parents.

Although Mutz probably would have preferred I do it at my desk, I remained seated in his office and read the traffic accident report.

The hit-and-run occurred on the small Michoud Boulevard Bridge that spans the Michoud Bayou, 764 feet north of Chef Menteur Highway. I knew the area well, and not just because I'd been born and raised in New Orleans. As a boy I'd fished for brim in the Michoud Bayou, and my parents had once lived nearby. The area, which had thrived before the interstates replaced Chef Menteur Highway as a major thoroughfare, had become seedy and industrial.

Traffic officers Dan Henderson and Louis Lesage reached the scene minutes after the hit-and-run occurred. An ambulance soon rushed Patricia Giesick, still alive but unconscious, to Methodist Hospital, some three miles away.

Time existed to ask a couple of questions of Claudius James Giesick, the husband of the victim, before he was hurried to the hospital to await his wife's fate.

"Can you describe the vehicle that hit your wife?" Dan Henderson asked Giesick.

"I believe it was a four-door, and it was a late-model vehicle. The lights were off on the vehicle. There was only one person in the car and he was dark. I really don't know what kind of car it was."

"Did you see what direction the vehicle went when it reached the Chef Menteur Highway?"

"No, I didn't. The vehicle didn't slow down. In fact, it picked up speed after it hit my wife."

Henderson directed more questions at Giesick when the vigil began at Methodist Hospital. I sat in Mutz's office reading the "police-ese" of the accident report, but I could imagine as clearly as if I'd been with Giesick and Henderson in that hospital waiting room the wrenching emotions each experienced. It had happened to me on a different case: the little boy had been twelve years old, an only child, and a drunk had hurtled through a stop sign and hit him. The parents, from their own backyard, *had seen this happen*. I felt like a character out of the Spanish Inquisition, asking questions as they waited for their son to die. Thankfully, I'd never been in the situation where the roles were reversed, but I could picture it plainly enough.

Giesick, on his honeymoon, for God's sake, had just seen his wife mowed down in the street. And as he waited for word whether she would live, hawk-eyed, desperately trying to decipher expressions on the faces of hospital personnel (does that nurse's smile mean Patricia is all right? does the grim visage that doctor wears indicate hopelessness?), the last thing he wanted to do was remember details. Some people so want to forget gruesome events they have witnessed that hypnotism is needed before they can recall.

Nor did Henderson enjoy torturing Giesick. If he had a whit of humanity he empathized, and from there it took just a short step to a reversal of roles and imagining *his* wife had just been run down. *He* wouldn't want to answer questions. Thoughts of revenge, justice, whatever you called it, against the hit-and-run driver wouldn't become dominant emotions until later.

A feeling of what's-the-use would also have assailed Giesick. He'd believe the odds were very long that his wife's assailant would ever be found, though on this point he would be wrong. Perhaps eighty percent of hit-and-runs are ultimately solved. Before this tragic morning was over, dozens of cars fitting the description Giesick supplied were stopped.

I think the idea that police become inured to violence, that they desensitize themselves to survive, is largely incorrect. If a cop does that he loses a critical edge. The fact that he does care and, almost like a little boy, can maintain a freshness, wonderment, if you will, which permits shock, abhorrence, and perpetual amazement, generates the enthusiasm and willingness to work hard that sometimes is needed to solve a case. Still, I knew how Henderson had to appear to others as he intruded himself into Claudius Giesick's worst hour. But what else could he do?

"Can you remember anything else that may help us in our investigation?"

"I believe the car was a late-model Cutlass or Malibu. It was dark in color. After the car hit my wife, I think it took a right at the highway. And another thing I remember was that it had loud mufflers."

"Can you recall anything about the driver?"

"He was dark and had light eyes. He looked young. He also had something on his head. I can remember this because the light hit what was on his head and it shined. It could have been a helmet."

"Can you tell us what took place immediately before the accident?"

"My wife and I were looking at the water near the bridge. We were standing by the tree next to the bridge, and we were getting ready to go back to our car, which was parked across the street in the shopping center, when my wife said, 'Let's race back to the car.' Then she began to run across the street. She didn't see the car, which was only a few yards away; its lights were off. The car was in the right lane, and when the driver saw my wife he started to swerve to the left; but it was too late and he hit her. The automobile never did slow down; in fact, it speeded up. When it got to the highway, I believe it made a right turn."

Patricia Albanowski Giesick died on January 16, 1974, at 11:35 A.M.. a little over nine hours after she had been run down. She never regained consciousness after being hit.

The Autopsy Protocol, signed by Assistant Coroner Monroe Samuels, M.D., listed with typical cold finality the injuries that killed her:

1. Acute craniocerebral injury
   a. Contusions of scalp
   b. Bilateral subdural hemorrhage
   c. Subarachnoid hemorrhage
   d. Multiple cerebral contusions
2. Fracture of pelvis
3. Abrasions and contusion of face, trunk, and extremities
4. Hemorrhagic pulmonary edema

I'd read it all, everything Mutz had handed me, and figured this was as far from a heater case as you got. I looked at Mutz and could see he knew it, too. I thought, *you know you're the natural guy to be dumped on, but this?* Mutz's secretary could handle it, and probably with a much lighter touch.

Henderson and Lesage had the case classified as a hit-and-run, and that was surely what had happened. Suspicion such as this from grieving parents was the rule. It's more likely in suicides—"My daughter just *couldn't* have taken her own life; she had so much to live for"—but occurs frequently whenever death is involved. All I could see that really required checking was the Albanowskis' insistence that the honeymoon couple's car was in the garage for repairs, while Giesick told Dan Henderson it sat in a shopping-center parking lot Patricia was racing to reach when struck down. A discrepancy like this could easily be cleared up. By anyone, with one phone call.

I didn't think the insurance money posed a problem. My wife and I took out life insurance when we married. That Giesick's first wife had died in a hit-and-run bore checking out, but probably it wasn't true. A mixup, somewhere. A misunderstanding. The wildest rumors inevitably abound, any homicide detective can tell you, when a death first occurs. If Giesick's first wife and infant child had been killed in a hit-and-run, and if it was suspicious, and if he planned the same fate for Patricia, why in the name of sanity would he ever let the news leak out? No, it had to be a mistake.

Commander Mutz had two things in mind in giving me this case: avoiding unpleasantness for the department, and keeping hassles away from himself. Destribats was a lawyer (maybe an important one—we didn't know), and lawyers could cause problems. They might even tell the press we didn't respond to the legitimate concerns of citizens. At the least Destribats would begin calling us, and better that I took the calls than Mutz.

Perhaps I should have been eager to rush out and check whether Henderson and Lesage had classified the case incorrectly. But I didn't think they had. Mutz knew, more surely than I did, how terribly distraught parents become when they lose a child. Where I had gone wrong was in telling Mutz I didn't have much work to do. Even if the victim in the French Quarter rape investigation picked the suspect out of a photo lineup, many long hours and days would still be required. An application for an arrest warrant and an arrest warrant needed to be prepared and executed; the suspect had to be located and arrested, often not an easy task in the teeming French Quarter; an application for a search warrant and a search warrant needed to be prepared, reviewed and signed by a judge, and served (if I found physical evidence, a crime lab would be summoned to photograph, fingerprint, and confiscate); other witnesses had to be located, their statements taken, and a physical, *not* photographic, lineup needed to be set up; a report had to be typed out, some fifty pages long if past experience served as a guide, and presented to the Orleans Parish District Attorney for review; and I'd have to appear before a grand jury.

"What do you want me to do?" I asked Lieutenant Mutz.

"Look, John," he said, able to read my thoughts. "Everybody up here is snowed under. But these are things that have to be done."

"It's not top priority?" I knew it wasn't.

"Whenever you get to it. In your spare time. Appease those people in Trenton."

So that was it. I got out of Mutz's office and negotiated the several steps to my desk. Nobody paid any attention. Certainly not Pascal Saladino, a big veteran homicide detective usually smoking a huge, vile cigar. Pascal was strong and tough, something you knew right away, even though a pleasant smile never left his face and his voice was highpitched.

Pascal was largely responsible for my becoming Homicide's youngest detective. He knew I'd been commended by the department: on my way to work as a patrolman, still in civilian clothes, I'd spotted a pair of tourists being mugged, chased the suspect (he was armed with a handgun), and was grateful I could capture him without using my own weapon; he turned out to be just fourteen years old.

Later I happened to secure several homicide scenes for Pascal and, being an eager beaver, pleaded with him to let me help with the investigations. He agreed, reluctantly perhaps, and seemed pleased with the work I did. I thought Homicide was the crème de la crème, told Pascal so, which made him laugh, but he later submitted my name for consideration on "the murder squad."

That's how it was done in 1970. A veteran would nominate a candidate; a single negative vote—a blackball—and the nominee was out. Homicide detectives took pride in being an elite, so getting accepted was no cinch; but largely because of the respect his peers had for him, Pascal obtained my acceptance.

There can be abuses in this kind of system. A person can nominate his brother-in-law, and if *all* the other detectives are corrupt, he conceivably could be accepted. This couldn't happen in New Orleans Homicide, where pride in the unit weighed heavily. A greater danger was a *single* blackball given for other than professional reasons keeping a candidate out.

Anyway, I owed a lot to Pascal. Moreover, like all the younger guys, I considered him a philosopher; ask Pascal for the time, and he'd tell you how to make a watch.

I could see Pascal wore his gold belt buckle. This was Homicide's "in" thing at the time, wearing a large gold monogrammed belt buckle—earlier the rage had been a trench coat and chapeau—and Pascal had the biggest buckle of all. Trouble was, the initials on the belt buckle were E.N. He'd bought it at a hock shop.

Pascal Saladino, tough without ever being macho, surprisingly sensitive in a business not known for the quality, would play an important and continuing role in the Patricia Albanowski case, which soon got promoted from a make-work assignment to an investigation of vast dimensions and complexity requiring methods bordering on the Byzantine.

Nor did Fred Dantagnan, my closest friend in Homicide, take note of my exiting Mutz's office and plopping down at my desk. I looked at Fred, seeking sympathy. He knew how much I wanted a case I could bite into. But Fred was busy griping out loud to nobody in particular (no one would have listened, anyway) that he needed to get to a crime scene and didn't have a car. Homicide was notoriously short of cars, and if a member of the first shift (us) needed one and if it was in use by someone on the third shift forced to work overtime, nothing could be done but wait. "Damn corpse will rot before I get there," Fred complained to an audience that didn't care. "I oughta call Pelican Ice and have 'em ice the guy down."

The best way to do a job you don't want is to get started, get it over. I could write Destribats a letter, which would hold him for a while, telling him I'd be looking into the points he and the Albanowskis raised. That seemed a little cold. If someday something happened to my daughter Amy, now one year old, I'd rather hear a human voice offering assurances than receive a letter in the mail. *Maybe you should call,* I thought.

A moment later the question became academic. Homicide didn't have enough typewriters, either, and for the first time I noticed mine was missing.

"Mr. Destribats, this is Detective John Dillmann with the New Orleans Police Department. I received your letter concerning the death of Patricia Giesick, and there are a few questions I'd like to ask."

"I'll help however I can," Destribats said. He sounded smooth and polished. I guessed him to be thirty-five or forty years old and successful. "But I really think you'd be better off talking to the Albanowskis. The information I passed on came from them."

"I'll get in touch," I said. "But you mentioned 'a large insurance policy.' How large?"

"I don't know. I'm repeating what the Albanowskis said. I can tell you they're terribly upset over the loss of their daughter. An only child, I believe. Being grief-stricken is understandable; natural, I would think. But I tell you, I've never seen anything like this. They're just demolished by what happened. You can almost reach out and touch the grief."

"You mentioned a previous hit-and-run involving Giesick's first wife."

"There's no substantiation. Evidently Giesick told this to Patricia, and she mentioned it to her parents."

"About Giesick's car being in a garage for repairs. Obviously it wasn't. He told the traffic officers he and his wife were going to race to it."

"It wasn't just the traffic officers. It was mentioned in an article about the death in the New Orleans *Times-Picayune*."

"I read the article," I said. The kind of story that stuck in your head. Not only was the honeymoon-couple angle played up, but it had been the first New Orleans traffic fatality of 1974. That in itself surprised me, made the story unusual. I didn't have statistics on such matters, but I had patrolled the streets of a pre-dawn New Year's morning.

The fact that Patricia's race to the car had appeared in two places—the traffic accident report and the *Times-Picayune* story—didn't seem significant to me. The news account almost certainly came from the police report.

"Yes, well," Destribats said, "the car is something I would think needs to be checked out. The insurance money and the alleged hit-and-run, they're probably what they appear to be, that is, nothing to be concerned about. Don't get me wrong, there's likely to be an explanation for the car, too. I can't emphasize enough how emotional and torn apart the Albanowskis are by all of this. But I questioned them closely before writing that letter. They're very definite on the point: they talked to Patricia just a few hours before she died, and she mentioned the car being in the shop for repairs."

"I'll call them."

"Please do." He gave me the number. "I'm sure your calling will mean a lot. If I had to guess, I'd say nothing will come of this. But if you could meet the Albanowskis, I think you'd want to allay their doubts."

I dialed the number Destribats gave me and Josephine Albanowski answered.

"Mrs. Albanowski," I said, "this is Detective John

Dillmann with the New Orleans Police Department. I want to . . .''

"Oh, thank God. I've been praying you'd call."

"I want to tell you how sorry I am about your daughter Patricia. I'm looking into her death, and I need to ask you a few questions."

"You ask whatever you want, Detective Dillmann. And thank you so much for giving your time. We've been afraid no one would care." Mrs. Albanowski's voice cracked, and she seemed on the verge of crying. I imagined because of Patricia's age—she'd been twenty-five—her mother would be about fifty, but the desperate pleading voice I heard sounded older than time.

"When did your daughter move to Texas, Mrs. Albanowski? And where?"

"In November of 1972. She lived in Richardson." Her voice quavered again.

"Where is Richardson?"

"It's a suburb of Dallas." She was openly crying now. Destribats had been right, this sort of grief was more than uncommon. It was something pitiful and palpable. The noises I heard might have come from a wounded animal, frightened and alone in the forest.

"Mrs. Albanowski, I'm sorry. I know how you feel." I really didn't. "Would you like for me to call you back in a little while?"

"Please. No. We've been waiting for you to call. Praying you would. How can I explain? Have you seen a picture of Patricia, Detective Dillmann?"

"No, I haven't."

"She was such a beautiful girl. Movie-star beautiful. I don't tell you that just because I'm her mother. Everyone said so. Strawberry-blond hair and the prettiest green eyes in the world. Oh, God. We loved her so much, Detective Dillmann. Our lives revolved around her. I'll never believe she ran out into the street in front of that car. She always held her daddy's hand when they crossed a street. Stan was very firm on this. And he made certain she always looked both ways.''

"When did Patricia meet Dr. Giesick?"

"About two weeks before Christmas." The crying stopped, but only from a determined effort. Now sobs punctuated Mrs. Albanowski's conversation. Involuntary intakes of breath. I wondered if life might never be all right for her again.

"And when were the two married?"

"January second. Patricia wanted to wait, but he was very anxious to go ahead. I advised her to wait. 'You've only known this man a few weeks,' I told her. But she was dazzled. He had a doctorate degree in psychology, spent a lot of money, said he wanted to buy her a new Monte Carlo automobile and take her on a Caribbean cruise for their honeymoon. That's where they were headed when the car broke down. To Miami, to take a cruise.''

"Tell me about the car breaking down."

"Patricia called us from her motel room about eleven-thirty. That's ten-thirty your time. Just a few hours before the accident. Her husband was out of the room. She specifically said the car—the one her husband bought her, the one they were taking to Miami—was in a repair shop. She'd just returned to the room from having a pizza. It was quite a long walk, she said, going to get that pizza.''

"You're sure of this?"

"I couldn't be more certain. They took that long walk to get the pizza because they didn't have a car." The last sentence was the first I'd heard where grief was not the predominant emotion. Something else. A call for justice?

What are you going to do about this, Detective Dillmann? was what she really said.

"Mr. Destribats mentioned 'a large insurance policy.' Do you know how much is involved?"

"About thirty thousand dollars, I think."

This did not seem to me to be a large insurance policy. Not to kill your wife over. But what did I know? I knew of an individual killed in an argument over a dollar bottle of wine.

"You found out about the insurance from Patricia?"

"She called and said she was afraid."

"Did she say why she was afraid?"

"No. But it's obvious, isn't it? Thirty thousand dollars is a lot of money."

I soon learned the Albanowskis had been working people their entire lives. Stanley Albanowski, fifteen years older than his wife, had labored thirty years in a factory. For almost twenty years Josephine had worked as a seamstress. To these people, and to their only child who was their raison d'être, thirty thousand dollars seemed an unattainable sum.

"I've heard about a previous hit-and-run. Can you tell me anything about that?"

"Only that Patricia's husband told her that's how he lost his first wife. An infant child also died. I believe it happened in Texas or Oklahoma."

"Did Dr. Giesick tell you this himself?"

"No. Patricia told me in one of her calls. You should remember, Detective Dillmann, that I only met Patricia's husband once. This was at her funeral. He didn't even get here in time for the viewing. And he only stayed a few hours. He was here and gone, almost in a flash." Again I heard the sobs, the anguish so absolutely convincing.

"After the marriage, how many times did Patricia call you?"

"Three. Shortly after her wedding. Just a few hours before she was kill—before she died. And one other time."

"When was that?"

"I'm not sure of the date. She called to say the Caribbean cruise was definite."

"Is there anything else you can tell me, Mrs. Albanowski?"

"I don't know. Everything is so horrible now that Patricia is gone. You'd have loved her, Detective Dillmann. She was young and honest and full of life."

"I'll be in touch with you as soon as I learn anything."

"Detective Dillmann?"

"Yes?"

"Please help us. Don't let our daughter's killer go unpunished."

Mrs. Albanowski's grief came from the core of her soul, and affected me deeply. No one, I thought, should ever have to be so utterly bereft.

That the Albanowskis loved Patricia Ann dearly was strikingly, startlingly evident even over a telephone. The Albanowskis literally worshipped their daughter. The sun rose and set on her. I believed they might even have been too selfless: every conscious action was dictated by what helped Patricia, what made Patricia happy.

It occurred to me that an individual would need an exceptionally thick skin not to be moved by such suffering and to fail to respond to pleas for help. Nothing could alleviate the pain from the loss of their daughter, but it need not be deepened by uncertainty over what had happened. At least the Albanowskis should know. They might not accept what was told them—people tend to believe what they want to—but nonetheless, they deserved the unvarnished truth.

The Albanowskis had my complete sympathy and a personal commitment not to give up until no questions remained. Despite the genuine sympathy, however, I really didn't think anything was going to come of all this.

Undoubtedly, there would be an explanation for the car that was supposedly in the repair shop but wasn't. What had changed for me, though it nowhere nearly approached what it would become, was the desire, kindled by Josephine Albanowski—Geesus, she could be *my* mother, talking to some other cop—to learn the truth.

I called the Seventh District and asked the desk sergeant for Dan Henderson. He wasn't on duty. I asked for Henderson's home phone number, figuring I wouldn't get it, and the sergeant said he'd call Henderson and ask him to call me. Within five minutes the traffic officer was on the line.

"How you doin', buddy?" Henderson and I weren't close friends, but cops tend to call each other "buddy." Dan and I had lifted weights together in the police department gym.

"I'm looking into that hit-and-run you handled out on Michoud Boulevard."

"The honeymoon couple."

"Right."

"That was a rough one. Goddam, having that happen on your honeymoon."

"Dan, the parents have asked us about the car the girl was running to. Did you see that car?"

"I handled the scene itself. But Sergeant Fayard went with the husband, who pointed the car out to him. It was across the street in a shopping-center parking lot. A brand new Oldsmobile Cutlass with no plates."

"Did you ask the husband about the car?"

"John, the girl didn't die until after 11:00 A.M. When I went to the motel to question him, he'd already checked out and left for Texas."

"Did he take the car?"

"I guess so. But it was funny. When I checked with the desk clerk, I learned he paid the bill with a credit card issued to a Dr. Charles Guilliam."

"Guilliam?"

"Right. The husband, Dr. Giesick, used a card issued to Dr. Guilliam. He told the clerk Guilliam was a friend of his, and the use of the card a honeymoon present."

"Have you talked with Dr. Giesick since he returned to Texas?"

"No. Giesick left a phone number where he could be reached, and I tried it once. He never called back. And I didn't try again. It was an obvious hit-and-run, and there's an A.P.B. [All Points Bulletin] out on the vehicle and suspect."

"Well, Giesick's phone number is in your report. I'll give him a call."

"Good luck."

What had I learned? That Dr. Giesick used another doctor's credit card. Well, I knew people who borrowed credit cards. That Giesick left for Texas shortly after his wife died. I couldn't imagine doing that myself—I would stay with my wife, accompany the body to New Jersey— but there could have been a good reason. Though he missed the viewing in Trenton, he made it for the funeral. And one other thing nagged at me. I couldn't put my finger on it.

I shuffled the notes I'd taken during the three phone conversations. Sure! There it was. Mrs. Albanowski said Giesick bought Patricia a Monte Carlo. The car Giesick showed Sergeant Fayard was an Olds Cutlass.

And something else bothered me. Something closer. I caught a flash of movement behind and turned my head: it was Bobby Egan, homicide detective, called Blinky because his eyelids always seemed to be moving with the rapidity of a camera shutter. Other things being equal (two men clean-shaven, wearing suits), a visitor to Homicide would peg Egan a murder suspect and the second man a detective.

Egan apparently had been standing there for several minutes. He bobbed back and forth on the balls of his feet, like a fighter, and looked impatiently at his watch.

"Damn, John, when you gonna be done?"

Homicide was also short of telephones. Egan, working the shift previous to mine, obviously had put in overtime, and needed to use the phone before he could go home.

"I just got one more call to make, Blinky."

"Let me slip in there first, will you?"

"No, sir. Wait your turn."

"Give me a break. I've been on since midnight."

"I know. Taking up a car we needed."

"Be a good guy. I'm so hungry my stomach thinks my throat's cut."

"Leave me alone, Blinky. Go away. Bother somebody else."

"You sonuvabitch."

And they called us the Homicide *Unit?*

I dialed Dr. Giesick's number in Dallas.

"Hello. May I help you?" The woman's voice was polished, professional.

"Could I talk with Dr. Giesick?"

"Dr. Giesick's not in right now. May I take a message?"

"Can you tell me when he will be in?"

"This is his answering service, sir. He usually checks with us twice a day. In the morning and in the evening. Would you leave your name and number?"

"Ask Dr. Giesick to call Detective John Dillmann with the New Orleans Police Department. Area code 504, phone number 822-2813. If I'm not in, have him leave his number with the secretary. She can reach me on the radio, and I'll be back to him in five minutes."

"I'll do that, sir."

"Blinky," I said. He stood in the center of the crowded room, looking desperately about, muttering to himself because no telephones had opened up. "You can use this one," I said.

"You're a good guy, Dillmann."

I scooped up some papers, grabbed my clipboard, and headed down to the third floor of the parking garage to get one of those previously unavailable cars. I carried with me six Bureau of Identification photographs (mug shots) to show the French Quarter rape victim, hoping she could identify the man I believed had committed the crime. A delicate business. I had to get six photographs of people who looked very much alike: an I.D. would never stand up if, say, I showed five pictures of individuals who resembled polio-vaccine discoverer Dr. Jonas Salk and one picture of a Charles Manson look-alike. You had to be careful. A defense attorney, and rightly so, would point out differences in the way the photographs were lighted. Never would you have a photo lineup where one person sported a mustache and the others didn't.

In this case the victim couldn't make an identification. Still, I really believed I had the perpetrator. As always, the temptation existed to prod the victim, make subtle suggestions to help her select the individual I suspected. Every detective, even relatively inexperienced ones like me, knew ways to "coax" a witness, guide her, without her knowing, toward the "right" identification. But such methods had to be avoided, regardless of the detective's feelings.

All wasn't lost in this investigation. It never really is. Another witness existed—the boyfriend, forced at gunpoint to watch the rape—and even if he couldn't make an I.D., it wouldn't be hopeless. If he did, however, there would be probable cause to pick up the suspect for a physical lineup. Of course, if the victim could never identify the suspect, there would be no case.

At 4:00 P.M., shift coming to an end, I started back toward headquarters. While driving, I received a radio message to call my friend Fred Dantagnan, the detective who earlier had been bemoaning his lack of a car.

"What's happening, Fred?"

"A smokin' gun in a bar." A homicide in a saloon, the suspect was under arrest, no Sherlock Holmes would be required to solve this one. "I'm up to my ass in witnesses. Most of them drunk. Could you take a few statements?"

"No problem."

At 8:00 P.M. I got home to Metairie, a New Orleans suburb. The kids—Todd, five, and Amy, one—were asleep, and my wife, Diane, had dinner waiting. We'd been high school sweethearts, and married at age nineteen. Diane has auburn hair, big wondering brown eyes, and likes everybody. She's a very pretty, very gentle person, who keeps my life from descending into barbarism.

Being married to a cop is usually tough. It requires a person of exceptional understanding. The cop is often in a foul mood, and the mate understandably wonders why she should have to be the one to suffer. The answer is, she shouldn't.

Most citizens can't comprehend the people our jobs require us to deal with day in and day out. You become discouraged, depressed, prone to despair. The majority of police officers become heavy drinkers. Those who don't must master the trick of living two lives, a difficult task indeed. Disaster awaits the cop who can't separate his existence on the street from that at home.

It helped that I could talk it out with Diane. Her sympathy for victims made my job seem worthwhile; her concern for the accused—was the individual really guilty, if so, why—kept me from becoming a vengeance-seeking Mike Hammer.

Over coffee she told me about her day, and I talked about mine. Diane zeroed right in on Mrs. Albanowski.

"I feel so sorry for that woman, John. I can drive myself crazy thinking about what might happen to Amy. She's suffering what I only fear. To lose your daughter, and not know. That would be the worst awful hell."

"I'll find out what happened."

"Do it tomorrow. Don't make Mrs. Albanowski wait."

2

"RIGHT. WE HAD that car."

Bill Gray, service manager of Bob McKinnon Chevrolet, had a repair order in his hand. When I reached headquarters the next morning, I looked in the Yellow Pages for Chevrolet dealerships, found the one closest to the Ramada Inn where Patricia and Dr. Giesick had stayed, and decided to gamble on a trip out there.

I studied the repair order and Bingo! Dr. Giesick had picked up the car—a blue 1974 Monte Carlo—at 5:22 P.M. on January 15. Some eight hours before Patricia had been run down on Michoud Boulevard. Yet Patricia, just three hours before her death, had told her mother they had no car. She'd talked about walking a considerable distance to get a pizza.

The Monte Carlo had been left at the dealership on January 14 for suspected transmission problems, but the only work performed was setting the idle. I took down the serial number of the vehicle, noting it had temporary Texas plates.

"I'd like to talk to the mechanic," I said to Gray, who already had agreed to make a Xerox of the repair order.

"He's over here."

The mechanic, covered with grease, offered to shake hands. I've never met a mechanic who didn't offer to

21

shake hands. It's their idea of a joke, like people telling the elevator operator, "Lots of ups and downs in your life, I'll bet."

"Do you remember," I asked, "working on a blue seventy-four Monte Carlo? It would have been about two weeks ago."

"I don't know. Maybe."

"Here's the repair order."

"I remember that one. Supposed to have transmission problems, but all I had to do was adjust the idle. It was strange. Looked like somebody who knew about cars got in there and jammed the linkage."

"Linkage?"

"That's it. Made the car so it didn't shift smooth. I fixed it just like that." I was amazed he could snap those gook-covered fingers.

"My mechanic would have charged fifty dollars," I said. "He'd have explained how much work was involved."

"Sometimes you get lucky."

As I drove toward the Ramada Inn I tried to sort out the confusion. The car business didn't make sense. Groping even for far-out possibilities, I couldn't find a reason for Giesick's not telling his wife the car was repaired. I could find plenty of motives, all of them dark, to point out the wrong car to Sergeant Fayard, but I quickly shoved those out of my mind. Being overly suspicious would be as wrong as going through the motions, assuming the Albanowskis were distressed, overwrought parents, and looking for a way to keep the case classified as hit-and-run. I knew one thing: I wanted to talk to Dr. Claudius Giesick. He hadn't answered my phone call, and I wondered about that.

I showed my identification to the front-desk manager (he'd been reading the newspaper—a story about President Nixon's State of the Union address, due that night) and asked to see Dr. Giesick's registration card. The bill, as I knew, had been paid with a credit card issued to Dr. Charles Guilliam, but Giesick had signed his name, not

Guilliam's. I asked if this was unusual, using someone else's card.

"Not really. Of course, we check to see if the credit card is good."

Before returning to headquarters, I went to the nearby Louisiana Cement Company to see if the rape witness could pick my suspect out of a photo lineup. He couldn't. The reason I'd zeroed in on this particular suspect was that three separate confidential informants had said he was the perpetrator (he bragged openly about this "hustle," a word I didn't think fit the crime). Well, a close eye would be kept on him. He was a French Quarter character, a crime wave all by himself, and not likely to stop suddenly. Some property had been stolen from the victim. If we could arrest the suspect on another charge, a search warrant could be obtained, and we might recover the property. A long shot, but not hopeless.

At headquarters I checked for messages (none from Dr. Giesick), and considered myself lucky to find my desk unoccupied—I had to share this tiny piece of furniture with a detective from another shift, and it required effort just to keep our papers separated. But anyone who wanted could and did use the desk.

"Hello. May I help you?" It was Giesick's answering-service woman from the day before.

"Right. This is Detective John Dillmann in New Orleans. Did Dr. Giesick get my message?"

"Yes. I gave him the message yesterday evening."

"Please give him the message again. Tell him to call right away. Say it's extremely important."

"I'll tell him, Detective Dillmann."

I was steamed. I got up from my desk and began to pace. Who did Giesick think he was? Maybe it was prejudice, but it seemed doctors were always hard to reach. Acted like they were doing an enormous (and expensive) favor when they deigned to talk to someone. I told myself to calm down.

But, hell, I had reason to be mad. If that were my wife,

I'd be burning up the lines between Dallas and New Orleans. For all Giesick knew, we'd caught the man who killed Patricia.

I went downstairs to get a cup of coffee. I needed some time to think: that business about the car made no sense. Even if Giesick planned to kill Patricia with the car, what difference would it make if she knew it was out of the shop? Certainly he wouldn't tell her he was going to run her down. Once she was dead, since he had to assume he'd be successful, it wouldn't matter that she'd known. But *not* telling her risked exactly what happened: she would talk to someone else, in this case her parents, and some detective would come sniffing around what otherwise would be an open-and-shut hit-and-run.

I still didn't think homicide was involved. There would be an explanation for the car, I believed. I'd have it as soon as Giesick called.

The police department snack bar, operated by handicapped people, is known as "The Rumor Clinic," a place where ideas that might have been initiated in outer space are bandied about as solutions to crimes: "It was the grandmother; she motorized her wheelchair, and . . ." But The Rumor Clinic also fosters the latest internal gossip, usually wrong, about who's going to be transferred, who's about to be suspended, who's having an affair with whom, etc. In this vein Betty Harper struck up a conversation. She was a clerk in the records room.

"Why all the interest in this hit-and-run accident?" she asked.

"What interest?" I didn't know anyone cared, besides the Albanowskis, me, and my wife.

"Yesterday Lieutenant Mutz asked for the report. That's unusual, the commander of Homicide being concerned about a hit-and-run. And today an insurance fellow came in and bought a copy of the report."

"Do you have his name?"

"I can get it."

"I'll owe you."

The man's name was John Webb, an insurance adjuster with Crawford and Company. I called him when I got back to my desk.

"What's your interest in this case?" I asked Webb, after I'd identified myself.

"Farmers Insurance Group out of Houston, Texas, has retained my company to investigate a claim filed by Dr. Claudius Giesick."

"How much insurance are we talking about?"

"A hundred thousand dollars."

"That much?"

"It's a fifty-thousand-dollar policy, with double indemnity for accidental death. You said you're with Homicide? Is there something I should know about this case?"

"No. I've just started to look into it."

"Well, keep me in mind."

"Do you have anyone at Farmers Insurance Group I could talk with?"

"Ron Gatheral. He's a branch manager. Supervises agents."

I called Gatheral.

"We gave the case to Crawford and Company," he said, "because of what we learned from the agent."

"And what was that?"

"I'd rather have you talk to the agent himself. But there was an indication Dr. Giesick also inquired about travel insurance. In other words, he wanted the life policy and the travel policy. In view of what happened, we'd be remiss if we didn't investigate."

"When was the insurance purchased?"

"January seventh."

Five days after the wedding. I thought Giesick would be doing himself a favor if he called me right away.

"What's the status of the claim?" I asked.

"It's classified as a hit-and-run accident?"

"Yes."

"We'll probably have to pay fairly soon. If you don't

come up with anything, and if Crawford and Company draws a blank, we couldn't very well withhold payment.''

''You'd have more time if the classification gets changed?'' If Giesick wanted that money quickly, he really would be smart to call.

''Oh, yes. No one would expect us to pay if there was an open investigation.''

''What's that insurance agent's name?''

It was Bud Gibson, and he sounded like a Bud, a good ole boy from Texas. He called me ''pahdnah.''

''Dr. Giesick phoned me on January third.'' *The day after the wedding.* ''I met him later that morning, and on January seventh went to his apartment in Richardson where he signed the papers. He said he and his wife were going on a honeymoon, and he wanted travel insurance, too. I told him Farmers didn't have travel insurance.''

''Had you done business with Dr. Giesick before?''

''No. The first time I heard of him was January third. He probably got my name out of the phone book.''

''What does Giesick look like?''

''A real smart dresser. Five feet ten with long sandy blond hair.'' Maybe the hair was long to Bud, but it wouldn't be to most people, or so I thought when I later saw a picture of Giesick. ''Wore horn-rimmed glasses and had sort of a baby face. Looked younger than twenty-four, know what I mean? Seemed real intelligent.''

''What do you mean, 'real intelligent'?''

''He spoke good, pahdnah. Hell, he's a consulting psychologist, so I guess he should be smart. Knew a lot about insurance. Had all the right questions. And when I gave him the answers, I got the idea he already knew them.''

''When did Dr. Giesick file his claim for the insurance?''

''January seventeenth. The day after the death. That caught my attention. That, and the fact the policy had just been written.''

''When do people usually file?''

''Well, pahdnah, I don't think we keep statistics on that. We do on everything else. But I'd say most of us would wait for the wife to be buried, and for things to settle down a little.''

Gibson gave me Giesick's address and social security number, and I told him I might get back to him. The address, 516 Tejas Trail, Richardson, Texas, had been Patricia's before the marriage.

I sat at the desk staring at the wall, my eyes glazed. I was getting hotter about Giesick not answering my calls, a fruitless exercise not designed to help anything, but in my mind I also heard the trembling voice of Mrs. Albanowski. Diane had been right last night. Human beings can adjust to anything if they just know. Not knowing, dangling in a void, was the most exquisite torture.

I could think of two reasons for Giesick's not calling: he had something to hide and hoped I would go away; or simple arrogance. He made a mistake if the former applied, similar to the error debtors commit when they try to avoid creditors. The creditor—or the cop—is not going to fade out of the picture, and it's wise to appear upfront about things (even if you're not) than to play hide-and-seek.

''You okay?'' It was my friend Fred Dantagnan. He must have been off that day and just come in for his paycheck, because he wore torn jeans and a bulky sweater. The sweater made him look almost not human. Fred is built like a tank. He's only five feet seven, but broad as a barn, almost supernaturally strong, and has legs like the stumps of oak trees.

Fred and I were the two least-experienced detectives in Homicide, which probably is why we liked each other so much. The veteran detectives tended to hang around with their own; their attitude toward the youngsters was wait and see. A lot of people didn't last long in Homicide, and the burden of proof was always on the new detective.

The stereotypical homicide detective drinks hard; has a mistress or two on the side; resembles more Clint Eastwood's Dirty Harry than Peter Falk's gentle, thoughtful Columbo; is plunging precipitately into a morass of despair because of the portion of the human element he most frequently encounters; and is a chain-smoking degenerating horse-race addict who drives a battered Ford and lives apart from his wife in a dingy beer-can-cluttered one-room walk-up illuminated by a single naked overhead bulb.

Fred Dantagnan wasn't any of these things. Masterfully he'd constructed two lives for himself. Calling him a model family man doesn't begin to describe his devotion to his wife, Bea, and his children, Ricky and Kelly. A good time for Fred involved taking his kids shopping. The ultimate was visiting Disney World. Seeing the way Fred lived, I tried to emulate him, but I wasn't always successful. Fred was so good-natured (you wouldn't think it, looking at this fierce, powerful bowling ball) that other detectives played practical jokes on him. He had a bald spot on top of his head, so he often received hair-growing solutions in the mail. His "friends" were always telling gung-ho marine recruiters he wanted to enlist, and these patriots are hard to shake when they think they're on the track of a good man.

Regardless, Fred's wife wouldn't recognize Fred at work. Until I got used to it, I didn't recognize Fred at home.

"The Mother gave me this," I said to Fred, handing him Destribats' letter.

He read a paragraph. "What's this all about?"

I told him what I knew.

"You've got to get hold of this asshole Giesick."

"I've tried. He won't return my calls."

"He won't answer your calls?" Fred's face turned red, and I knew what he thought. No business is more serious than murder. "He'd answer your calls if he was in New Orleans."

"He's in Texas. I think."

"Call Texas. Have him picked up for something." Fred, always a man of action.

"I don't know, Fred."

"You think he killed this girl?"

"I don't know. The Albanowskis think so."

"I know how you can get him to call."

"How?"

"Call his answering service. Say the insurance company's given you the hundred thousand to hand to him. He'll call."

"I got one thing I can do."

I walked the few feet to Commander Mutz's office and peered in. His tan-and-green tweed sports coat clashed with his sky-blue tie. He nodded for me to come forward.

"About that hit-and-run," I said.

"Yes?" His voice filled with hope. He figured I'd ironed out the discrepancies and one less case existed among the mind-numbing volume.

"I've got problems," I said.

"Oh," he said. The smile that had started to form magically curled downward.

"The car that was supposed to be in the repair shop: it wasn't. Dr. Giesick had taken it out. And it was a blue Monte Carlo. Not the Olds Cutlass he showed Sergeant Fayard."

"What does Giesick say?"

"He hasn't answered my phone calls. Another thing: the amount of insurance is a hundred thousand dollars."

"What else?"

"He filed for insurance the day after his wife died. The body wasn't even cold yet, and he's looking for money."

"What do you intend to do?"

"Dr. Giesick needs to be interviewed. If the mountain won't come to Mohammed . . ." I thought this clever, but Mutz just looked impatient. "I think I should go to Texas and talk to him. Give him a few more days, but then, definitely, go to Texas."

"Go to Texas, huh?"

"Yes, sir."

"Is it a crime not to tell your wife your car is out of the repair shop?"

"No, sir."

"Is it a crime to purchase a hundred thousand dollars of life insurance?"

"No, sir."

"Is it a crime to be greedy and want your money right away?"

"No, but . . ."

"Have you located any witnesses to indicate something other than a hit-and-run?"

"No."

"Do you have any physical evidence? Any physical evidence at all?"

"No."

"John, you don't have anything to justify a trip to Texas."

"The girl was afraid, Lieutenant. Her parents told me she was afraid."

"And that's no crime, either. Look, keep trying to get hold of Dr. Giesick."

"I'd like one favor," I said.

"What is it?"

"This is classified as a hit-and-run fatality. I'd like it unclassified. List it as an open investigation."

Mutz rubbed his forehead, frowning. "I'll give the coroner a call," he said. "You go see him."

"I'll do that."

"And keep trying to reach Giesick."

I wanted to give a cheer for Mother Mutz. I'd scored just a small victory, and some of the churning in my stomach subsided. Giesick would find out he no longer occupied the driver's seat.

The coroner had the say on reclassifying an investigation, but if Mutz recommended it, this became a formality. What Fred Dantagnan had jokingly suggested would be the stark reality: I'd be holding Giesick's insurance money. Farmers Insurance, which would *have* to pay with the case listed as a hit-and-run fatality, wouldn't release a penny with the investigation classified as open.

The coroner's office is in the huge Criminal Courts Building on South White Street in midtown, two miles from the French Quarter, a mile from the Superdome. I talked to the coroner himself, Dr. Franklin Minyard, a man with enormously impressive medical credentials and a deservedly excellent national reputation. Dr. Minyard breathed in the same rarefied atmosphere as Dr. Thomas Noguchi in Los Angeles (the model for Quincy) and Dr. Milton Helpern in New York City. All three were more than forensic scientists. They were medical detectives.

Known in New Orleans as Dr. Jazz, Dr. Minyard is a vastly gifted trumpet player. He often appears with Al Hirt, Pete Fountain, and the Olympic Brass Band. The first time I saw Dr. Minyard he was leading a Mardi Gras parade.

Dr. Minyard told me Commander Mutz had called, but if I'd thought he would rubber-stamp something, I was mistaken. He wanted to know about the case, and I found myself once again reviewing what I'd learned. When I'd finished, he asked his secretary to bring him the pathologist's report.

"There's no doubt she was hit by a car," he said, when he'd finished reading the document.

"Yes, sir," I said. What could I say?

"If you'd like," Dr. Minyard said, "I'll check with some of my medical friends in Texas. See if they know anything about this Dr. Giesick."

"I'd appreciate that."

"You can consider this an open investigation."

I didn't think it the smallest victory. And it seemed larger when I got back to headquarters and learned Giesick still hadn't called.

After being shuttled around the credit card company's switchboard, I finally got the right person: John Hunt. I gave him Dr. Guilliam's credit card number, and he located the address: 8602 Tuxford Drive, San Antonio, Texas. Hunt told me Dr. Guilliam had bank accounts in Scottsdale and Phoenix, Arizona. Best of all, he had Guilliam's phone number.

"Dr. Charles Guilliam, please." The voice on the other end belonged to a young woman.

"He's not in right now. This is Mrs. Guilliam. May I take a message?"

"This is Detective John Dillmann with the New Orleans Police Department. Could I have Dr. Guilliam's office number?"

"He's in Dallas for the next few days on business."

"Have him call me, please. It's important." I gave her the number.

I called the San Antonio Police Department and talked to a Detective Jaraz. I asked as a favor if he'd see whether Dr. Claudius Giesick had a record. Almost as an afterthought, I asked him to check on Dr. Charles Guilliam. I repeated the procedure with the Richardson, Texas, police, talking to a Sergeant Taylor. Being impatient, I gave the requests an importance they perhaps didn't deserve.

Next I talked to the local FBI. This always required a certain delicacy. FBI agents tend to view homicide detectives as clumsy Neanderthals, while the detectives generalize the FBI men as inexperienced know-it-all kids straight out of college with degrees in business administration. By sounding respectful and impressed that I could actually be talking with the mighty FBI (I *was* impressed by their equipment and technology—with our limited budget, we were a horse-and-buggy carryover in the Space Age), I received not the slightest hassle when I asked for a national check on Drs. Giesick and Guilliam.

Spurred by the momentum of zeal, I walked down to the records room on the second floor and sent a message over the NCIC (National Crime Information Center) teletype. It occurred to me Dr. Guilliam was paying for the sins of Dr. Giesick. If Guilliam had been at home or in his office, his name wouldn't be rattling around in computers. Well, it wouldn't hurt him. No one keeps records on detectives checking someone out.

With nothing to do but wait (the paperwork on the two suicides held no appeal for me, and I didn't want to get more swelled up about the nonresponse from Giesick), I decided to offer what reassurances I could to the Albanowskis. They were entitled to know someone was doing something. This time I talked to the father, Stanley.

"You were right about the car," I said. "It was checked out of the garage before Patricia talked with you."

"Both Jo and I are grateful you're taking your valuable time for this." The voice was soft but deep. It reminded me of my grandfather's voice.

"Well, you have the right to know what happened. I intend to find out."

"We wish we could thank you in person." It was a worker's voice. Strong. Good timbre.

"The insurance money was more than you thought."

"How much?" This trip will be through hell, the voice said, but nothing else is appropriate.

"One hundred thousand dollars." I didn't add, maybe more. Maybe Giesick found a company that sold travel insurance.

"Is there anything else?"

"Some good news. He won't be getting that hundred thousand, at least for a while. I've had the case reclassified from a hit-and-run accident to an open investigation. The insurance company won't pay as long as the investigation's open. The thing is, Giesick hasn't returned my calls. It's stalemate right now."

"Please don't give up on this."

He really feared I would. He couldn't be sure a voice on the phone could be trusted to see how important this was. I'd have feared the same thing. And Mr. Albanowski couldn't know the depth of my empathy for him, how much I found myself touched by his plight. I wished I could find more adequate words to tell him.

"I won't give up."

"You know, Detective Dillmann, we haven't heard from him, either. Saw him just that once. At the funeral. But not a word since."

The information I'd requested on Drs. Guilliam and Giesick began to come in as I said goodbye to Mr. Albanowski. Nothing. Neither had a record in San Antonio or

Richardson (Dallas). The NCIC had no information about a previous hit-and-run involving Giesick's first wife and infant child. The FBI, the last to check in, had no record in their super state-of-the-art computers.

Quitting time came. The weather outside, cold and gray and drizzling, matched my mood. I'd do the paperwork on those suicides at home.

What I really wanted to do was accomplish something with this case. Keep calling Giesick, Mutz said, but Mutz, I figured, was a cautious bureaucrat who didn't want to rock the boat. I could call Giesick forever and, if he didn't answer, I would never move off dead center.

Pascal Saladino was also preparing to leave. No bureaucrat, Saladino. He'd been around. He'd know what to do in a case like this. I'd bet no hotshot psychologist would jack him around.

"Sal," I said. "Could I talk with you for a few minutes?"

"Get away from me, Skinny." Pascal called everybody, including Dantagnan, Skinny.

"It won't take long." Pascal had a reputation for helping younger detectives.

"I've got important business, Skinny." Actually, I was fairly muscular. Had 190 pounds on my five-foot-eleven-inch frame. Lately I'd been working with weights.

"I really need help." I'd drive Diane and myself crazy doing that paperwork.

"I told you, I've got important business."

"I could buy you a drink. We could talk over a drink."

"Why didn't you say so? Wear your coat. You'll catch cold without it."

"Let me make one phone call."

I expected once again to be made angry, and wasn't disappointed. "Hello. May I help you?" I'd gotten to know this voice.

"This is Detective Dillmann in New Orleans. Has Dr. Giesick called in again for his messages?"

"Yes, he has. I told him it was important to call you, Detective Dillmann."

"Add something to that message next time, will you?"

"Surely."

"Tell him it's Detective Dillmann with Homicide."

We went to a bar called Miracle Mile, a police hangout on South White Street. Not a place to take your wife. About the size of an average suburban kitchen, poorly lit, smoky, a jukebox (country music) and cigarette machine the only extras, Miracle Mile's clientele, besides police, consisted of an occasional assistant district attorney or judge. Not many judges at all. Many policemen view judges as misguided bleeding hearts, and the mixture of the enforcement arm of the law with the sentencing arm, over drinks usually unmixed, can be explosive. Assistant district attorneys normally felt more at home, except those thought to rely too heavily on plea bargaining. But the district attorneys, as a whole, could be more law-and-order than the cops. Rightly or wrongly, they felt a good conviction record helped their careers. Later, as defense lawyers, they would exhibit the same determination in a different direction—and probably not be so welcome at Miracle Mile.

I had trouble breathing in the packed bar. A person could take up smoking in self-defense. Saladino's big cigar, usually a room clearer, made barely a dent in this environment. I had a beer, Saladino an amaretto (considered a sissy drink by some of the super-macho patrons, who nonetheless wouldn't say anything to the hulking Pascal), and I told him everything I knew about the case.

"You think this guy Giesick killed his wife?" Dantagnan had asked the same question. I gave the same answer.

"I don't know."

"What do you think? Come on, Skinny, pretend your life depends on it. You gotta guess. Don't matter if you're right or wrong. But if you don't guess, you're dead."

"I'd guess he did it." There! I'd come out and said it, surprising even myself. It was just a feeling I had, one that until now went unacknowledged even in my own mind. It was instinctual, intuitive, something, but I knew it was quite strong.

"Prove it," Saladino said. And thinking that funny, he launched into his high-pitched laugh.

"I told you, I can't even talk to the guy. I figured you might have an answer to that. Mutz is looking at the case from the administrative end. You see things different."

"Mutz is right. You got nothing. And you're wrong. Talking to this asshole is no panacea. He'd bring his lawyer along with him, and then where would you be?" Pascal liked to answer his own questions. "You'd still be up shit creek."

"What would you do, Sal?"

"I'd look for physical evidence. You probably won't find any. I wish I had twenty dollars for every guy I know is a murderer and can't prove it. Now I'll make a guess. I'll guess you don't break this case. And you won't be any damn good for other investigations if you let it eat away at you. Give it your best shot, that's all you can do, and try to figure out when to walk away from it."

Sal had been laughing through all of this. A strange bitter laugh that said he'd been through it all himself.

I finished my second beer and got up to leave.

"Physical evidence, Skinny," he said. "Get physical evidence. Something you can take to the grand jury. That's the edge you've got. Get 'em in front of the grand jury and let 'em lie their asses off. Goddam lawyers won't help in there."

Driving home, I couldn't get my mind off Dr. Claudius Giesick. The more I thought, fantasized, the more sinister my imagination made him.

Sinister? I would find out I didn't know what sinister was.

— 3 —

THE DELTA AIR LINES flight arrived at Dallas–Fort Worth
Regional Airport just after 9:00 A.M. on February 2, and
Lieutenant Jack Burleson of the Richardson Police Department's Dallas Metro Squad met me at the gate. Burleson,
in his early forties, soft-spoken, wore a gray suit and had
salt-and-pepper hair, and if he resented assisting a young
detective on what might be a wild-goose chase, it didn't
show. Burleson had worked his way up through the ranks,
and didn't make me feel like a neophyte dealing with a
bigshot lieutenant. I soon learned he was assigned to the
Greater Dallas Area Organized Crime Task Force, and had
known Jack Ruby, the nightclub owner who killed Lee
Harvey Oswald. Never having been in Dallas and having
no authority there, I'd asked the Richardson police for
someone to show me around, and they turned me over to
Burleson. I didn't even know where Dr. Giesick lived, so
Burleson, whose territory included Dallas and its suburbs,
might be a godsend.

This marked my fifth day on the case, and nothing much
had happened in the previous two: more fruitless phone
calls to Giesick's answering service, another talk with the
Albanowskis, and a key discussion with Diane.

Giesick still hadn't called, and I committed a foolish
error; I got mad at the answering-service woman. Giesick's

refusal to answer calls wasn't her fault, but I vented my frustrations on her. It's like getting mad at a telephone operator for what is the phone company's responsibility or chewing out the grocery checker for high prices the owner charges. I did learn from the answering-service lady that she had never seen Giesick, she "wouldn't know him from Adam"; he was simply a voice on the phone, a customer who paid his bills.

My talk with the Albanowskis had been difficult for the three of us. There was nothing disingenuous about them, and I hated the role I felt obliged to play: pretending something was happening. Especially with these people. Just from telephone calls I liked them, wanted very strongly to ease their hurt.

The discussion with Diane had been the key. She called the Albanowskis "those poor souls," and insisted I had a duty to "help them." Well, I said, I could go to Texas, but Mutz wouldn't pay for that.

"We'll pay it ourselves," she said. My salary as a homicide detective was $14,000 a year, and we had two kids and a mortgage. But we had managed a little savings, I had two days off coming up, and I could take a vacation day.

Diane's very unusual suggestion made me realize again why I could count myself as lucky. But it was the kind of thing I'd come to expect from her: people were in trouble and she saw a way to help. My own reaction was one of delight. The case was eating me up, and I welcomed any suggestions, no matter how offbeat they were.

On the drive to Richardson, where Burleson had checked me into a motel, I told him what I knew about the case. I watched his expression closely, to see if he thought me crazy, but he remained professionally noncommittal.

"I figure the thing to do first is find Giesick," I said.

"You've checked the phone book?"

"Right. No listing."

"Let's check all the area phone books."

But sitting in the Ramada Inn room, phone books stacked

knee-high, we drew a blank. A prospective client wanting psychological help from Giesick would have a tough time reaching him.

We drove down crowded Central Expressway to the Bureau of Vital Statistics in downtown Dallas. The businesslike, gentlemanly Burleson pointed out Dallas landmarks as we went. I stared long and hard at the Dallas Cowboys' offices (we were caught in a traffic jam), as if staring would somehow materialize three of my football favorites, Tom Landry, Bob Lilly, and Roger Staubach.

We made a side trip to Dealey Plaza, where President John F. Kennedy had been assassinated. "Geesus," I said.

"Smaller than you thought, isn't it?" said Burleson.

"Like a fishbowl. A shooting gallery."

"It looks like that 'cause you know what happened. But everybody expects something bigger."

Dallas seemed to be a city on the move, bright, bristling modern construction projects everywhere, a cosmopolitan metropolis bursting at the seams, a can-do place with none of the defeated pessimism I imagined existed in much of the East, where such dreams were already failing. New Orleans didn't race breakneck speed to modernize, either, the way Dallas did, but the reasons were an entrenched elite satisfied with the status quo and a genuine desire to preserve the city's wonderful cultural and historical heritages. If New Orleans ever did modernize, I hoped it wouldn't be with hard rock replacing jazz and McDonald's substituting for French, Cajun, and Creole cuisine.

But some things are the same everywhere. The records room at the Bureau of Vital Statistics matched anything New Orleans had for being drab. I expected dust to flurry up. The people in the records room seemed to have been there a long time, frozen in amber, their movements lifeless and automated. A pretty young woman would look old and tired in here.

Burleson obtained Patricia's marriage certificate and handed it to me. The certificate listed Giesick as a widower, and his address as 24 North Commerce Street,

Ardmore, Oklahoma. The marriage had been witnessed by T. Rogers and C. R. Lee, and the ceremony performed by the Reverend Samuel Corey, pastor of Southwest Calvary Grace Christian Church. I handed the certificate back to Burleson, who read it.

"I guess," I said, when we were back in the car headed for the Ramada, "I looked in the wrong place for Dr. Giesick. He lives in Ardmore, Oklahoma."

Burleson didn't answer. Previously the most friendly and courteous of men, he'd become tight-lipped, his face set in stone. It was such an unexpected, remarkable transformation, I wondered if I'd said something wrong.

I made two other lighthearted remarks to Burleson as he crept north on Central Expressway, but he was somewhere else. I concentrated on hoping the unconscious section of Burleson's brain, the part doing the driving, wouldn't get us involved in an excuse-me fender-bender on this race-track for snails.

When we reached the Ramada parking lot, Burleson seemed to have arrived at some understanding with himself. Grim-faced, he suggested we talk in my room.

"Sam Corey," he said, when I was seated on the bed. He occupied the only chair.

"The minister who performed the ceremony," I said.

"Right," he said. I thought it amazing the sarcasm and venom this mild man could put into one word.

"What about Corey?"

"It's going to take all night."

"Go ahead."

"I'll tell you just a little. I don't have the stomach for all of it. You can read the rest tomorrow when I take you to the Intelligence Division."

"Tell me."

"Corey is a preacher who lives in San Antonio and owns a string of massage parlors in both San Antonio and the Dallas area. They're blatant fronts for prostitution. Corey commutes on a daily basis between San Antonio and here, and is thought to be involved with organized crime. Right now he's fighting a war with other massage parlor owners. There've been threats and extortion. Some shootings. People from Hawaii, rough sorts, have gotten into the dispute, on the side opposing Corey." Burleson paused for breath.

"Is he legally allowed to perform marriages?" I asked.

"He's a certified minister. I guess he is."

"Sounds more like a career criminal. What's the connection between him and a psychologist?"

"Maybe none. Maybe Corey just performed the marriage. Why, I can't imagine. And I can't even guess about possible connections. Look, John, instead of my relying on memory, why don't I take you to Intelligence tomorrow? I guarantee you'll get an eyeful."

First thing in the morning we again fought Central Expressway traffic to reach downtown and the offices of the Greater Dallas Area Organized Crime Task Force. Burleson drank coffee while I read. The material on the Reverend Sam Corey could fill a book.

The first impression I got of Corey, looking at his picture, was his enormous size, five feet nine inches and 350 *pounds*. I studied the picture for a long time. I'd gotten a description of a man with such a build having been seen with Giesick in New Orleans.

I couldn't take my eyes off Corey's picture. He had a blank, malevolent stare, thinning brown hair, a shapeless, lumpy, unattractive face. His stomach could have had a giant beach ball pumped up inside it, and the beach ball had somehow wrinkled, resulting in layer upon layer of flesh. Corey's behind was massive, broad, and thick.

Without reading the entire file, I might have viewed Reverend Corey as a harmless buffoon. He ran for mayor of San Antonio using the slogan, "Let's put the nitty-gritty before the city," and promised that if elected he would hire a girl in hot pants to chauffeur the mayoral limousine. He also promised to introduce austerity into government and to lead by personal example. Corey vowed to live " poverty," just as he once had "successfully lived in the days of monastic existence as a Brother of Mary."

Several of Corey's masseuses ran for city council on the same ticket. The campaign, doomed to defeat, provided a bonanza of publicity for the massage parlors, but what struck me was that Corey had been serious. He loved the publicity (no matter that most of it made him appear grotesque), and mistook the barbs his small audiences hurled at him for affection that would translate into votes. The preacher thought he could win.

Further reading contained no such whimsy. I found it remarkable that such characters as Corey exist. Still, I couldn't locate a connection with Dr. Giesick. Finding that address in Ardmore had filled me with hope, but no Giesick was listed in that town.

Sam Corey ("the Reverend" part stuck in my mouth), told investigators he was born in Mansfield, Louisiana, in 1933, and moved in 1939 to San Antonio where he'd lived ever since. He said he'd graduated from Central Catholic High School in 1950, and the next year became a novitiate in the Society of Mary teaching order. He stated he had acquired a B.A. from St. Mary's University in San Antonio as a Catholic priest, earned an M.A. from Trinity University, San Antonio, and been a professor of American history at San Antonio Junior College for two years.

This piece of "biography" didn't ring right to me. Diane is a Catholic, and I thought I remembered her saying it took more than a B.A. to be ordained a priest. Maybe different orders had different requirements.

In 1965 Corey and his wife Rita opened the Arm of Mercy nursing home. I would have loved to know more about that outfit, but the fat file on Corey told me nothing else. And what about his wife? I understood from Diane that getting married brought automatic excommunication for a priest. I supposed that didn't deter the massage parlor operator.

In 1970 Corey opened his first massage parlor, the Tokyo House in San Antonio, and his wife was his first employee. He currently owned an entire chain of massage parlors, having expanded to Richardson, Irving, Garland, and Oklahoma City, Oklahoma.

At the moment Corey was under indictment for felony theft and free on $10,000 bail. Earlier his Roman Holiday Massage Studio in Irving had burned down, a clear case of arson, but whether Corey himself did it for the insurance money, or a competitor trying to put him out of business, wasn't clear. A rival owner's masseuse named Betti said a tough-looking character had visited her and said: "You'd better padlock your places real quick and not turn on your ignition. I'm one of Papa Sam's boys and I'm after you." A rival parlor owner, Susie, said her ten-year-old child had been shot at the day before she testified on the felony theft charge against Corey. Another masseuse, whom Corey's Tokyo House reportedly tried to recruit, reported a burly visitor telling her: "I hear you have a pretty little boy. You must think a lot of him. And you must have heard of everything going on about the Tokyo House. If you value your life and your little boy's, you'll come talk to us." Another rival massage parlor owner, whose association with a Miss America contestant caused her to be eliminated from the competition, said he had received funeral wreaths in the mail and threatening phone calls, including someone saying a bomb had been planted in his driveway, had found a dead cat on his lawn, and had been sent notes indicating he'd been targeted for death. Informants for the Task Force said Corey had backing from organized crime, which provided him with muscle and money.

Corey's massage parlors seemed to be profitable. The Tokyo House alone grossed as much as $1,000 a day, which allowed plenty left over to pay the $150-a-month rent. The masseuses, who did all the work, received thirty percent of what they brought in.

Corey believed in advertising. The following ad, similar to ones Corey ran, had appeared in Dallas-area newspapers:

There was more, much more, about massage parlors,
and massage parlor owners, and wars between massage
parlor owners, but I didn't want to read it. Frankly, it

made me sick. I looked over to Jack Burleson, leaning against a counter chatting with a clerk, and shook my head.

"Corey's something, huh?" he said.

"The Massage Parlor King." Indeed, *Texas Monthly* magazine would use that exact phrase to describe him.

"You can see why I wanted you to come here."

"A Catholic priest." I still couldn't make sense of that. "Running a whorehouse."

"Don't let it get to you. This is Texas. Look, I can make you a bet. Give you a hundred to one and still be stealing from you. The priest business is a tax dodge. You wouldn't believe the people we have here who call themselves preachers. Mostly they're the mail-order variety, and real low-life. They send ten dollars to a post office box and a 'school' mails them a diploma. Damned if the government doesn't let them get away with that dodge. But legitimate preachers back the phonies. They're afraid the next step is for the government to remove *their* tax exemption."

"But they're not Catholic priests."

"Didn't you read that marriage certificate?"

"You're right. Southwest Calvary Grace Christian Church. I'll check to see if it exists."

Before we left the Crime Task Force offices I gave Giesick's answering service another call, but whether I was phoning from Texas or Louisiana the result never varied. I thought of going to the answering-service offices and planting myself there until Giesick called in for his messages, but that might do more harm than good. Pascal Saladino said Giesick might agree to meet me with an attorney present, and from then on I could be butting up against a stone wall. For now, I figured it best to learn as much as I could about Giesick, gather information that might give me an edge.

If anything, I was hotter than before over Giesick's not returning my phone calls. After this length of time even a pesky salesman would have gotten an answer, if only to tell him to back off. I was involved with an investigation into the possible murder of his wife, and he had to judge it serious because New Orleans Homicide (no matter how unofficial I might be) had come to Texas to pursue the matter.

Driving back to Richardson, I attempted to think as Giesick would, a task made more difficult because I'd never met the man. So I tried to imagine myself in his shoes. If my wife had been killed in the manner Giesick said, I'd want to cooperate with the police. I believed any citizen would. Even if he didn't care a whit for his wife, or the police, cooperation represented the best approach. Otherwise the husband guaranteed exactly what was occurring: a detective dredging up every piece of background information possible. Who needs that?

On the other hand, if I had something to hide concerning my wife's death, I'd probably act precisely as Giesick did. He didn't have to talk to me, and I couldn't force him. So why should he? No warrants or indictments had been issued; there hadn't even been any accusations. Giesick could gain no advantage by talking to me if he had something to cover up. As a psychologist, he probably possessed a logical mind, and reasoned that for the present he didn't need a lawyer. A lawyer might further arouse suspicion.

If Giesick had something to hide—and I couldn't come up with any other reason for his actions—life was no stroll in the park for him right now. He might figure he'd committed the perfect crime, but he could never be sure. *What could go wrong?* he'd be worrying over and over again. Unfortunately, I knew what could go wrong for me and the Albanowskis. Hadn't Saladino fantasized about being a rich man if he had twenty dollars for every murderer he knew and couldn't prove the crime?

Burleson and I found Pat Garrick, manager of the Tejas Trail apartments where Patricia had lived, on the premises. I asked if Dr. Giesick still lived in the apartment.

"No," Garrick said. "Ever since the accident—I heard

about it from Trish's mother, she wanted her daughter's personal belongings returned—I haven't seen Dr. Giesick, and don't think he's been back. It seems a bit cold, but I've had to initiate eviction proceedings against him. The rent is long overdue, and there hasn't been a sign of him.''

So it is, I thought. Giesick could make a ghost envious. Except for cameo appearances (at the funeral, the auto repair shop, the motel, the hospital, the insurance agent's office), no one could get the slightest fix on him. I wondered again about psychologists. Didn't their clients need a way to reach them?

''Can you describe Dr. Giesick?'' I asked.

''Short brown hair.'' Not to insurance agent Bud Gibson. ''Maybe five ten. Neat dresser. Seemed like a bright guy. I really didn't have much to do with him.''

''How about Patricia? You called her 'Trish.' Did you know Patricia pretty well?''

''No, I didn't. Everyone called her Trish, though. I do know she was close to her next-door neighbor, Joseph Richardson. And I could give you the number of her former roommate, Nancy Queens.''

''That would help.''

Garrick produced the lease Patricia had signed. She'd been living at the Tejas Trail address for a year before her death, with Giesick moving in when the two got married, fourteen days before the hit-and-run in New Orleans. Patricia listed her employment as a bookkeeper-typist with a large local carpet company.

Garrick let us into Patricia's apartment, a nice two-bedroom, immaculately maintained. It could have been a model apartment shown to prospective occupants: not a dish out of place, not a scrap of paper left lying around, not a stick of furniture even slightly askew. The apartment had been put in apple-pie order, awaiting the honeymoon couple's return from their island cruise. I felt I knew the answer but I asked Garrick anyway if he'd cleaned the place up, and he said he hadn't touched it, nor had Patricia's belongings yet been returned to her parents. Like me, he'd been waiting to hear from Giesick.

I stared for a moment at a portrait photograph of Patricia. If possible, she was even more beautiful than Mrs. Albanowski had described. The dead girl's hair had been an almost luminous strawberry-blond, cascading over her shoulders, and her striking green eyes sparkled, haunted. Patricia had high cheekbones and a pretty upturned nose, and looking at the model-perfect face made it easy to imagine the rest of her. She'd have long elegant legs and a slender shapely figure to make men gasp.

I poked around the apartment, deftly, having to fight the impulse not to disturb anything. I felt a vague sense of eeriness. The place had the aura of being timeless, as if it had been this way forever, and now I had to rummage about, to learn what I could about Patricia and her husband.

Very little of Giesick could be found in the place. A couple of suits, a couple of shirts. No men's razor, no men's toiletries, no sign, really, that any permanence had been anticipated. I didn't think it fruitful to dwell on that point. Nice as the apartment was, it belonged to Patricia, and the couple had probably planned to move elsewhere.

I came across a big thick leather-bound scrapbook, three-quarters full, maintained as meticulously as the apartment. Burleson and I sat at the dining table, Garrick standing behind us, and studied the moments Patricia herself wanted to remember.

She'd graduated from Notre Dame High School in Trenton, New Jersey, and from King's College in North Carolina. Even in crowded shots of her classmates, pretty coeds and bright-eyed adolescents, Patricia stood out, like a magnet drawing the gaze to her. All the photographs showed a happy young girl and woman, laughing and clowning, surrounded by friends. Of her year in Texas, nothing.

I asked Garrick to take me next door and introduce me to Patricia's friend Joseph Richardson. The way things had been going I didn't expect him to be in.

He was in his late twenties and filled with wonder about

the police involvement. This often happens. The person being interviewed can end up as the interrogator if the detective isn't careful, with disastrous results. First of all, Richardson might be a friend of Giesick's (how could I know otherwise?) and relay everything I said. Second, it wasn't impossible that an ill-advised remark of mine at this time could come back to haunt at a later court proceeding.

"I understand you were a close friend of Patricia's," I said, once I was in Richardson's living room.

"I think I was."

"Were you close to Dr. Giesick?"

"No. I only met him once or twice and he was very quiet."

"Do you know how Patricia met Dr. Giesick?"

"It was in December—1973—about two months ago. She came home excited and happy. She'd met a psychologist who'd asked her to marry him. He told her he was going to buy her a hundred-thousand-dollar home and a yacht. I do know he bought her a brand new Monte Carlo as a wedding present."

"What else did she say?"

"She just went on about how happy she was. I couldn't help being a little suspicious: love at first sight, Prince Charming, all that. Of course, I hoped it was true. I cared a lot about Trish. A really good kid. But it seemed odd she could reel in such a catch at a massage parlor."

"Massage parlor?" I shot a glance at Burleson.

"You'd have to know Trish to understand. She was the girl-next-door type, very pretty but oh so naive. Naive, totally and completely, describes her best. She was the person you sold the Brooklyn Bridge to."

"But what about the massage parlor?"

"Would you believe? She thought the place gave massages. She believed a bookmaker worked in a bindery, a cat burglar stole cats. It was touching, in a way, someone being so simple and trusting. And surprising. She *looked* so elegant and sophisticated. Still, if you cared about Trish, you worried something bad would happen to her.

Anyway, she'd lost her job. I guess she worked too slowly, or something, and this was fast-track employment. Probably Trish should have taken more time to find other work, writing to her parents for help to tide her over while she searched, but she was too proud to do that. She wanted to show she could make it on her own. So she applied at the massage parlor. Her upbringing was very strict and religious, and she felt there was something wrong taking that kind of job, though she didn't know what the job really was. She was caught in a tug of war with herself. She didn't want to ask her parents for help, and she didn't want to get mixed up with the massage parlor, which seemed the only other immediate solution. Of course, the massage parlor creeps had to be delighted when she walked in off the street. I don't imagine you find girls that beautiful in the type of places we're talking about.''

"What was the name of the massage parlor?"

"The Geisha House."

I looked at Burleson. He knew I wondered whether Corey owned it. He shook his head.

"How long did Patricia work at the Geisha House?"

"Just long enough to find out what it was. Three or four days. It took that long before she was faced with what was expected of her. Like a little girl, she was shocked by what she'd gotten into, but full of hope and optimism about the new man she'd met.''

"She didn't wonder what he was doing at a massage parlor?"

"I don't know. But Trish would buy any story he gave her. She was dazzled by Giesick. The young, successful psychologist, interested in her, promising her the moon.''

"What were your impressions of Dr. Giesick?"

"I'm not qualified to give an opinion. He was a classy dresser. Very quiet. Appeared successful. I just hoped Trish had found Mr. Right.''

"Has he been back to the apartment since Patricia died?"

"I haven't seen him."

"What more can you tell me about Patricia?"

"Only that what you saw was what you got. Nothing devious about Trish. Like all of us, maybe more so, she wanted to be happy, and she associated happiness with marriage. But she was going to need luck. She'd fall for anything, especially if enveloped in rainbows and fairy-tale castles. I only hoped things would work out for her."

"You spent a lot of time with Patricia?"

"I didn't take her out, if that's what you mean. But, yes, we had many long talks. I liked her a lot, as I guess you can tell. Just listening to what she wanted from life, which was modest enough, I had to cheer for her. She would have been damn great for somebody."

"Did she ever express fear of Dr. Giesick?"

"No. He had her walking on clouds."

Well, Patricia had been afraid, if the Albanowskis were to be believed, but indications of this first occurred after Giesick began buying insurance. Perhaps there'd been other causes, private ones between the newlyweds, and I might never learn what they were. But the reasons for Patricia's fear must have been overt and tangible. From what I'd discovered so far she wouldn't have discerned subtleties.

Burleson drove me back to the Ramada, and I went over in my mind what I had: a naive girl who worked briefly in a massage parlor, quitting when she found out the nature of the job; a psychologist who for reasons unknown visited the parlor, swept the girl off her feet, and married her; and a preacher who owned massage parlors, though not the one where Patricia worked, performing the marriage ceremony. I had connections to make, but they escaped me. However, plenty of time remained. Forever, actually. I decided if I got discouraged, I'd remember the voices of the Albanowskis and Diane, or concentrate on the arrogance of Giesick, and discover plenty of incentive.

Jack Burleson, ever helpful when he thought it appropriate, along merely to smooth the way for me in a strange jurisdiction, did not intend to offer advice unless I sought it. The case belonged to me, he figured, and some detectives guarded that prerogative, so if I wanted an opinion I could ask. I wanted one. Burleson knew more about police work than I did, and it would be foolish and negligent not to seek his help.

"Should I get Corey out of my mind?" I asked.

"Just the mention of his name should put you on your guard. I consider Corey a dangerous man. To answer your question, no, you shouldn't put him out of your mind."

"How deep do you think I should dig?"

"You have to follow where you're led, and he keeps popping up. I know it's fascinating to speculate on possible connections between Giesick and Corey or Corey and the girl, but right now you don't have a shred of evidence worth anything in court. It's not much help to tell you to keep working, but that's all I can do. Your job's not any easier with Giesick and Corey in Texas and you based in Louisiana."

Evening approached—4:00 P.M.. February 3, 1974—when Burleson deposited me at the Ramada. I had a couple of phone calls to make and some thinking to do. This was the end of my second day in Texas and, at most, I had one more. Maybe in the morning I'd visit the Geisha House.

A concerned Nancy Queens started asking questions the moment I identified myself over the phone. Patricia's former roommate had taken her friend's death hard.

"When did you move in with Patricia?" I asked.

"March of 1973. It was a matter of economics. Neither of us alone could afford such a nice place, but together we could."

"And when did you separate?"

"Around Christmas. Trish had met Jim Giesick, and the two intended to share the apartment after they married."

"Can you give me any background information on Patricia?"

"She's from New Jersey. She came to Dallas a little more than a year ago. That's when I first met her, when she worked as a secretary for a carpet company in Richardson."

"Why did she come to Texas?"

"In New Jersey she'd met a guy from Dallas she thought she was going to marry. She came here to be close to him. He was a typical big talker—Trish fell for that stuff, especially the romance part of it. He promised her the moon, and when it suited him he took off. Trish was hurt, of course, but the embarrassment was worse. She didn't know what to do; she didn't feel she should go home. She decided to try to make it here."

So Giesick hadn't been the first with the promises.

"How long did Patricia work for the carpet company?"

"Nine months, I think. I guess her work wasn't satisfactory. She took another job, this one with a manufacturing firm in Dallas, but it didn't last long either. Trish was made to be a wife and mother, not a big hit in the business world."

"When did she go to work at the Geisha House?"

"That was something, wasn't it? Well, it was toward the middle of December. Trish'd been out of work for six or eight weeks; she just hadn't been able to find anything. She intended to keep looking in her spare time, but when she found out what she'd gotten herself into, she quit, and at that point everything happened at once. She met Jim Giesick, there was the whirlwind courtship, and Trish, I can tell you, was one happy girl."

"What do you know about Dr. Giesick?"

"Practically nothing. I only met him once."

"You call him 'Jim.' "

"That's what Trish called him. It was always Jim promising her this, or Jim with plans for that. She ate it up. It hadn't been easy for Trish in Dallas, but now she thought all of that had changed."

"Why was Dr. Giesick moving into her apartment? Why didn't she move in with him?"

"It was a temporary arrangement. He was going to buy her a beautiful house. Trish said he always seemed to have plenty of money, that he was a prosperous psychologist. The one time I saw him he dressed the part."

"Do you remember what he talked about?"

"Actually, he was very quiet. He didn't come on like a big shot. We have a lot of those in Texas. Mostly with oil wells. Every guy in Texas has drilled an oil well, or is about to. I guess Jim's being modest helped me believe what he told Trish. She was one naive girl, Detective Dillmann, I want you to know."

"I've heard that before."

"Take it to the bank. A very pretty girl, a darn nice kid, but not equipped to get through the singles jungle."

"She had a college degree. She knew how to dress and how to keep an apartment. I've been to your old place. It's in perfect order."

"I'm talking about being gullible. Trish was a complete innocent. There's a difference between street smarts and book smarts, and Trish wasn't street smart. It's a shame we have to be."

"Do you know where Dr. Giesick lived before he met Patricia?"

"I sure don't."

"Did you meet any friends of his?"

"No. I met him that once, and he and Trish were alone."

"Did Patricia express any fear of Dr. Giesick? Did she have any reservations at all about him?"

"Not that I knew."

I thanked Nancy Queens and said goodbye. I hesitated a moment, then called Homicide in New Orleans.

"What's happening, buddy?" I said to Fred Dantagnan.

"Where the hell you been?" he asked. I hadn't told anyone on the force I'd gone to Dallas. "I've been calling your house trying to get you. Diane won't say a thing. Some best friend you are."

"It's not important where I've been." I didn't want to get in a lengthy discussion about it. I could catch him up later. "Why have you been calling?"

"I've got news that will make your week."

"Giesick called."

"Who's Giesick?"

"Dammit, Fred, I told you about that case. The honeymoon couple. You're only interested in your own little world."

"Be cute, asshole, and I won't give you the news."

"What you got, Fred? Tell it to me. I don't have all day. I'm talking long distance, and on my own dime."

"Where are you?"

"Just tell me what you have."

"You know that jerk you were looking at for the French Quarter rape?"

"Right."

"He's history. About 1:00 A.M. he jacked a tourist on Toulouse Street, then made the mistake of pulling his piece on a uniform. Got himself shot."

"How's the uniform?"

"Okay. Shook up a little."

"You're right. My week is made."

I've never known what to think of this kind of attitude, but most cops have it, that's how it is. I was sure this rapist (and I knew I couldn't prove in court he was a rapist) had a mother somewhere who loved him, and maybe other people. I simply felt relief that he was gone. What worth did he have? I believed there were women in the world who, though they'd never know it, had been spared a terrible and possibly fatal future encounter. I didn't see any cause to mourn.

In my mind this death closed the rape case. I had three exceptionally reliable informants who in the most unequivocal terms named the man shot dead on Toulouse Street as the French Quarter Rapist. This information already sat in the case file, but the file would remain open, listed as an unsolved crime. To ease the pain and anxiety of the rapist's victim, I would tell her (without any specifics, in the most general manner) that the man who assaulted her was off the street, no woman need ever again fear being brutalized by him.

"Anything else going on?" I asked Fred.

"Nothing. Except I guess you're behind in your insurance premiums."

"What does that mean?"

"There's an insurance guy who calls here every hour wanting to talk to you. Insurance guys are never that eager unless they're selling something, or you owe them money. I figured you're not buying, so . . ."

"Or unless you can save them some money," I said.

"What?"

"Never mind. Give me his name and number."

His name was Mick Hanson and he was director of special services for Mutual of Omaha. I called him at the company's home office in Nebraska, identified myself, said I was returning his calls, and held my breath because I had a hunch what was coming.

"I understand," Hanson said, "from the Orleans Parish Coroner's office, that you're investigating the death of Patricia Giesick. Could you give me any information on the status of your investigation?"

"Well, Mr. Hanson, I'd like to know why you're interested in the case."

"Dr. and Mrs. Giesick purchased a two-hundred-thousand-dollar travel insurance policy just prior to her death, and . . ."

I didn't hear the rest. My mind was too busy adding numbers, which might add up to a motive: $100,000 from Farmers Insurance Group plus $200,000 from Mutual of Omaha came to $300,000 total. And there might be more. The $300,000 could be only what I knew about.

"I'm sorry," I said to Mutual of Omaha's Hanson, "I didn't catch that last part."

"I said Dr. Giesick has filed a claim for the money. I'm trying to learn the status of your investigation. Anything you've discovered would be appreciated."

"When did Giesick file his claim?"

"January seventeenth. He didn't wait long, did he?"

No, I thought, he didn't. The same held true with Farmers Insurance Group, and I had trouble making sense of it. If the murder was the most cold-blooded possible, that is, if he'd courted Patricia with the intention of killing her—and I suspected as much—then careful planning was indicated. But it just made sense to play the role of grieving husband for a while. Instead, Giesick rushed forth to collect the money. To me this didn't jibe with a crime that had taken weeks, perhaps months, to put into operation.

"My investigation," I said, "is open. I don't have anything substantial."

"I'll be looking into the case also."

"That's fine. I can tell you now you're not the only insurance involved."

"Really?"

"There was a fifty-thousand-dollar life policy with Farmers Insurance Group. Double indemnity. You guys are unlucky. He tried to buy the travel policy from Farmers, but they don't sell that coverage."

"Wonderful."

I'd thought that would make *his* day, in a reverse direction. What I found interesting was Dr. Giesick's determination to purchase insurance. It hadn't been a one-time urge for him. Rejected by Farmers Insurance Group, he'd sought out Mutual of Omaha. I didn't know if some phobia existed that applied to your wife's being accidentally killed, but I doubted it.

"You said you're planning your own investigation," I said. "What do you have in mind?"

"Giesick purchased our travel policy at Dallas–Fort Worth airport. At a Tele-Trip counter. I thought I'd start by coming to Texas to interview the people who sold the policy."

"Could you hold off? I'm in Texas now, headed back to New Orleans to regroup, but I think I'd like to be with you at the airport." I figured the time approached when I'd have to look more closely at those insurance policies, and cooperation would be easier to obtain with Hanson along. That director-of-special-services title was impressive.

"I'll wait to hear from you."

Good, I thought, *and when we do get together in Texas, I don't think I'll be paying for it.* The additional insurance money involved and Giesick's eagerness to collect it should at least persuade Mutz to release department funds. My own savings account could ill afford another depletion jolt.

What I'd said to Hanson about regrouping was true. I needed time to think, preferably in the quiet of my home. I also needed to get back to my job. I didn't know how Mutz would react to my going to Texas, but I cringed thinking about what he'd say if I missed work.

I called Lieutenant Burleson, thanked him for his help, and told him I would fly back to New Orleans the next morning. On the flight home, February 4, the day after Patricia—Hearst—was kidnapped, the words "find Giesick" kept hammering in my head. Mutual of Omaha hadn't helped. Hanson told me the address on the policy was the one on Tejas Trail, and of course the phone number belonged to that answering service.

Find Giesick. But how? I'd tried the front door and been rebuffed. It was time to look for a back door.

—4—

"LET ME READ from my notes. It will be easier for you to understand that way."

February 16, twelve days since I'd returned from Texas. The caller was Detective Walter Dennis of the San Antonio Burglary Squad.

"Detective Dennis," Dennis read from his notes, "was contacted by Claudius Giesick on Friday, February 15, 1974, at about 3:00 P.M. Giesick stated that his home had been burglarized and he was not satisfied with the sheriff's investigation. Later in the day at Dennis' office, Giesick admitted fabricating the burglary story as an excuse to see Detective Dennis. Giesick said that in July of 1972 he and his wife, Kathy, had moved to Tucson, Arizona, to hide from the Zents, three brothers who were smuggling gold bars from Panama into the United States. He said he had informed on the Zents to the U.S. Secret Service; subsequently Bill Zent had threatened his life. Giesick said the intense pressure on him from the Zents had caused the breakup of his marriage to Kathy. He then told Detective Dennis he had met a girl in Dallas named Patty and they were married in January. He went on to say that Patty was killed in a hit-and-run accident in New Orleans and the police were investigating the accident as a possible homicide. He stated Patty had taken out a travel policy for about $300,000 before they went on their honeymoon. He added he did not want her to take out the policy, but she insisted. Giesick asked Detective Dennis to call the New Orleans police and tell them he had given information to the Secret Service, prompting his disappearance for two years. Detective Dennis informed Giesick he would contact him later in the evening. Detective Dennis ran a computer check on Giesick and learned he was currently wanted under warrant #72-1699, relative to bad checks. Detective Dennis later met with Giesick and arrested him under the above-mentioned warrant.''

"You mean you've got him?" I said.

"Locked down safe. For the moment.''

"What do you mean, 'for the moment'?''

"It's a bondable charge. He hasn't posted bond.''

"Is there anything you can do? Shift him around from jail to jail? Hide him? Anything? Until I can get there.'' The almost two weeks since the trip to Dallas had, if anything, increased my desire to meet Giesick. He was key to the entire case, the sine qua non, and at last I had the chance to confront him. I had a staggering number of questions to ask this ghost, plus a major act of self-control to perform while asking them. I boiled with anger and frustration, this being the one-month anniversary of Patricia's death and the nineteenth day he'd refused to answer phone messages.

"Christ, brother,'' Dennis said. "I can't start moving the guy around. He's been in front of the judge and the bail's been set. But you may be okay. I don't think he can raise the money, at least real quick. If he had the cash he'd have posted it already. Plus it's a weekend. I think he'll sit here a few days.''

"Let me get this straight,'' I said. "He came to you hoping you could take the heat off from New Orleans?''

"That says it. He thought being an informant would cut some ice.''

"What's this business about bad checks?''

"You've got me there. It was there in the computer, so

I grabbed him. Evidently he hung NSF paper, and warrants were issued.''

"I had your computer run him down a few weeks ago. There wasn't anything.''

"This is probably something new.''

"Why did Giesick come to you?''

"He came to me earlier about the Zents. I passed him along to the Secret Service. I guess he knew the Secret Service couldn't help him, so he came back to me. God knows what people imagine our jobs are.''

I felt more relief than satisfaction. I'd come to think Giesick a character of mythic proportions, at least where lack of fear and icy cool under pressure were concerned, an antagonist who'd tax the ingenuity of the great fiction detectives I'd read about as a boy. But he was human, after all. The constant pressure applied to him had finally forced a move: the wrong one. Actually, until now, Giesick had been winning. Maybe he still was, but the odds had shifted. So long as he refused to talk to me, and I continued to draw blanks looking for physical, eyeball, put-your-hands-on-it evidence, he remained in the clear. I couldn't touch him. I could mope around New Orleans, letting myself be eaten up because Giesick had gotten away with the cold-blooded murder of an innocent girl, but there wouldn't even be the satisfaction of a public trial, where some fingers would be pointed and the more alert among the citizenry could see beyond the bluster of lawyers and the technical correctness of a jury verdict to brand in their minds what this man had done.

My major hope had always been to meet Giesick, question him about the case's several inconsistencies (most important, why Patricia thought the Monte Carlo was in the repair shop), and probe for areas of investigation he might inadvertently provide. If he stayed away from me—and I couldn't ever imagine not pursuing him, as long as questions needed to be answered—he was safe, assuming I got no breaks in the case in some other unforeseen direction. I'd thought he understood this. His refusal to return my calls, which numbered more than fifty, seemed to attest to a basic awareness that nothing good could come from talking to the police. But now he'd made an error, gotten himself locked up (I knew no army of detectives had been out, night and day, beating the bushes for him on NSF check charges—people in relatively minor trouble are usually picked up for something else, perhaps speeding or DWI), and I had my opportunity.

"Is Giesick a psychologist?" I asked Detective Dennis.

"You mean, a real live one with a degree?"

"Right."

"Geesus, I wouldn't think so. I thought he fixed cars. But who knows?" There was a hesitation on the other end of the line. "A psychologist? That would be something. He's got a good line of bullshit, so maybe, but I understand he's a mechanic."

"Well, I'll learn more when I get there. I want you to know I'm grateful. You accomplished what I couldn't."

"I'll be seeing you soon."

"As soon as a plane can get me there."

The Delta jet—the fare this time paid by the department—cruised just a half hour from San Antonio, and the excitement gripping me gave no sign of abating. I had butterflies in my stomach, like it had been before a high-school football game. Interviewing Giesick had been my primary goal for an entire month, and I didn't want even to think what I'd do if he told me to take a walk. Instead I went over in my mind what had transpired since I'd returned from Texas the first time. It had been little enough, considering that the case had dominated my thoughts.

I'd talked to the Albanowskis twice. Their attitude remained one of gratitude that someone had concerned himself with the case. It was my job, I said, and I'd be remiss if I didn't press forward. This was the simple truth. The high amount of insurance money and Giesick's purposeful elusiveness demanded resolutions of the questions they raised.

Time hadn't dulled their grief. I'd gotten the impression from the very first the Albanowskis would never recover from their loss, and nothing had occurred since to alter this estimation.

Mainly in these conversations with them I learned more about Patricia. She had loved to swim and sun on the Jersey beach, and she adored pet animals. Giesick, they remembered, had bought her a Saint Bernard puppy as an additional wedding present. I hadn't heard about the dog before, a surprising fact since the Albanowskis said Giesick and Patricia brought it to New Orleans. Could you take a dog on a Caribbean cruise?

Also, since I'd returned from Texas, I'd located Ricky Mock, the teenager Giesick flagged down to call the police after the hit-and-run. Mock said he'd dropped his date off and was headed home when he saw Patricia lying on the Michoud Boulevard Bridge with Giesick leaning over her. Giesick waved for him to stop. He said his wife had just been struck by a car and exhorted Mock to call the police. This the good Samaritan teenager did, returning to the scene to learn the injured woman had already been rushed to Methodist Hospital.

I hope what happened to Ricky Mock didn't sour him on helping others. The next evening, concerned about Patricia's welfare, he went to the hospital to inquire of her condition. Told she had died, he proceeded to the parking lot, started his car, and was promptly collared by a security guard. The car Mock drove had a loud muffler, and in other ways fit the vehicle Giesick had described as the hit-and-run automobile. New Orleans traffic division police were summoned, and treated Mock as a suspect until his story could be verified. Regardless, I thought the teenager added another small piece to the overall mosaic of the investigation. Giesick, I suspected, under self-imposed pressure he imagined came from the traffic officers, felt he needed to come up with a quick description of the hit-and-run vehicle. He said the first thing that came to his mind, which described the last car he'd seen: Mock's. Mock's vehicle fit the hit-and-run automobile to a tee: dark, a four-door, late-model, with a loud muffler.

I'd had several conferences with Commander Mutz, whose attitude toward the case had undergone a sea change. Previously he had viewed the investigation as make-work, public relations, undertaken to pacify the inquisitive Destribats. But the high amount of insurance ($300,000, and perhaps still counting), Giesick's eagerness to collect it, Giesick's refusal to answer calls, and the discrepancy of the Monte Carlo's not being in the repair shop, combined to force an adjustment in Mutz's appraisal. He'd gone from a small headache (assigning make-work) to a big one. For, like Pascal Saladino, he suspected that from the department's point of view, we had the worst kind of murder on our hands: one we wouldn't solve.

Mutz said he wished he could assign six men to assist in the investigation, but Homicide's caseload made that impossible. He told me to keep digging in my "spare time." "Life goes on," he said, a questionable assertion. He did say department funds would finance any of my future trips if they showed promise. Giesick's being in the San Antonio cooler definitely qualified.

Detective Bernard Koby of the San Antonio Police Department's Intelligence Division met me with bad news at the airport late Saturday night. He insisted we have a drink in an airport lounge. A delay in getting to Giesick was the last thing I wanted, but Koby wouldn't take no for an answer. When he delivered the news I drew the alarmed attention of the bartender by kicking over a stool.

"Giesick made his bail," Koby said.

"On a Saturday night?"

"I haven't told you the part you won't like."

"You already have."

"Sam Corey put up the money."

This struck like a thunderbolt, and when the noise subsided I let the information knock around in my head for a while. Except for Corey's performing the marriage ceremony, it represented the first genuine link I'd discovered between the preacher and Giesick. With Corey's putting up the money for Giesick's bail, I suspected there were plenty more.

I asked the San Antonio detective to tell me more about Corey, and I received the latest on the massage-parlor-owning preacher, all of it unsavory. It seemed Corey had embarked on a busy expansion period, eager to dot the state of Texas with his emporiums. Rival massage parlor owners opposed him, and the war escalated with more arson and gunfire.

"Do you have Giesick's address?" I asked Koby.

"I'm sure it's on the arrest record."

"How about Corey? Do you know how to reach him?"

"I've got his home phone number at the office."

I thought it would be best to talk with Corey first, learn what I could from him about Giesick. At the moment I knew practically nothing, a big disadvantage when questioning anyone.

"Do you think Corey will talk to me?"

"Why don't I call him in the morning? God knows, his business and mine mean we've talked often enough before. I'll come up with a pretense to get him to headquarters, and then you can pop right in. Will he talk to you? I don't know. But right away he'll let you know one way or the other."

I stayed in a Holiday Inn not far from downtown, and was surprised to find out that the Alamo, Texas' shrine, sat right in the heart of the city. I'd always pictured it in some outlying field. From what Koby told me about the Lone Star State's Third City, it seemed similar to New Orleans, with its old and character-packed architecture.

I didn't sleep a wink at the Holiday. The frustration of getting nowhere, not only of being unable to talk with the key individual but with anyone who even knew the key individual, left me in a frenzy of anticipation. I knew I should get some rest, and tried, but sleep didn't come that night.

Koby handled the introductions smoothly the next morning.

"Oh, by the way," he said to the Reverend Samuel Corey, as I made my way into the Intelligence Division office, "this is Detective John Dillmann from the New Orleans Police Department. He has a few questions he wants to ask."

Corey remained unruffled. I caught just a flicker of alarm in his eyes, but then it vanished and he bounded to his feet shaking my hand and asking how he could be of help. My own reaction couldn't have been as smooth. Nothing I'd read or heard could have prepared me for the Reverend Samuel Corey. Dressed in civilian clothes—slacks and shirt, loafers—he was fat the way exceptionally obese people who are about to die are fat, a big round moon face, layer upon layer of flab underneath the chin, wide mammoth behind that made his walk a waddle, a stomach hideously jutted out so far it defied gravity merely for him to stand. Various police reports listed his height as five feet nine inches, which might have been right, but 350 pounds seemed an underestimation. I'd never before seen anyone of Corey's proportions.

He appeared saccharine-sweet. Cloying. I asked if I should call him Reverend, and he said Sam would be fine.

"Mr. Corey," I said, "I want to ask you a few questions about Dr. Claudius James Giesick."

"Fine."

"How long have you known Dr. Giesick?"

"Since December seventh, 1973."

"How do you remember the exact date?"

"I was involved in an automobile accident with Dr. Giesick. His car ran into the back of a car I was driving. Surprisingly, we became friends after that. Dr. Giesick has done some contract work for me in my business." Corey talked smoothly, without effort, no need to grope for words.

"What kind of business is Dr. Giesick in?"

"He's a consulting psychologist."

"What work did he do for you?"

"He developed preemployment tests for potential employees."

"I understand you own the Tokyo House massage parlor, among others, here in San Antonio."

"That's correct." He answered questions as a witness might, one who had been coached by an attorney, briefly and to the point. I couldn't get out of my mind how grotesque he was.

"And Dr. Giesick has developed tests for possible employees?"

"Yes."

"What kind of tests?"

"I told you. Preemployment. Psychological stuff."

I didn't want to push. More important questions demanded answers, and Corey felt uncomfortable talking about Giesick's "work." "Did you know Dr. Giesick's wife, Patricia?"

"I also met her in December of 1973, several weeks before they were married."

"What were the circumstances of your meeting the future Mrs. Giesick?"

"Dr. Giesick introduced me to Trish. He said she was a secretary who'd previously worked in a massage parlor, and wondered if I had any part-time positions available in one of my places. I said I didn't use part-time help."

"When was the next time you met Patricia Giesick?"

"Several days before they married. I was with the two of them when they informed me of their plans. It seemed to me she wanted the wedding more than he did. She said she was looking forward to having children." This volunteered information contrasted with his previous way of answering questions. He had a reason to want me to believe Patricia pushed for the wedding.

"I understand you performed the marriage."

"Yes. I'm an ordained minister with the Calvary Grace Christian Church of Faith. The parent church is in Fort Lauderdale, Florida."

"Where did the ceremony take place?"

"At Trish's apartment in Richardson."

"Who attended?"

"Two of Trish's friends. I don't remember their names, but they witnessed the ceremony."

"When was the last time you saw Mrs. Giesick alive?"

"I had dinner with them two or three days before they left on their honeymoon. I understand New Orleans was one of the stops they intended to make before going on a Caribbean cruise."

"Do you know how they got to New Orleans?"

"They went in their new automobile. They picked the car up when they drove me to the airport so I could catch a flight to San Antonio. This was a few days before they left on their trip."

"Can you give me a description of their car?"

"It was a two-door Monte Carlo."

"Do I understand correctly that the only contact you had with Dr. and Mrs. Giesick after the wedding was when you ate dinner with them several days before they went on their honeymoon?"

"I believe that's correct."

"When did you first learn of Mrs. Giesick's accident?"

"On the morning of January sixteenth I received a phone call from Trish's mother in Trenton, New Jersey. She said Trish had been in an accident. But she was very incoherent, and I couldn't understand her very well. She put her husband on the phone, and he told me Trish was in a New Orleans hospital. I called several hospitals in New Orleans, finally got hold of Dr. Giesick, and he said his wife was in critical condition. He told me they had been out walking, that she had been looking at ducks just before she'd been struck. Dr. Giesick called back later in the day, said his wife had died, and that he was returning to San Antonio as soon as he could make funeral arrangements."

"Mr. Corey, where were you when you received the phone call from Mrs. Albanowski?" The business about the call from New Jersey seemed a fantastic lie, but he delivered it without skipping a beat.

"I was in my studio on Blanco Road."

"Your studio's at the Tokyo House?"

"Yes."

"When did you next see Dr. Giesick?"

"In the latter part of the evening of January sixteenth. I picked him up at the airport and he spent the night at my home."

"Do you remember what airline Dr. Giesick came in on?"

"No."

"How long did Dr. Giesick stay with you?"

"Several days. Until his wife's funeral. I accompanied him to Trenton, New Jersey, for the service. We arrived on a Sunday night before the Monday morning funeral."

"How long did you stay in New Jersey?"

"We left that evening."

"Mr. Corey, you said Dr. Giesick flew from New Orleans to San Antonio. Do you know what happened to the Monte Carlo?"

"He must have returned and got it. I've seen him driving it since we got back from New Jersey."

"When was the last time you saw Dr. Giesick?"

"Last night. I bailed him out of jail here in San Antonio about nine-thirty."

"Do you know where Dr. Giesick currently resides?"

"Not the street address. But it's in Irving, Texas."

"Mr. Corey, when was the last time you visited New Orleans?"

"Several months ago. On business."

I doubted the truth of this answer. People I'd interviewed said they saw a man of Corey's description with Giesick in New Orleans. How many people fit Corey's description?

"What type of automobile do you drive?"

"I lease two cars. A 1973 Buick and a 1973 Cadillac."

"Mr. Corey," I said, gripped with tension, "you wouldn't

mind, would you, signing a statement to the effect of what you've told me?''

"No," he said, the word sliding off his tongue to damn him. "Whatever you need. I'm more than happy to cooperate."

Maybe so. But as I began to type up our conversation, Sam Corey started to squirm. He wriggled all over his chair. And sweat. The sweat started as a trickle, but soon it popped out of his pores, drenching him, and the odor became so trenchant I had to clamp my jaws tight and hold my breath for fear I'd vomit. The smell threatened to overwhelm. I needed to act as if this were routine, keep tap-tap-tapping at the typewriter as if this was the most ordinary thing in the world. I wanted to go faster. Corey got to his feet, pacing, agitated, trailing his nauseous scent from one end of the room to the other. I could almost hear his mind working, *how the hell do I get out of here, gracefully, without signing any damn statement? Especially this statement.*

My own adrenaline flowed just as fast, and I had to will my fingers to function slowly. I needed a poker face, a body that appeared relaxed and at peace with itself: in short, to look exactly the opposite of how I felt. All of what Corey had told me couldn't be true, and it might be extremely important later to be able to confront him with his lies.

Again a critical question, and again suspense that could only have lasted a moment, but in my mind stretched on and on. "Would you review this statement very carefully," I said, "and sign it if you find it true and correct?"

Corey sat in a chair right next to where I'd typed up the statement, and his reading was agonizingly slow. He concentrated on every word. The sweat gushed forth, as though from a fountain, and if he intended to control his facial expressions he failed. When he'd read the entire statement his chin slumped onto his chest, his eyes closed, he slowly shuffled the several pages as he might a deck of cards. He'd tried so hard to be cooperative, to appear upfront to this detective from New Orleans, never dreaming a statement would be taken, and now he needed to fish or cut bait. The debate going on inside him showed all over his face. In the end he signed, I think, because he didn't have the courage to look into my eyes and say no. Whatever his reasons, they were not good ones where his own welfare was concerned.

He signed, but in a way I'd never seen before. He wrote "Sam Corey," and then added, "with the right to make a change if I should recall something different."

When Corey left, his scent lingering behind, I sat with Detective Koby in his office, reading the statement again and again, wondering what I had. Surely not the entire truth. The business about the Albanowskis calling on January 16 didn't sound right at all. They'd never mentioned a Sam Corey to me, nor I to them. But why would he lie about such a thing? I asked Koby if I could make a long-distance call, and he said to go ahead.

"Mr. Albanowski," I said, "did you or your wife call the man who married Patricia and Dr. Giesick, a man named Sam Corey, on the morning Patricia died?"

"No. Of course not. We didn't know Reverend Corey existed until the day of Patricia's funeral."

"Why didn't you mention him before?"

"It never came up. I hope we haven't done something wrong."

"No. Not at all. I'd just like you to tell me everything, no matter how unconnected or unimportant it seems."

"Well, this Reverend Corey showed up with Dr. Giesick. He wore a Roman collar, and everyone assumed he was a Catholic priest, though we've had some doubts lately. He accepted money from mourners to say masses for Patricia."

"He asked for money?"

"No. It was given to him. To say masses. This is a common practice at a Catholic funeral."

I didn't know whether to laugh or be revolted. I settled on being revolted, an emotion I'd always be able to summon up when I thought of Sam Corey at that funeral: the

Massage Parlor King accepting donations from friends and relatives of the deceased to say masses.

Detective Koby thought it hilarious. No place existed, he said, where Corey couldn't work a scam.

I didn't see how he'd worked one on me. I had a signed and notarized statement from him in which he'd lied. The Albanowskis had not called him; they hadn't even known of his existence. What else did Corey say that wasn't true?

The preacher asserted Patricia was more eager than Giesick to be married. I doubted this. Corey claimed the witnesses at the wedding were friends of Patricia's, but if so, who were they? Joe Richardson, Patricia's neighbor and good friend, and Nancy Queens, the former roommate, had no idea who these witnesses, these "friends," might be.

I wondered also about those preemployment tests Giesick allegedly gave to prospective masseuses. I hadn't pressed Corey on the matter, for fear of warning him off, but I strongly suspected hanky-panky. And why had Corey bailed Giesick out of jail on the bad-check charges? The two, according to Corey, had only met in early December 1973, and this through a rear-end automobile accident. That accident needed checking. Plus—if they became such good friends in so short a time, was it likely Corey wouldn't know Giesick's home address?

But all this was nothing compared to Corey's assertion that he hadn't been in New Orleans for "several months." Upon returning from my Dallas trip, I'd gone to the Ramada where Patricia and Giesick had stayed. I interviewed every motel employee I could find. I found three who, on January 16, at 9:00 A.M., *two hours and thirty-five minutes before Patricia died* at Methodist Hospital, remembered Dr. Giesick's having breakfast in the motel dining room with an "enormously fat" man. The description I obtained fit Corey exactly. And how many people looked like him? I'd never met one.

I thought those three witnesses would identify Corey when shown a picture, thus placing him in New Orleans on the day Patricia died. What did this mean, I wondered, especially with a signed and notarized statement from Sam Corey to the contrary? Not much, perhaps. I could hear Mutz's voice telling me successful murder prosecutions got built on much stronger foundations than this.

What to do next? I hadn't accomplished the sole purpose of this trip, the interview with Giesick. I thought briefly of contacting Lieutenant Burleson in Dallas, asking him if I flew there would he help me look for Giesick in Irving. That seemed a long shot. Giesick had just been released from jail. He might not be home yet. He might not live in Irving, for that matter, all I had to support this being Sam Corey's word.

"Would you give me a lift?" I asked Detective Koby.

"Where do you want to go?"

"Eight six oh two Tuxford Drive. Dr. Charles Guilliam's home. Giesick used his credit card in New Orleans. Today's Sunday and I figure we might catch him in."

The neighborhood, a nice one, featured manicured lawns and spacious brick houses. Upper middle class. Just the kind of place you'd expect a doctor to live. I rang the doorbell and it was answered by an attractive woman in her mid-twenties with shoulder-length blond hair.

"Is this the Guilliam residence?" Koby asked.

"Yes, it is."

"I'm Detective Bernard Koby with the San Antonio Police Department. This is Detective John Dillmann with the New Orleans police. We'd like to speak with Dr. Guilliam."

"He's not home right now." She looked flustered. Her feet shuffled and one hand went to her hair. "I've got the kids in the tub right now. Could you wait a second?"

Her "second" lasted twenty minutes. Koby and I stood on the porch making small talk and shuffling *our* feet.

When she reopened the door she was smiling, her composure regained, and she invited us inside and asked if we'd like coffee. She called over her shoulder, "My name's

Katherine,'' and led us to a comfortable den with a big soft sofa and a large color TV.

"When will your husband be home?" I asked.

"Not until tomorrow. He's in Dallas on business." She sat primly with hands clasped in her lap.

"Do you have a phone number where I can reach him?"

"No, I don't. But could I know what this is all about?"

"I'd like to ask him some questions about a Dr. Claudius Giesick. Do you happen to know Dr. Giesick?"

"He's a business associate of my husband's."

"What kind of doctor is your husband?"

"He's a consulting psychologist."

"I understand Dr. Giesick is a consulting psychologist."

"Yes. As I've told you before, he's a business associate of my husband's."

"Mrs. Guilliam, did you know Dr. Giesick's wife was fatally injured in a hit-and-run accident a month ago in New Orleans?"

"I'm sorry. I didn't know."

I removed a photograph of Giesick from my clipboard. "Is this Dr. Giesick?" I asked.

"Yes, it is. Listen, Detective Dillmann. That is your name, isn't it? Could you tell me what the problem is? Why do you want to talk to my husband?"

"It seems, Mrs. Guilliam, that Dr. Giesick used one of your husband's credit cards while he was in New Orleans. I'd like to know if it was used with permission."

"I'm sure it was."

I stood up from the sofa, stalling for time to think, and ambled to the doorway to the kitchen. I could see out the kitchen window to the backyard, and what I spotted meant the case would never be the same again. It didn't take even a moment for the truth to hit. My eye saw and my mind recorded and it was there.

Out in the backyard were two Saint Bernard puppies!

Giesick had given Patricia a Saint Bernard puppy as a honeymoon present, and the dog accompanied them to New Orleans. What had happened to the dog after that?

Well, it played in Guilliam's backyard. I knew there could be other explanations, and in due time they'd probably be forthcoming. But I didn't think they would hold up. Giesick had a Saint Bernard puppy. Guilliam has a Saint Bernard puppy. *Giesick is Guilliam.* I knew it in the pit of my stomach and in the clearest part of my brain. All the rigamarole about two consulting psychologists added up to nothing more than a scam.

I had to control my excitement. I didn't dare turn away from the kitchen and let Katherine Guilliam-Giesick see me. Hadn't Giesick's first wife, the one he "divorced" because the marriage couldn't stand the pressure from the brothers Zent, been named Kathy?

It took effort to bring myself under control. "Do you have any pictures of your husband?" I asked, returning to sit on the sofa. I suspected Mrs. Guilliam, or whatever her name, would soon try to get us to leave, more difficult to accomplish with a person sitting down.

"I'm afraid I don't," she said testily.

No pictures of her husband? Come to think of it, I hadn't seen any in the den, or when I'd come through the house. Maybe that's what she'd been doing, removing pictures, while we'd been cooling our heels on the porch? And perhaps calling her husband?

"Could you describe Dr. Guilliam to me?"

"Look," she flared, "I don't know what this is all about. I'm not going to answer any more of your questions. I don't want you around here. If you leave your phone number, I'll have my husband call you when he gets home, but right now I think you should just get out." Her anger, masking fear, made her voice rise with every word; she was screaming when she finished.

We left as requested, but as we went two well-scrubbed little girls, aged perhaps three and five, came rollicking through the house, saying "Mommy! Mommy! Mommy!" and throwing their arms around Kathy Guilliam-Giesick's legs. But I'd learn that even this touching, unrehearsed, warm domestic scene was not what it appeared, that it too was tinged by tragedy and evil.

"What do you think?" I asked Koby, when I settled back in his car.

"I don't know. But she sure was nervous."

I told Koby I thought Guilliam was Giesick, and I gave him my reasons. The detective kept nodding his head, but didn't volunteer his own feelings. His lack of reaction seemed strange to me.

We decided that the next day—this was Sunday with much of San Antonio closed—we could start an in-depth background check of Dr. Charles Guilliam, with the specific aim of proving he'd married Patricia bigamously and in fact had led two lives. This would effectively kill any hope Giesick had of collecting insurance money, but again I could hear Mutz's voice in my head, and I knew I remained light-years from establishing murder.

Koby dropped me at the Holiday Inn and I spent the rest of the day reading the Sunday *San Antonio Light,* a paper filled with Watergate stories. Earlier in February the House of Representatives had voted 410 to 4 to grant broad constitutional authority to the Judiciary Committee to pursue its impeachment inquiry. The authority included the power to subpoena anyone, including the President, and regardless of whether Nixon testified, the hearings in Washington were shaping up as the year's major story.

I needed sleep that night, but knew it had to be timed carefully. If I fell asleep too early, I'd wake up too soon and not be at my sharpest in the morning. I planned to get a solid eight hours, with plenty of time left over in the morning to shower, shave, and have breakfast. But about 8:30 P.M. Detective Koby called.

"John," he said, "I just got a call from one of our uniforms. Jim Giesick called him about an hour ago. We must have stirred up some real shit with Katherine Guilliam, because it looks like Giesick is panicking. You're not going to believe what he's got to say."

"Giesick?"

"The uniform. His name is Patrick Kilough."

"Give me what you've got, Koby. Don't keep me on the edge of my seat." Actually, I was in bed.

"Giesick wants you off his back. Look, Kilough is on his way over to my house right now. We'll come to your room and he can give you the story himself."

Kilough—he and Koby arrived about nine-fifteen—was an eleven-year veteran who said he'd known "Jimmy" Giesick for six years. They'd met at Rizner's Drive-In Restaurant in San Antonio, and shared a mutual interest in auto mechanics. The two became good friends until some time in 1971 when Giesick vanished. Kilough didn't see him again until November 1973.

"How did you happen to see him in 1973?"

"Just ran into him. He invited me over to his home on Tuxford Drive and I met his wife Kathy again. Jimmy said she'd been threatened, and for that reason they were living under the name of Guilliam. He said he worked as a consulting psychologist with school children."

"So Kathy Guilliam is really Kathy Giesick?"

"Yes."

"Tell me about the phone call today."

"He called me at home. I could tell by his voice he was worried. He said he needed my help. He told me he'd been in New Orleans and witnessed an automobile accident, and a New Orleans detective had come to town investigating what happened. He asked if you contacted me, I not tell you he was using the name Guilliam."

"Why did he think I might contact you?"

"I have no idea."

It didn't make sense. But a lot of times in murder investigations, things don't. A sensible person wouldn't commit murder in the first place. I could only figure Giesick suspected I was close to learning about his double identity, and decided to head me off. Illogical as it seemed, this seeking help from a police officer against another police officer, I had to concede Giesick had been effective so far. Despite my considerable efforts since entering the case, I'd had difficulty locating anyone who really knew him. Things popped right now, I thought, because of the general accumulation of pressure (the constant calling of his answering service, the reluctance of the insurance company to pay, etc.) and specifically, today's interviews with Sam Corey and Kathy Guilliam. I had no doubt he'd talked this over with both of them. Nor did I doubt his being filled with anxiety: his approaching Officer Kilough proved that. Perhaps his panic would open doors that forever would have remained closed if he'd stuck to his original plan, ignoring me.

I'd relearned a lesson, one I shouldn't have permitted myself to forget. In my eagerness to accomplish something, I'd allowed myself to become depressed by lack of progress. But in truth, I had been making progress. I should have put myself in Giesick's shoes, thought his thoughts; if I had, I would have been so worried, because no matter how confident he might be that homicide couldn't be proved, doubts would surface. The doubts could lead to fear, panic, mistakes. The contest is never as one-sided as either the hunter or the hunted suspects, not until the genuine denouement. My error had been in overestimating Giesick; he could very well be making the same error. In his mind I might have assumed the fear-inducing, crazed-eyes, menacing specter of Charles Bronson bent on vengeance, operating with the inexorable efficiency and logic of Hercule Poirot.

"What else did Giesick say?" I asked Kilough.

"Said he was in a hurry. Asked me to call his wife, Kathy, and said she would explain further."

"What did Kathy say?"

"She told me Jimmy had been in New Orleans and witnessed an accident, the bumper of a car had struck a woman and she'd been seriously injured. She said Jim was so shook up he gave the police the wrong name. She asked me to tell you, if you contacted me, that as far as I knew she and Jim had been divorced for several years."

"What did you tell her?"

"I told her I'd like to help them, but I wasn't going to lie. Let me ask you something, John. What is this all about?"

"Why did you call Detective Koby?" I asked.

"Jimmy's call made me curious. I got hold of the detective bureau and asked a couple of the dicks up there if they knew of anyone from New Orleans in town asking about Jimmy Giesick. They gave me Koby's name."

"The girl," I said, "that Giesick said he saw being struck by a car bumper was his wife. She's dead."

"His wife?"

"What do you think? Giesick told you to call his wife, didn't he?"

"He sure did."

"Then the girl in New Orleans wasn't his wife."

But the moment I said it I couldn't be sure I was right. Not legally. You hear about men having two wives. I did know that Giesick wouldn't be collecting any insurance money and that the marriage to Patricia had been bigamous, against the law.

"You say Kathy Giesick told you her husband gave the wrong name to the officers in New Orleans?"

"That's what she said."

"What name should he have given? Guilliam?"

"I imagine that's what she meant."

"Christ," Koby said. "Let's have a drink."

I kept a bottle of J&B Scotch in my suitcase. It saved money, not having to buy bar drinks. I rounded up ice from a machine and we made cop talk for a while. Later I took a signed statement from Pat Kilough, and then it was very late and I knew sleep couldn't be postponed any more.

"I'll call you in the morning," Koby said. "We'll get started on that background check."

That will be fine, I thought. *Koby can be my alarm clock.*

— 5 —

MY WAKE-UP call came instead from Claudius James Giesick. For a few moments I thought it a dream. My voice was sleep-filled, I could barely see, and a moment passed before I could read my watch: 7:15 A.M. But the message provided the best possible stimulant, one guaranteed to jolt me awake.

"Detective Dillmann, this is Dr. Jim Giesick. I understand you want to talk to me."

"Yes. I've been trying to reach you for several weeks. I need to ask you questions about your wife's accident."

"Is there some problem? Did you come all the way to Texas just to talk to me?"

"As a matter of fact I did."

"Why? Have you found the guy who did it? I don't know if I could pick out the driver, but I'm sure I could identify his car."

Giesick had chutzpah, and words flowed smoothly and effortlessly off his tongue. I wanted to tell him, *yes, I've found the guy who did it, it's you, you son of a bitch, you murdered your wife in cold blood.* I wanted to say that, but it would be crazy to scare him off. I'd listened to Sam Corey tell a story I considered fantastic, and so too should Giesick be stroked.

"No. We haven't found the driver who killed your wife.

81

I understand, Dr. Giesick, you left New Orleans under a lot of emotional stress. But you have to understand my position. There are questions that haven't been answered.''

"Well, we could meet somewhere."

Terrific. How long had I waited to hear this?

"Are you in San Antonio?" I asked.

"I'm in Dallas."

"I'll come to Dallas. I'll see you later in the day."

"There's a better way. I have to come to San Antonio this afternoon on business. We could get together there."

"How about at my motel?"

"I'd rather not. I'm meeting with a business associate in San Antonio. I could see you at his office."

Here comes the lawyer, I thought. But I was wrong. Throughout this case I would consistently underestimate the depravity of the principals.

"What's your business associate's address?"

"Four two one eight Blanco Road."

The Tokyo House massage parlor. Giesick's "business associate" was the Reverend Samuel Corey!

"What time?"

"Eight-thirty tonight?"

"I'll see you then."

Things were rolling now. Perhaps it was activity for the sake of activity (surely Giesick wouldn't make a Perry Mason–type confession), but I felt better. Doing nothing, like it had been in New Orleans as the case ate away at me, was pure torture. Now at least I could get busy, and from that might come something positive.

I wondered how Giesick knew where to reach me. Diane didn't even know I was at the Holiday Inn. I believed Giesick had talked with his wife, Kathy, and with Sam Corey, that my interviews with them persuaded him to come forward (it turned out I was dead wrong about his motives), but I certainly hadn't told either of them where I was staying. So who did know? Who could have given him the information?

Detective Koby called at 8:30 A.M. and said he was on

his way. After coffee in a nearby diner, we went to the Bureau of Vital Statistics. The marriage certificate said Claudius James Giesick wed Katherine Ann Kaiser on September 12, 1969, in Bexar County (San Antonio). We found no record of a divorce, though there wouldn't be unless the divorce had been granted in Bexar County. I made a Xerox of the marriage certificate, and Koby and I headed for the Tuxford Drive area.

Again, my feeling of being sure and my ability to prove it were two separate matters. I needed more evidence. Officer Pat Kilough knew the Giesicks by both that name and as the Guilliams, but I wanted additional proof.

"Do you recognize this man?" Detective Koby dutifully asked two neighbors, as I showed them Giesick's arrest photo on the bad-check charge. "Oh, yes," was the reply from both. "That's Dr. Charles Guilliam." One of the neighbors added that the Guilliams drove a new Monte Carlo. *Right*, I thought. *Would I like to get my hands on that car.*

"Do you agree with me?" I asked Koby. "Giesick is Guilliam?"

"I don't see anything else it could be."

"So we've got a bigamous marriage?" I was thinking about something larger than bigamy, though. I had just the embryo of an idea.

"I'd say we do," Koby replied.

"But how do we prove it? Geesus, how do you check every county in America to prove a couple *hasn't* been divorced?"

"Don't think you have to, buddy. Here in Texas we recognize common-law marriages. You can show the Giesicks have been living together as man and wife. Over a considerable period of time, several months at least on Tuxford Drive. Therefore, in Texas, you could argue, they *are* married."

"I think they are, anyway."

"I do, too. But what we think doesn't count for squat. I believe a judge will buy your common-law argument."

"Well," I said, putting bigamy out of my head, "I've got that meeting with Giesick tonight, and I can hardly wait."

"What time do you want me to pick you up?"

I thought it over. "Koby, I think it's better if I go alone."

"You want to meet this guy alone in Corey's massage parlor?"

"Giesick is antsy as it is. I don't intend this to be an interrogation. I want to give him enough rope to hang himself." I hesitated a moment, my mind racing back to that early-morning phone call from Giesick. "Besides," I added, "I doubt if he'll show up."

"Why's that?"

"I think he got talked into this by Corey or Kathy, or both. I could understand if he was going to have an attorney along, but what can he gain talking to me? I'd guess he'll mull it over and decide to become a ghost again."

I arranged for Budget Rent A Car to deliver an automobile to the Holiday Inn, and showed up on time at the Tokyo House massage parlor. It was the size of a three-bedroom suburban home, and the front door opened into a small carpeted waiting room peopled by two young women I assumed were masseuses. Each wore low-cut leotards, lots of makeup, and smiles as fake as their mascara-laden eyelashes.

"Can we help you, baby?" said the one with red hair. "The girls will be fighting over you."

"Right," I said. "I . . ."

"Would you like to take a look at our menu?"

"I'm . . ."

"I'm the manager here, but for you . . ."

"What I'm trying . . ."

"You're not shy, are you, baby? We'll get you over that, real quick."

"I'm supposed to meet a Dr. Giesick here," I said

quickly. The other masseuse, a brunette, had come up behind and kneaded my shoulders.

"Oh. Are you a friend of Jim's?"

"I wouldn't call myself a friend."

"He wouldn't mind waiting if you went in back."

"Thanks. But, no. I think I'll wait for him out here."

My paranoia worked overtime. This seemed too obvious for a setup, but I couldn't be sure. I had other reasons for staying clear of involvement, but the one that first came to mind made me laugh. I could picture Mother Mutz's frown as he shuffled pictures of me in baby clothes taken by Giesick's hidden cameraman.

The elusive psychologist arrived at 8:45 P.M.. fifteen minutes late, which made me happy because I'd convinced myself he wouldn't show at all. Giesick didn't walk in, he bustled, brusque and businesslike, scarcely broke stride to nod and say, "Mr. Dillmann," open another door, and motion for me to follow. Giesick moved with the quickness and sureness of Sammy Glick; his aim, I decided, was to make me feel guilty about wasting his valuable time. It was ludicrous. We were in a massage parlor, not the War Room of the Pentagon, with the button about to be pushed, every moment critical.

"I'm in a hurry," Giesick said, as if I couldn't tell, when we were alone in the new room, which was small and I figured served as an office. "Gotta catch a plane back to Dallas. I can only give you a minute or two."

"I understand," I said, taking a seat and crossing my legs. Giesick looked spiffy in coat and tie. He had clean-cut features, with a pudgy boyish face topped by brown hair that I'd call medium-length. I'd heard women call men with looks and a build similar to Giesick's "cuddly" and "teddy-bearish."

"In my business," Giesick said, "you gotta keep movin', gotta keep makin' it. I wish I could sit back and relax. Have a civil service job like yours: eight hours a day and then home with the wife and kids. Though," he said, looking at me and remembering the time, "I guess sometimes you have to work extra hours, also."

"Dr. Giesick, do you . . ."

"Call me Jim."

"Do you recall . . ."

"Wait a minute. This seems too formal. Let's undress and let the girls give us a massage. A freebie. We can talk while they work." His suggestion, delivered as casually as offering coffee, made me blink.

"I'd rather talk here in the office. I need to take notes."

"Notes? You're going to tape notes?"

"Take notes. So I can remember what you say. I'm not going to tape anything."

"For all I know, you could have a tape recorder on now. I'd feel more comfortable if we undressed and I knew for a fact you weren't recording this conversation."

"Dr. Giesick," I said, feeling the law had to be laid down here, "I've attempted to contact you for several weeks through your answering service. I've been unable to talk to you until this morning, when you finally condescended to call. I could have asked you to meet me at San Antonio police headquarters, but instead invited you to my motel. I thought you'd be more comfortable there. I agreed to your suggestion of the Tokyo House, and now you want me to undress, lie on a table, and interview you while we're being massaged. All because you're afraid I'm going to tape our conversation. Well, there are certain questions about your wife Patricia's death that need to be answered. Since you were the only one there, only you can answer them. If you'd like to answer my questions now, that's fine. It will be fine the other way, too." It really wouldn't. I was bluffing. "But I'd think you'd rather talk to me than a grand jury. If you want to talk in a professional manner, let's do it. Otherwise I can leave. But you're fucking nuts if you think I'm going to get buck naked."

Giesick didn't seem shaken. "Well, okay," he said. He looked at his watch. "But I really don't have much time. I've got that plane to catch."

"I need some background information. What's your current address?"

"Three oh six one Walnut Lane, Irving, Texas."

"I understand you're a doctor of psychology."

"That's correct." He looked at his watch again. He possessed the mannerisms of an important businessman whose time was being wasted.

"Where were you educated?"

"I studied at the University of Sao Sebastio in Rio de Janeiro and at Munich University in West Germany. In December of 1972 I received my Ph.D. from the University of Mexico in Mexico City."

Geesus, I thought. Talk about conflicting versions! The Burglary Squad's Detective Dennis, whom I suspected probably gave the more accurate one, believed Giesick to be an auto mechanic. Talking to the well-dressed, articulate Giesick, I had to admit he could pass for either.

"Prior to your marriage to Patricia, had you ever been married before?"

"Yes. Twice. The first was in 1966. I married a young woman named Linda Perry. The marriage lasted less than a year, and we were divorced in Austin. In 1969 I married a lady named Margaret Hope Miller. We were married in Winter Haven, California, and had the marriage annulled three days later in San Antonio."

Winter Haven, California?

"When did you meet Patricia?"

"About six months ago in Dallas. We didn't start dating until the first part of December. We were married in January. For some reason she was very anxious that we be married."

"I've read the police report, of course, but I wonder if you could tell me the circumstances surrounding your wife's death."

"Our car broke down in New Orleans. We were on our honeymoon, on our way to take a cruise from Miami. We . . ."

"What was the matter with the car?"

"Transmission problems. I was pissed off because it was brand new. I'd bought it for Patricia as a wedding present."

"Did you have the car repaired?"

"Yes. I took it to a Chevy dealership."

"When did you get the car out of the shop?"

"Early in the evening before Patricia was killed. We picked the car up and drove to a pizza place for dinner. Since it was late, we decided to spend another night in New Orleans and head to Miami in the morning. Later we decided to go for a ride. While we were driving, I remembered this bayou we'd walked over the day before. I parked the car in a lot across the street, and we went to see if the family of ducks we'd seen was still there. Trish loved animals. I thought seeing the ducks would make her happy."

"Then what happened?"

"It was pea-soup foggy. Trish was in a playful mood, laughing and jumping around, and suddenly she said, 'C'mon, I'll race you back to the car.' Before I could answer, she darted into the street and was hit. I mean, it happened just like this." He snapped his fingers. "One moment she wanted to race, the next moment she was running, to get a head start, I guess, and the moment after that she lay in the street. The car just loomed out of the fog. The driver tried to swerve, but he had no chance. The car rolled over Trish after it hit her. I was horrified. I didn't know what to do."

Giesick seemed about to cry. He moaned and covered his face with his hands.

"What make car did you drive that night?" I asked.

"Why, Trish's new Monte Carlo, of course."

"I don't understand. The vehicle you pointed out to the traffic officer was an Oldsmobile Cutlass."

"No, it wasn't! It was the only car in that parking lot. Helluva traffic officer if he can't tell a goddam Olds from a Monte Carlo!" Remarkable how quickly Giesick shed his grief. His flare-up had been sudden, volatile; an instant later he reverted to the looking-at-the-watch routine.

"Dr. Giesick, I understand this isn't the first time one of your wives has been killed in a hit-and-run accident."

"Where did you hear that?" He smiled engagingly.

"From Patricia's parents."

"Oh, so that's what this is all about?" He laughed, a laugh filled with relief. He lifted his arms toward the ceiling, stretching, tension flowing from his body. "You're concerned because you thought this happened before? Well, it didn't. Shit, you've been around, you know how it is with guys and broads. I told Trish that story to get sympathy. Works every time with women. I also told her I'd been married to Miss Texas. It was to impress her, to make me look special. But, hell, you can check with my two ex-wives. There's nothing dead about them." He smiled, stretched again. "I'll be damned. I don't mind saying you made me nervous with all those calls. I didn't do anything wrong—Christ, I'm a victim, I lost my wife—but with no witnesses, no telling what you suspected me of."

"Do you still have the Monte Carlo?"

"Yes, at my place in Irving." Giesick's assumption that Homicide's involvement stemmed from the rumor of a previous hit-and-run had a soothing effect on him. It might also make him careless. Con men, a group in which I strongly suspected he held membership, often let their thinking become sloppy. They get spoiled by easy successes. I kept thinking about Winter Haven, California. If he didn't bother to get that right—Winter Haven is in Florida, I've been there—I figured plenty of other loose ends existed.

"You left New Orleans rather abruptly after your wife died," I said.

"Yes. I'm very sorry I did that. I was in shock. I'm trained to deal with emergencies, but I couldn't handle this. I couldn't think. I didn't know what to do. I had to get away, let someone else see to the details."

"That was the Albanowskis."

"Yes. I panicked. I couldn't bring myself to tell those people their only child was dead. There was a preacher at the hospital. A Reverend Kolemay. I asked him to call and break the news. Then I drove the Monte Carlo to the airport, left it in a parking garage, and flew to Houston. I spent the night there."

Sam Corey said Giesick had spent the night with him.

"Where did you go from Houston?"

"The next morning I flew to Dallas. That was the seventeenth of January."

"When did you stay at Sam Corey's house?"

"The night of the seventeenth."

It had been the sixteenth, according to Corey. One of them made a mistake or lied; it didn't seem a point you'd make a mistake about. I looked at Giesick, fresh and chipper. I guess he didn't know about Corey's statement, though actually, he did. He figured the statement no longer existed, that it had been stolen.

"When did you pick up your car from the airport parking garage?"

"On the eighteenth. I flew back to New Orleans. I'd also left my clothes behind at the motel, and I picked them up. Then I drove back to Dallas."

Corey said he didn't know when Giesick picked up the car. He claimed Giesick had stayed at his house until the two flew to New Jersey on Sunday the twentieth. Surely Giesick couldn't have gone to New Orleans without Corey's knowing it.

"When did you hook up with Sam Corey to go to the funeral?"

"I stayed two days alone in Patricia's apartment, after picking up the car. That's how I think of it, as Patricia's apartment, but it belonged to both of us. Those were the worst two days I've ever spent, surrounded by all those memories of her." He seemed about to break down again, and I wondered how the act would fly in front of a jury. "After two days I couldn't stand it anymore. I tell you, all the tears were drained out of my body. I was still crying, but they were dry sobs. I flew to San Antonio and asked Sam if he'd accompany me to New Jersey."

Astounding, I thought. Did he believe the Massage Parlor King of Texas would lend a touch of dignity to the last rites? Actually he'd collected donations to say masses. Regardless. I didn't think Giesick had spent two days in that apartment. Patricia had left it in the condition I'd seen.

"Do you have any identification?" I asked. "Something with your name on it."

Giesick tensed slightly. Again a flicker of wariness appeared in his eyes. His voice was casual and steady, though, as he said, "Sure," and reached for his wallet.

He handed me an Oklahoma driver's license issued in December to Claudius James Giesick, birthdate October 11, 1947, current address Ardmore, Oklahoma. I held the license longer than I had to, taking notes, and could see Giesick looking at his watch again. The issue of identity seemed to guarantee a nervous reaction from him.

"According to the motel records, you used a credit card issued to Dr. Charles Guilliam. Who is Dr. Guilliam?"

Giesick got to his feet, once again the busy young doctor in a hurry. He stared impatiently at the watch, then at me, pacing faster and faster in quick little circles. "Dr. Guilliam's a friend of mine. A business associate. Look, I've really spent longer with you than I should have. I'm going to have to break the speed limit to catch that plane. You won't alert any of your cop friends, will you?" He chuckled, and put his hand on the doorknob.

I wanted to arrest him right then. I would have, too, if we'd been in Louisiana, but in Texas I had no more authority than the average citizen. The bigamy charge was serious enough—a felony in Texas, he'd likely get five years—but my real purpose was finding a legal means to lay hands on the Monte Carlo. If the physical evidence Mutz said we needed actually existed, it likely would be found on the hit-and-run vehicle, and the most obvious car was Giesick's "wedding present" to Patricia. Pop him with bigamy and the law says there's probable cause to impound the Monte Carlo.

Giesick had the door open. "Check with my ex-wives, ya hear?" he said. "You won't find any previous hit-and-run, and both of us can stop worrying about this."

"We'll probably be seeing each other again," I said.

"Loosen up," he said. He cast his eyes around the adjoining reception room. "Have some fun. There'll be plenty of real murders to solve." Then he was out the door and outside and gone.

Despite his poses, the mention of Guilliam had driven Giesick out. He feared that connection most, which gave me the exact area to investigate next. But did he fear only the uncovering of bigamy? Five years can scare anybody. Or did the unmasking of Guilliam lead to murder?

Likes and dislikes shouldn't play any role in a criminal investigation, but personal impressions and judgments can't be avoided. I didn't like Giesick, and would happily have arrested him in the massage parlor if I could have. He seemed to me a poseur of the first rank, and I thought of Patricia and felt I got an insight into the meaning of naive. Then again, *I* had reason to be suspicious. Patricia hadn't. Nor had her friends, Joseph Richardson and Nancy Queens, found cause to warn her.

I didn't like Giesick? The word "like" soon became so mild it lost all meaning. Hate is closer, but not close enough. And fear. Gut-wrenching, sickening, helpless fear. The absolute worst kind of fear.

I returned to the Holiday Inn. When I opened the door, my room looked like a blue norther had blown through, and the red flashing message light on the phone, bright and insistent, blinked an ominous warning.

— 6 —

"HE'S GOING TO kill our kids?"

I knew tears glistened in Diane's eyes, and her hands trembled, but she maintained more control than I did.

"He didn't say that, John."

"What did he say? Tell me exactly." Geesus, a third degree of my own wife.

"He said, 'I understand your kids are sick, but they're going to get sicker.' "

"Diane, here's what I want you to do. Call your father and ask him to pick up you and the children right away. Pack a few things, just enough for two or three days, and go stay with him. You'll be okay in your dad's home."

"Why can't you come back?" It wasn't a question. She was telling me as strongly as she could.

"Honey, this is connected to the Albanowski case. That's the only thing it could be. And I'm pretty sure I know who made that phone call." I could picture his fat face. For all my days I'll be able to picture it. "The best way to deal with this is to stop it. Cut it off right now. Sweetheart, I can't spend the rest of my life guarding you and the children. I want to come home. Please believe me. I love you and Todd and Amy. But you'll be okay at your dad's home. I'll make sure of that." But how can you ever be sure? "I'll be home as soon as I can—just a couple of days. I'll fix this so we won't ever have to worry about that man."

"Be careful, John."

"You'll be okay, Diane. I'll be home soon. You and the kids will be safe."

I was trembling when I hung up the phone. It was good Diane couldn't see me. I slammed a fist into one of the pillows on the bed, overwhelmed by frustration, helplessness, and rage. My mind began transmitting terribly unwelcome scenarios of what could happen to my wife and children—even what life would be like for me without them. I knew it would be intolerable. The individual threatening my family, I thought irrationally, forced me to realize, ponder, how much I needed that family.

Do something, I urged myself. *You've been trained not to get paralyzed by a crisis.*

I called Fred Dantagnan and told him about the phone call Diane had received. My hands were cold and the story took longer than it should have to relate. I kept thinking about the Reverend Samuel Corey and organized crime, and figured every likelihood existed that the Massage Parlor King could carry out his vicious threat. Jack Burleson in Richardson, not a man given to dramatics, said Corey currently was embroiled in a war, a war featuring some very tough characters.

Fred got right to the point. "That scumbag Corey don't understand. I could go see him." He chuckled. "Take Bruno along. Bruno speaks his language."

Fred's own children might just as well have been threatened, so close were our two families (he was Amy's godfather), but any cop would have been just as angry. When he said Corey didn't "understand," he meant the unwritten, rarely voiced, but very real law governing the code of conduct between criminal and police: you never threaten a cop, and you absolutely never harm one, or his family. The criminal knows it brings too much grief. Police officers, often feeling isolated from the rest of society, which they believe doesn't understand them and can even be hostile to their efforts, tend to become clannish and protective toward one another. This "us versus them" mentality, plus the fact that there are more police than any criminal gang could ever muster, makes it unwise to threaten, or do harm to, a cop or his closest loved ones. The Mafia understands this perhaps best of all. No matter how harsh and brutal this criminal outfit might be to its enemies, it is unfailingly polite to police, never using or threatening force. Professional criminals understand that eliminating one cop guarantees five will take his place, getting rid of five brings twenty-five, and so on, they'll just keep coming. All of which didn't comfort me. It would be no solace if my children were harmed by someone who didn't understand the rules.

I thought nothing could have been more heinous than threatening my family—except for the carrying out of the threat. Or, potentially, more effective. I couldn't imagine a police officer backing off from a threat aimed at him. I know I couldn't. You'd have to get into a new line of work if you backed off, or remain on the job haunted by the knowledge that you didn't have what it takes. But your family? What written or unwritten law required your family to be in danger? Thinking about harm coming to Diane and the children was too much to bear.

"I'm worried about my kids, Fred," I said. He was still thinking, and chuckling, about his and Bruno's having a tête-à-tête with Corey.

The Bruno Fred referred to was Bruno Drury, former uniform on patrol, now assigned to traffic court. A man who resembled television's Fred Munster, but without Munster's sunny disposition. Drury had collected so many brutality charges (he hated everybody, regardless of race, color, or creed) the police brass transferred him to the rather unprovocative atmosphere of traffic court. Bruno could have been fired, I suppose, but who needed him loose on the street?

"I know you're worried, buddy. And I wish I could tell

you to rest easy. But I'll keep a close eye on your family, and I'll spread the word around here."

I knew this was no idle promise. It wouldn't have mattered if Fred were an enemy rather than my best friend. You don't threaten a cop; worse, a cop's kids. "I appreciate your help."

"Bullshit. You want me to send Bruno to Texas to talk to Corey?"

"I'll take care of Corey."

I'd been sitting on the motel room's rug, on the only spot not littered by clothes and papers. Someone—Corey himself, I suspected—had turned the room inside-out, and not bothered to conceal the fact. He wanted me to know. My suitcase was open and upside-down, dresser drawers and their contents scattered across the floor, even the mattress had been pulled off the bed. The ransack job was total.

I didn't have to strain to figure out why: the statement I'd taken from Corey. A tapestry of lies. Something he never should have signed. The fact he hadn't found it was a triumph of sorts, and owed to my conservative approach to being a detective. I'd figured even when I got the promotion I might not be a super sleuth, able to sniff out the most esoteric clues and from them build rock-solid cases, but with caution I could avoid bumbling and mistakes. Attention to detail was something I wanted to be second nature. I'd feared a fire, a maid accidentally scooping it up, whatever; as soon as I had Corey's statement, I deposited it in the San Antonio Police Department's property-and-evidence safe.

Giesick's meeting with me now made sense. Corey must have ordered it. He would have realized a conference with the elusive Giesick was the one thing guaranteed to get me away from the motel. So Giesick really had a reason to hurry: once he saw I'd kept our appointment, he knew Corey had plenty of time to break into the room and find what he wanted. No reason for continued questioning.

Only the con man's love of chatter and belief in the magic of his own persuasive powers kept him around.

Getting into the room posed no problem. Such locks are easily picked or jimmied, and a person skilled with a butter knife, credit card, or other piece of plastic or steel can enter as quickly as turning the knob. Countless victims have made the mistake of leaving money or valuables in a locked motel room, thinking them safe.

I couldn't fathom how Corey's mind worked. What possibly could he hope to gain by threatening my children? Adding an exclamation point to the threat by making it clear he'd broken into my room? Such actions showed a total misunderstanding of a cop's nature. The cop couldn't conceivably focus his attention elsewhere, give in, or run away. He'd have to resign not only from the police force but from the human race. Corey had made a mistake signing that statement, but a bigger one with his threat. Fred Dantagnan would indeed spread the word around the department; ultimately it would filter up to Commander Mutz. If the case called for more manpower, he'd see to it. It wouldn't be people just doing a job. No one is more fanatical than a police officer summoned to help an officer in danger.

Dumb, dumb, dumb, I thought, the more I considered that threat to my children. But most criminals bear little resemblance to Arthur Conan Doyle's arch villain, Professor Moriarty. I'd seen a murder in the French Quarter, the victim with his head sawed off, no clues left behind, the motive robbery. No way in the world I'd solve that case, it seemed. But two hours later—two hours—the murderer tried to sell the stolen jewelry to an alerted pawnbroker.

No cause existed to be grateful for Corey's lack of understanding about how things worked. Quite the opposite. Being bold and unstable enough to make such a threat, a sure demonstration he adhered to no normal constraints, might mean he'd carry out the threat. No matter how conscientious and determined Fred and other officers would be, I had no certainty a clever killer could be stopped. All the resources of the Secret Service and the United States government hadn't kept John Kennedy alive.

It didn't help to think about Todd and Amy and Diane, though I couldn't avoid it. Cold, empty fear filled me. I knew stopping Corey and Giesick would end the threat, and I had to concentrate on that end to keep from going crazy. But with all my thoughts about Corey's mistakes, I couldn't prove anything against him. Nor was I closer to connecting Giesick with murder: in that critical area I'd so far been outwitted. *Physical evidence,* I told myself. That could only mean Giesick's car.

"I've got some problems," I said to Jack Burleson, when the operator put me through to him in Richardson. I still sat on my little island on the floor.

"I thought I might hear from you again," said the veteran lieutenant. "You made a case on Giesick yet?"

"Not for murder. For bigamy. You remember my mentioning Dr. Charles Guilliam?"

"The guy with the credit card?"

"Right. Well, Guilliam's Giesick. Or Giesick is Guilliam." *Geesus,* I thought, *you sound like a bad comic.* "Giesick is living a double life. He's Giesick in Dallas. As Giesick, he married Patricia Albanowski. In San Antonio he's Guilliam. He was already married when the ceremony with Patricia took place."

"Can you prove it?"

"Yes. I have a copy of the certificate of his marriage to Katherine Ann Kaiser. I don't know if they divorced, but they're still living together. I hear that's a common-law marriage in Texas."

"You heard right."

"I've got two I.D.'s from neighbors saying Giesick is Guilliam. Also, a written statement from a San Antonio police officer showing the same thing."

"What can I do for you?"

"I need a warrant for Giesick's arrest."

"You'll have to testify."

"How soon can we set it up?"

"Catch a plane first thing in the morning. I'll work on it in the meantime, and pick you up at the airport."

"I want to get out tonight." I told Burleson about the threat to my children and the ransacking of the room. I said I wanted to move quickly.

"You think Corey went through your room?" I hadn't mentioned Corey to Burleson.

"Who else?"

"That's right. Who else?"

"I got a signed statement from him, Jack. He didn't waste time telling the truth."

"Come as soon as you can. I'll meet you at the airport. There's a motel right there, and I'll have you registered under a different name."

The next morning, February 19, I testified in the court of Justice of the Peace Robert Cole, Dallas County, Texas, and he issued an arrest warrant for Claudius James Giesick on the charge of bigamy. Burleson at my side, I found the nearest phone and called Koby in San Antonio. I told him about the arrest warrant, and asked as a favor—one cop to another—if he'd collar Giesick quickly. Most important, I said I wanted the Monte Carlo impounded and the car, particularly the undercarriage, given a thorough examination by the crime lab.

What happened during the accident had been unusual. I'd questioned a number of New Orleans traffic officers and they told me that when a vehicle strikes an individual, the person, if struck center-hood, usually flips onto the top of the car; if struck off-center, the victim catapults up and away from the automobile. Not always. Usually.

Patricia had been run over. This, I learned, rarely happens without the involvement of a second car. The first vehicle splays the victim onto the pavement, and a second car does the running over. Since the hit-and-run auto passed over Patricia, crushing her, any physical evidence would likely be on the undercarriage.

I made three more calls before leaving the courthouse. First, to Diane, staying with her parents. She said she and

Todd and Amy were fine. A brave front. Diane had taken an interest in the case from its inception, identifying with the Albanowskis' grief, and I'd used her as a sounding board for my conjectures. Thus, she knew almost as much about the Reverend Samuel Corey as I did, and the knowledge couldn't be comforting to her.

Second, I called Fred Dantagnan. "That's some father-in-law you've got," he said.

"Mr. Walzer?"

"He's got spirit. Was over to your place when he moved Diane and the kids. I don't think they saw me. He packed a rusty old handgun, looked like he meant to use it if he had to. Warmed my heart to see a father out protecting his brood. Doubt if that gun would shoot, though. Geesus, it was old."

"You're keeping an eye on my family?" I knew he was.

"A lot of us are."

"I really don't know how to thank you."

"That's bullshit, buddy!" He hesitated a moment. "How about Corey? You hooked him into the girl's death yet?"

"No. But I got a statement from him. It's filled with lies."

"Well, keep on him. Keep on him good."

Third, I called Mick Hanson. The Mutual of Omaha director of special services heard me out, then said he'd fly into Dallas the next morning.

That afternoon Burleson and I managed to locate the Chevrolet dealership where Giesick had purchased the Monte Carlo. I obtained the motor number from the dealer—Johnson Chevrolet—and checked with Bob McKinnon Chevrolet in New Orleans verifying it as the car Giesick had brought in for repairs. I also needed the motor number when the San Antonio police impounded the vehicle. I had high hopes the crime lab could connect the Monte Carlo with the hit-and-run. Routine drudgery, and I kept apologizing to Burleson for dragging him along (we went to four dealerships before finding Johnson Chevrolet), but such details can win or lose convictions. Already complicated (I had no idea how the hit-and-run vehicle got introduced into the killing), the business about the car merited close attention.

The new Dallas–Fort Worth Regional Airport, virtually a city in itself, had its own security building and police force. Mick Hanson, Mutual of Omaha's man, gray-haired, conservatively dressed, in his early fifties, radiated competence and professionalism, and predicted his company would fight Giesick's claim "all the way." Hanson arranged for us to conduct our interviews in one of the rooms of the airport security building.

We first talked to Judy Martin, aged twenty-six, a sales representative for Tele-Trip, a subsidiary of Mutual of Omaha. I conducted the questioning.

"Judy, did Dr. Giesick purchase this insurance from you personally?"

"No. I believe he bought it on January thirteenth. I talked to him on the tenth."

"Where did the conversation take place?"

"At Love Field in Dallas. At our Tele-Trip counter. Dr. Giesick and a friend came in and asked about travel insurance."

A friend?

My heart beat a little faster. I'd told Hanson nothing about the Reverend Samuel Corey, so he had to be surprised when I diverted the thrust of the questioning away from Giesick.

"Do you remember anything about this friend?"

"Remember him? I'll say I do. He was enormous. Not tall. Obese. Terrifically obese."

"How was he dressed?"

"Slacks, a shirt and tie."

"Is this the man?" I handed her a picture of Corey.

"Yes. Hard to forget him, isn't it? He stood just a few feet away from me, but I'd remember him from a crowd."

"Let me get back to Dr. Giesick and January tenth. What did he want to know about travel insurance?"

"Dr. Giesick asked if the policy would cover a hit-and-run accident. He told me he had a friend this happened to and the insurance company didn't pay off."

"Judy, you're sure Dr. Giesick specifically asked about insurance that covered a hit-and-run?" I wanted her to say it twice.

"Positively. He zeroed in on it. He wanted to know if Plan C of our policy covered him while riding in an automobile and also as a pedestrian. I said Plan C would cover him as a pedestrian on any public street or highway and in any automobile or scheduled public carrier."

"He said he wanted the insurance for himself?"

"Yes, particularly coverage for himself as a pedestrian. He indicated he had plans for a trip to Africa. He talked about the narrow roads over there, and his fear of being hit."

"How much coverage did he want?" I thought about the brazen Giesick. Sao Sebastio University? A trip to Africa?

"The maximum. I told him two hundred thousand dollars. He said he'd think it over and left."

"I want to thank you, Judy. Before you sign a statement, would you look at this picture?"

"That's Dr. Giesick."

Next we talked with David Merrick, aged twenty-one, also a sales representative of Tele-Trip. I had to give Mick Hanson credit. Without his having everyone we needed lined up, the interviews could have taken days. As I conducted them, part of my mind wondered what progressed in San Antonio toward grabbing Giesick. Surely there wouldn't be the same maddening difficulty I'd experienced reaching him on the phone, and I'd told Koby how to contact me when the bust came down. No word had arrived yet. I understood the anxiety of citizens who made pests of themselves by calling every few hours to learn the progress of a case. I wasn't sure I could keep resisting the temptation to call Koby.

"David," I said to sales representative Merrick, "you

were present at Love Field when a Dr. Claudius James Giesick made inquiries about a travel insurance policy? I believe this was January tenth.''

"Yes, it was."

"Did you speak to Dr. Giesick?"

"Yes."

"Both you and Judy Martin talked with Dr. Giesick?"

"That's right. But she was away some of the time. With another customer. I think she probably talked to Dr. Giesick when I got called away."

"Was anyone with Dr. Giesick?"

"You mean the first time? On the tenth? I saw him again on the thirteenth, you know. When he bought the insurance at Dallas–Fort Worth airport. His wife accompanied him then. At Love Field on the tenth a man was with him."

"This man?" I handed over the picture of Corey. All of this could be critically important later: showing the cold-blooded nature of the crime, that Corey had been along shopping for the insurance.

"You use a wide-angle lens for this?" I could see Mick Hanson stifle a grin. He didn't know why I had an interest in Corey, but he could see the mass of flesh peering out of the picture. Neither of us suspected young Merrick had such a sense of humor. "Yes," he said, "that's the man I saw with Dr. Giesick. What does he do, if you don't mind my asking?"

"Religious work," I said. "He used to run a nursing home." *That's right*, I thought, *the Arm of Mercy nursing home*. I didn't know whether to laugh or shudder. "Did Giesick's companion say anything to you?"

"To be honest, I thought he was Dr. Giesick's attorney. He never said anything to me. He told Dr. Giesick what questions to ask. All of them had to do with hit-and-run coverage. Very specific questions. If this or that sort of hit-and-run happened, would it be covered?"

"Did Giesick ask about any other type accident besides hit-and-run? Did he wonder about coverage if his car collided with another car? If an airplane crashed? If he was struck by an automobile, but the driver of the auto didn't leave the scene?''

"None of those. Every question related to hit-and-run. That's a phrase, by the way, that doesn't appear on any insurance policy.''

I looked at Merrick and thought how pleasant it would be to hear him tell his story to a jury. Talk about cold blood! Corey and Giesick personified icy tundras, frozen antarctic glaciers, Siberian blasts of frigid wind so chilling they could bowl a person over flat, quick-freezing forever what an instant before had been warm and alive.

I wanted to see the faces of those jury members. Watch as they let young Merrick's words sink in. While Patricia tidied her apartment for their return and dreamed of a warm Caribbean cruise, her lover, accompanied by the grotesque preacher, asked detailed, probing questions about big-money hit-and-run insurance coverage.

But Merrick would be just part of a piece, if I did my job well. The Giesick-Corey murder conspiracy surely had begun earlier than the January 10 meeting at Love Field. It truly would add up to murder in cold blood.

"Were you present on January thirteenth,'' I asked Merrick, "when the insurance was purchased?''

"Yes. It was at the Dallas–Fort Worth airport, on the day of its grand opening. That's why I was at D-FW, to help handle an expected big crowd. Dr. Giesick's wife, Patricia, was with him, and it surprised me that she purchased the insurance. I'd gotten the impression on January tenth that the coverage would be for him.''

"Was Giesick's friend along on January thirteenth?''

"I didn't see him.''

"What was the face value of the policy Mrs. Giesick purchased?''

"It was two hundred thousand dollars. He originally wanted three hundred thousand, but a problem came up and he settled for the lesser amount.''

"What kind of problem?''

"I really don't know. You'll have to ask Pat Bailey, the manager on duty. Actually, she sold the policy to Mrs. Giesick."

Patricia Bailey, aged thirty-five, remembered the Giesicks very well, and not because Patricia Albanowski was so attractive, a genuine head-turner, but because she'd been so nervous.

"What do you mean by nervous?"

"Two things. As she filled out the policy application, I asked if she had other insurance with Mutual of Omaha. Dr. Giesick interrupted, saying he had two hundred thousand dollars' worth. Then Mrs. Giesick said, 'No, three hundred thousand, the same amount you want me to buy.' She seemed flustered by the amounts of money being discussed. The second time I noticed her nervousness was when she wrote in the name of the beneficiary. Her hand shook something fierce as she wrote her husband's name. Only one line was provided for it. She hesitated, her hand trembling like someone with palsy. Then she printed, underneath the beneficiary's name, the names of Stanley and Josephine Albanowski. I don't know what good she thought that would do. Dr. Giesick was listed as beneficiary. I don't understand, either, the dispute—and it was a sharp one—over whether Dr. Giesick had two hundred thousand or three hundred thousand in coverage."

I could make a guess. Remembering Giesick in the massage parlor, I could almost hear him telling his bride: "Look, sweetheart, I've taken out insurance for you. God forbid something should happen to me, and we can't spend the rest of our lives together, but if it does you'll be taken care of. By the same token, not that I'll ever need money, nor that money could ever replace you, but it just seems right, togetherish, that you do for me what I've already done for you."

I suspected that's how Giesick persuaded Patricia to take out the insurance, and knew I'd be very surprised if any policy existed on Giesick. I didn't understand the numbers game debate—two hundred thousand or three hundred thousand dollars—but that became clear with the answer to my next question.

"Exactly how much insurance did Mrs. Giesick buy?"

"It was two hundred thousand. When the couple approached the counter, Dr. Giesick told me his wife wanted to purchase a travel policy. He specifically stated she wanted a three-hundred-thousand annual policy, Plan C. I explained that two hundred thousand covered vehicles, common carriers, and scheduled air travel. I said the remaining one hundred thousand would cover only common carriers and scheduled airlines. Dr. Giesick seemed surprised. He asked if the additional hundred thousand included automobile accidents. I said no. He then said he didn't want the extra hundred thousand."

So that's how it had been, I thought. Giesick and Corey believed they could buy three hundred thousand dollars of coverage, not realizing only two hundred thousand dollars would apply to hit-and-run accidents. Relying on misinformation, Giesick told Patricia the coverage for which she was beneficiary amounted to three hundred thousand dollars. Of course, he refused to pay a penny extra for something he knew he wouldn't need, so he scuttled the extra hundred thousand dollars that didn't apply to a hit-and-run. A jury, hearing Patricia Bailey, would face deciding whether Giesick possessed a gift of seeing the future or if his interest only in hit-and-run coverage meant he had already sealed his wife's fate.

The fourth and last person Mick Hanson arranged for me to interview was Dolly Johnson, aged forty-nine, a Tele-Trip employee on duty at Love Field on January 12, two days after the first visit by Corey and Giesick, the day before Giesick and Patricia actually purchased the insurance.

"Did you talk with Dr. Claudius Giesick last January twelfth?"

"Yes. He came to the Tele-Trip booth at Love Field. He inquired about our annual travel policy, Plan C. I took out the rate sheet, and showed him the two-hundred-thousand-dollar coverage. I told him Plan C would cover him in his vehicle or as a pedestrian on a public street or highway. I informed him that by adding a one-hundred-thousand-dollar rider to Plan C, he could get the total to three hundred thousand.''

"But the extra hundred thousand wouldn't cover him as a pedestrian.''

"Right. I guess he didn't understand that. Anyway, he was very interested in the policy. He said he'd be back later that night to sign the papers. Not until then did he tell me he wanted the policy for his wife. At this time his friend suggested we draw up the policy in advance and have it waiting when the Giesicks returned to sign.''

"Who was this friend?''

"I don't know his name. But he hovered close, listening to everything. He seemed to be prompting Dr. Giesick when he thought questions needed to be asked.''

"Could you describe the friend?''

"You better bet I could. A fat man.'' She thought for a moment. "A *very* fat man.''

Mick Hanson and I had lunch in the airport. I couldn't sit still. I squirmed in my chair, crumpled napkins, absent-mindedly started to sprinkle salt on the side order of ham I'd asked for with my scrambled eggs. "I can't wait any longer,'' I said to an uncomprehending Hanson. I went outside the coffee shop to a pay phone.

"How you guys doing?'' I asked Koby. I wanted to chew him out for not having arrested Giesick yet. Indeed, I was experiencing the frustration any citizen does when, not knowing what is going on, he decides the police are loafing. Of course, the sane part of my brain told me, what's important for one person may carry an extremely low priority for another. Thoughts of Giesick filled my mind, but the San Antonio police might figure they had larger game to bag than a bigamist.

"I was about to call you,'' Koby said. "We grabbed Giesick.''

So much for police loafing. But he couldn't read my mind, so I didn't apologize. "Did you get the car?''

"It's being towed to the crime lab for processing.''

"When will we get word?''

"Should be later today."

"That's impressive," I said. The guilties attacked me, pangs of conscience that usually strike during a hangover. To hell with them. Why should I confess to Koby? "Did you pop Giesick yourself?"

"No. He was picked up by a couple of uniforms. He pulled up to the Tuxford Drive address in his Monte Carlo, but when he spotted the uniforms he fled. High-speed chase and all of that, but he didn't get far."

"He gonna get out on bail again?"

"You know the rules, John. Money walks, bullshit talks. Bigamy is a bondable offense. If he's got the money, he's walking."

"Helluva world." I didn't want to think about the connections between money and justice, either. "Well, you've got the car," I said cheerily. "I'll call you later today for the results."

I phoned just before 5:00 P.M. "I've got good news and bad news," Koby said.

Geesus. "Give me the bad," I said.

"Giesick made bail."

"Corey?"

"Corey."

"Lay the good on me."

"The lab guys found scrape marks on the frame of the Monte Carlo. They also picked a strand of hair off the right side of the radiator."

"No blood? Clothing?"

"Just the hair. And the scrape marks. The car hit something."

"The hair might be enough." I thought about what needed doing. "Look, Koby, do me one more favor. Have the crime lab put the hair in a petri dish, tape it, initial it for identification purposes, and shoot it off to the FBI lab in D.C. You'll need a cover letter to the FBI telling them what we want: whether or not the hair is human, and anything else they can tell by microscoping it. As I'm sure you know, the criminalist who removed the hair has to handle all the paperwork. Preserve the chain of evidence. Finally, ask that the results be sent to me in New Orleans.''

"I'll do it, buddy.''

I knew it would be a week before I heard from the FBI. Well, it was past time to get home to take care of my family. And plenty else I could do in New Orleans, like accumulate the thousand-and-one fractions of evidence needed to construct an airtight murder case.

— 7 —

"YOU WANT ME to hammer a murder indictment through the grand jury?" First Assistant District Attorney John Volz leaned back in his big leather easy chair, clasped his hands in his lap, and smiled condescendingly. A patient man, he'd take the time to explain the facts of life to this kid detective.

"That's right," I said. "Hammer through a murder indictment. What I've given you a blind man could see."

"You're wrong," Volz said in a soft voice. He was in his middle-thirties, but his striking good looks and sterling reputation combined to give him a dignity usually associated with a much older man. Six feet two and elegantly slender, hair prematurely gray, always impeccably dressed, the handsome, cosmopolitan Volz had for years been D.A. Jim Garrison's most trusted aide. Both Garrison and Volz were big, impressive men not given to a lot of words, and you needed only to see them enter a room to be enticed by their charisma. The phrase "commanding presence" came to mind. With cases always well prepared, these articulate, deep-voiced prosecutors were spellbinders in front of a jury.

D.A. Jim Garrison was on his way out of office at this time. Thanks largely to the adverse publicity he'd reaped from his prosecution of Clay Shaw, the wealthy head of the New Orleans International Trade Mart, for conspiracy in the assassination of President John Kennedy, Garrison lost the November 1973 election to Harry Connick, and the changing of the guard to Connick was currently in progress. Volz stayed around to make the transition a smooth one. Soon he would be U.S. Attorney for the Eastern District of Louisiana, a big step up.

Like every police officer in New Orleans, like much of the country, I'd closely followed Garrison's prosecution of Clay Shaw. It seemed an astounding number of people in Shaw's circle had dealings with Lee Harvey Oswald. Knowing Garrison, and the spectacular percentage of convictions he had obtained, I thought (and so did my friends on the force) he probably had Shaw dead to rights, but then his case disintegrated, torpedoing his career and making him a laughingstock in much of the press. Except for the Shaw case, Garrison's prosecutorial record compared favorably to anyone's.

But the Shaw case was far from my mind as I sat in John Volz's office trying to get grand jury action on Patricia Albanowski's murder. February 25, I'd been back from Texas five days, and I thought the case against Corey and Giesick was strong. Why didn't Volz see it? Had the D.A.'s office become conservative after the Shaw fiasco? Did the outgoing administration not want to prosecute a case which, though winnable, had no foregone conclusion? This last, I thought, touched closest to the truth. Most district attorneys, even the best, possess a streak of laziness, and may try to avoid cases promising a lot of work as reward. Also, they realize much of their future chances for career advancement hinge on the record they build in office: why handle a case you might lose when so many easy pickings exist elsewhere to keep the winning percentage up? In just such a manner, like football athletic directors, do some prosecutors think.

I couldn't change the overall nature of the beast, but in this instance I wanted action. My reaction to the threat against my children, the nerve of it, the sick cruelty, had changed from fear and near-panic to a hardened resolve to remove two menaces from society. The touching plight of the Albanowskis and the terrible fate that had befallen their daughter provided extra impetus for me, but subsequent events had conspired to turn the momentum into obsession.

One example: I'd done an additional, painstaking investigation at the Ramada Inn where Giesick and Patricia had stayed in New Orleans. Corey and Giesick were having breakfast in the Ramada coffee shop when told of Patricia's death. When they thought they were unobserved, they rose from their chairs, hugged, and in each other's arms did a little dance of joy.

I looked at Volz, an intimidating presence in patrician clothing; not a man to raise your voice to, not him. "I told you," I said levelly, "about Giesick and Corey in ecstasy when they heard Patricia was dead."

"You believe it was ecstasy. Your witness believes it. How do you define ecstasy? What makes the two of you experts at recognizing ecstasy? Look, if I have to play devil's advocate with you, I will. But you should understand, John, we have different jobs. You gather evidence. I have to determine if the evidence can convict. How does the happiness of these two men over your victim's death prove murder?"

"It doesn't. Not by itself. But you can't just look at one tiny part of the picture. If you study everything we have, it adds up to murder. A reasonable person couldn't see it any other way."

"Tell me again what you have." Volz leaned farther back in his leather easy chair, a faint smile still playing on his lips. I knew he was a busy man, but I wouldn't let him hurry me along. Busy or not, I wanted him to change his mind, and intended to take as long as necessary. I believed twelve jurors good and true would convict Corey and Giesick in the blink of an eye.

"Okay. Let's look at what we have," I said. "It can't be anything else but murder. Giesick and Corey set this girl up to be murdered. The motive is three hundred thousand dollars of life insurance. Giesick's a con man living two lives. No problem proving this. He resides with his wife Kathy under the assumed name of Guilliam in San Antonio. He's the swinging playboy bachelor Dr. Giesick in Dallas. Doctor, my ass. He's an auto mechanic. I hate having to check out stories I know beforehand are lies, but I do it anyway. Giesick never attended any of those high-class schools he talked about. Then there's Sam Corey. Reverend Corey. You'll love this guy. A mail-order minister who'd graduated to being the Massage Parlor King of Texas, with a stop in between for a stint as a nursing-home operator. Corey's involved with organized crime. He's fighting a gang war right now.'' I took a break to draw breath, and Volz, not a hair out of place, seized the opportunity.

''John, I'm sure they're bad guys. But everything you've told me so far is circumstantial. I can't convict Giesick of murder because he's a con man and a bigamist. I can't convict Corey of murder because he owns bordellos.''

''The whole picture,'' I said earnestly. I'd gone over this in my mind and had it indelibly etched there. ''Shortly after Giesick marries Patricia, Giesick and Corey make two trips to Love Field to talk about insurance. Hit-and-run insurance. That's all they talk about: hit-and-run, hit-and-run, hit-and-run. You can prove this. I've got signed statements. All Corey and Giesick wanted to know about was hit-and-run insurance. Lo and behold, after the insurance is bought, less than three days after the hit-and-run insurance is bought, Patricia is killed in a hit-and-run.''

''Circumstantial.'' I didn't know it that instant, but I would grow to hate that word. ''John, circumstantial evidence is effective only when no other reasonable hypothesis can be offered to explain the facts.''

''What else can explain these facts? Geesus, they set the girl up and murdered her for the insurance.''

''A decent defense attorney could find five ways to explain away your facts.'' Volz was composed, in contrast to the inner turmoil I was experiencing. ''I won't bother to tell you what the defense attorney would say. You should think on it. You'll see. Other scenarios can be found to explain away what you've told me.''

"I haven't told you half of it. I don't think it can be waved away, no matter what kind of pretzel the defense attorney twists himself into. I have a sworn statement from Corey saying he wasn't in New Orleans when Patricia was killed. He was here, all right, and proving it's as easy as rolling off a log. There's the Ramada employee who saw him doing the dance with Giesick. By the way, there's no chance of any of these identifications being mistaken. Corey sticks in a person's mind. Fay Keller, a desk clerk at the Ramada Inn, saw Giesick and Corey having breakfast together the morning Patricia died. Later, Fay Keller saw Corey and Giesick loading Giesick's clothes into a white-over-maroon car. Giesick asked if he could leave his Monte Carlo in the parking lot—he said he was returning to Texas—and pick it up later. But the next day when Fay Keller looked, the Monte Carlo was gone. Mary Alexander, Ramada's restaurant hostess, also saw Corey and Giesick having breakfast. The day before, she'd talked with Patricia. Patricia told her she'd been out walking with her husband in the early-morning hours of the fifteenth. Patricia told Mrs. Alexander it was very foggy and she'd been frightened. Read this any way you want, but it looks to me like this first early-morning stroll was a trial run. A way to find a place to do the job the next morning.''

"Circumstantial. Maybe Giesick likes to take walks at night.''

"Then there's Mary Weaver, also a desk clerk at the Ramada. She talked with Patricia at one-fifteen P.M. on the fifteenth. Patricia asked her to recommend a restaurant within walking distance because of the car's being in the repair shop. This was true enough. McKinnon Chevrolet had the Monte Carlo. *But there was nothing wrong with it.* Someone tampered with the linkage—remember, Giesick is an auto mechanic—and it took only a couple of minutes to fix. Now, at ten-thirty P.M. on the night of the fifteenth,

Patricia spoke to another Ramada employee, Elaine Harrison. Harrison said Patricia seemed lonesome and upset and just wanted someone to talk to. Patricia said she was on her honeymoon and everything had gone wrong since arriving in New Orleans: the TV had broken, the laundry had not been returned, and the car was in the repair shop. She asked about the availability of cabs to take her and her husband around the city the next day. This was ten-thirty P.M. Giesick got the car out of McKinnon Chevrolet at five-twenty-two P.M. Dammit, what reason could he have for not telling her?''

"I can think of a couple. And they'd sound very plausible.''

"Get this. I talked to Carla Earl, a maid. She not only can place Giesick and Corey in the Ramada restaurant, but she remembers Corey as the same big fat man walking around the parking lot of the Quality Inn, right next door. I checked at the Quality Inn. Corey rented a room there in the early-morning hours of the fifteenth." I grew agitated. "Balls o' fire, what's all this telling us? The preacher who performs the marriage, a marriage he knows is bigamous —we can prove Corey knows Kathy Giesick—shows up twice in Dallas with Giesick asking about hit-and-run insurance, then appears in New Orleans just before the hit-and-run takes Patricia's life.''

"I'm telling you, John, it's circumstantial." Volz was a rock, or maybe a sponge. He could survive any blow, or at least absorb it, and remain unmoved. Next to him the Sphinx would seem outgoing. Well, he hadn't heard the best yet.

"Then there's E. J. Swindler, the night desk clerk at the Quality Inn. He said that early in the morning of the sixteenth Corey came through the lobby of the motel. Corey claimed he had a headache and asked where he could purchase some aspirin. He added he hated to drive in the fog, but the headache was a bad one. Swindler remembers Corey returning twenty-five minutes later. So what do we have? You know much better than I do. Motive and opportunity. The insurance money is the motive, and Corey had the opportunity. He left his room about the time Patricia was killed.''

"Circumstantial."

"Circumstantial, shit!" Sassing a district attorney couldn't endear me to the city law-enforcement hierarchy. And it could get me in trouble. One phone call from Volz to Mutz and I'd be on the carpet for a chewing out. But I was hot, and frustrated, too. The circumstances (Geesus, *I* was thinking that word!) couldn't add up to anything else but murder, and the slick, debonair Volz seemed monumentally unmoved. I looked at him and wanted to muss his hair, shake his shoulders, something. He knew he could indict on the evidence we had. Give it a shot, anyway. What was the alternative? And how could we live with what the alternative implied? Permitting Giesick and Corey to walk meant allowing them to get away with murder. But more. It could mean sentencing another Patricia to death. I didn't think they would hesitate to kill again for money.

None of this impressed John Volz, who sat stationary and relaxed in his leather chair, hands clasped, wearing his patient schoolteacher smile. The only way to reach him was through reason, the tack I thought I'd been employing.

"John," I said quietly, "I can't produce an eyewitness to a case when there isn't one. And I can't produce physical evidence if there isn't any. Granted, the evidence is circumstantial, but you won't find a stronger circumstantial case. I know prosecutors have convicted on a lot less than I've given you.''

"That's your opinion." He hesitated. I marveled at how a person could converse without any gestures. "It's not mine. From what you've presented to me, we might—just might—get indictments, but never a conviction. Let me explain, again, why: for every reason you've given me to suspect Corey and Giesick, a defense attorney could fashion an alternative explanation. One factor influencing you— and myself also, I admit, and I have to fight it—is that you know the background of these individuals. The jury probably won't know. The state has to prove its case beyond a reasonable doubt. If the defense attorneys decide a defense isn't needed, that the case hasn't been proved, then Corey and Giesick won't take the stand. We won't be able to delve into their backgrounds. Hearsay evidence is admissible in grand jury proceedings, but not during trial. Thus, all the lies Corey and Giesick told you might never be heard by the jury. And the background information you've dug up, which, it's clear, reveals what low types these two are, probably won't be admissible. The fact that they're shady characters has no relevance to whether they murdered Patricia Albanowski.''

"I believe I could testify about what Corey told me. That he wasn't in New Orleans when Patricia was killed. That wouldn't be precluded by the hearsay rule. Then, you could call Fay Keller, Mary Alexander, Carla Earl, E. J. Swindler, and others I haven't even told you about yet to testify that he was in the city. I can give dozens of examples like this. Giesick told me he's a doctor of psychology. Witnesses can be called to prove he isn't. Corey said he was in Texas when he learned of Patricia's death from Mrs. Albanowski. How's that going to look? Remember, he signed a statement to that effect. Who do you think a jury will believe, Mrs. Albanowski or Corey?''

"I don't think any of this would be admissible.''

"Well, I do.'' I knew as soon as I spoke how presumptuous it sounded. Volz was the lawyer, a highly respected one. Nevertheless, although it probably would be a fight to get everything admitted, I believed it could be done. I suspected Volz viewed the case in a different manner. He could very well be thinking in terms of money. Trying Giesick and Corey could be expensive. The extradition proceedings alone would cost plenty. And, if we lost the case, a possibility, there would be a Niagara Falls cascade of criticism. So what? Let the criticism come, I felt. Letting Corey and Giesick get away with murder without a fight seemed far less acceptable. "Look,'' I said. "You haven't even heard all I've got.'' *Is there something the matter with me?* I wondered fleetingly. What I saw so clearly elicited only doubt and negative reaction from Volz.

"What else do you have?"

Didn't this man ever move? To get the kinks out? Scratch himself? Well, I'd tell him what I had, by law the road to justice passed through him, and I'd do it reasonably, in a soft voice, because emotion occupied no place in Volz's professional makeup, and it was important he be made to understand so the crime would not go unpunished.

"The Reverend John Kolemay," I said. "He's the chaplain at Methodist Hospital. At seven o'clock on the morning Patricia died, Reverend Kolemay was called to the hospital to render solace to the husband whose wife was critically injured. After talking with Kolemay, Giesick said he was returning to his motel room, and gave Kolemay the phone number where he was staying. Giesick also gave him the number of 'a salesman friend' he'd met. This salesman friend, of course, was Sam Corey, and the number was for Corey's room at the Quality Inn. Later, after Patricia died, Giesick returned to the hospital and talked with the Reverend Kolemay. Corey came along. Giesick introduced Corey as a salesman."

"Circumstantial. What does that have to do with Patricia's death?"

"Plenty. When tied to everything else."

"Most of your 'everything else' would never be heard by a jury."

"I think you could get it in."

"I don't. Where does that leave us?"

"You want an eyewitness. I can't give you one. The crime was planned so there wouldn't be an eyewitness."

"John, I don't think we can win this case. If I'm right, and we lose, then where are we?"

"I don't believe we'll lose." I really didn't think we would.

"That's why we're talking. To find out if one of us can persuade the other. But in the end we both know where the decision rests."

I guess he didn't have a diplomatic way to word it. It was just so frustrating. I knew Volz couldn't be pleased with the role he played, and did what he felt right. No matter I felt he was wrong.

"We've got Corey locked up, down, and sideways on the issue of being in New Orleans. Steve Lamartiniere, a security guard at Methodist Hospital, saw Corey about five A.M. on the sixteenth in the hospital parking lot. Corey drove up in a big black car, and Giesick went out to talk to him."

"I never doubted for a moment you could put Corey in New Orleans. That doesn't make him a murderer." I started to object but Volz gave a small wave to indicate he wanted to go on. "What we need is physical evidence. I know you're sick and tired of those words, but that's the way it is. Have you heard from the FBI on Giesick's car?"

"Not yet. I'm . . ."

"What about the black car you say Corey drove?"

"It's his personal vehicle. I checked the credit card receipt from Corey's stay at the Quality Inn. Then I contacted the credit card company and learned the charges Corey had made on the card in the last month. One charge was on January thirteenth—he was on his way from San Antonio to New Orleans—at the Belmont Motel in Lake Charles, Louisiana. I spoke to the manager and got Corey's license-plate number from the motel registration. The Department of Public Safety in Texas confirmed that the car—a 1973 black Buick—was registered to Sam Corey. But I haven't been able to impound the car for evidence. No probable cause." I drew a breath, smiled. "How about that? We could indict him for murder, but we can't impound his car." At least not until we had indicted him for murder. "I realize Corey's Buick could have been the murder vehicle. As for Giesick's car, I haven't heard from the FBI yet. I'd love it if the FBI turns something up, but we can succeed without that."

"John, I hate to keep saying it, but we disagree. That's all. I'm afraid you'll have to accept that."

I didn't see how. I was too deep into the case, too personally involved on several levels. "Let me tell you a little more about Giesick," I said. "Do we really want him walking away from this? Probably with his share of more than three hundred thousand dollars? We can prove he passes himself off as a psychologist. That Patricia, right to the end, believed he was a psychologist. I'll tell you what he really was. In 1969 Giesick was employed as an electromechanical apprentice at Kelly Air Force Base in San Antonio. In 1970 he was an auto mechanic with the C & J Speed Shop, also in San Antonio. In August 1970 he went to work as a manager-trainee for American Wheel and Brake Company. November 1970 he took a job with Tom Brown Chevrolet as a manager-trainee. When applying for credit in 1972, he listed his occupation as talent agent. Later in 1972 he and his wife, Kathy, moved to Arizona, and changed their identities to Guilliam. They obtained new drivers' licenses, credit cards, social security cards, the whole nine yards. When they returned to San Antonio in 1973, they moved into the Tuxford Drive house, and auto mechanic–car salesman Giesick was Dr. Giesick. Or Dr. Guilliam. Take your pick."

"All of that could be helpful," Volz said.

"Good," I said.

"At a later date."

"Oh."

"When you've got an eyewitness. Or, more likely, some useful physical evidence."

"Look, I . . ."

"You look, John." His voice hadn't gone up even a fraction of an octave. "Without an eyewitness, without physical evidence, you're riding a dead horse." Volz's voice softened. "If it's any consolation to you, I think those two murdered the girl. But I'll also tell you I don't think we'll ever prosecute. You'll probably have to find a way to live with that. I hope you know I'll be very distressed if my gloomy assessment proves right."

Not as distressed as I already am, I thought, as I walked

out of the Criminal Courts Building, crossed South White Street, and headed the block and a half to the desk I shared at police headquarters. It was cold and damp, typical late-February New Orleans weather (I've heard people from Wisconsin, a real winter icebox, complain about our cold, saying our forty-five degrees is worse than their zero degrees), cutting like a machete straight through clothes to chill backbones and freeze feet, and I was going head-on into a relentless wind off the Mississippi River, gray and turbulent, making progress a struggle, perfect companion to mood and case. Depression more than the environment hunched my shoulders and lowered my head.

Cursing Volz beneath my breath, sick at the thought that Corey and Giesick might prevail, convinced that someone else might die if they did, I foolishly comforted myself thinking matters couldn't deteriorate further: the only direction events could move was up, after the storm comes sunshine, etc.

Matters got worse, of course. Two days later, on February 27, my spirits descended to their nadir with the arrival of the FBI report from Washington, D.C. The FBI lab microscopic analysis, with which there could be no argument, revealed that the hair removed from the radiator of Giesick's car belonged to an animal.

I slammed a fist down on my desk and zipped an empty coffee cup across the room, the cup popping like a .22 when it exploded against the wall, the shards tinkling as they bounced, coming to rest broken and irreparable, destroyed as utterly as my case.

No one in the crowded homicide office raised a head or blinked an eye. Routine continued. I did hear someone, probably Saladino, say, "Shit, our checks are late again."

That night and the next I lingered late at Miracle Mile rotting my brain and my stomach with too much alcohol. The only thing worse than the failure and the feeling of failure was having to tell the Albanowskis that their daughter's killers would go free or that it had been a hit-and-run after all and I was sorry. Which? And Pascal Saladino, trying to help, trying to tell me what awaited every homicide detective down the line, not helping at all by saying there'd always be injustice. The worst, no, not the worst, was almost getting into a fist fight with a young uniform in a senseless argument I provoked.

The worst was seeing the disappointment and hurt in Diane's eyes the two mornings after.

And nothing got accomplished. I told myself I drank to forget the case, but each morning, bleary-eyed, bloodshot, feeling as if *I'd* been run over, I found the investigation still there in front of me, waiting for a resolution.

I'd been told by the sages at Miracle Mile "to stick it in the bottom drawer," the euphemism for forgetting it, letting it remain as an open investigation, an unsolved case, moldering, at least theoretically, forever.

Even that onerous possibility seemed preferable to what I feared would happen: a lawsuit by Giesick to change the murder's classification back to "hit-and-run," and then a second legal action to free the insurance money. How could I stop it? If the case was not a hit-and-run, where were the murder charges?

But that's not why I refused to stick it in the bottom drawer. I'd keep going—where?—because I wanted those two to pay, and because talking to Josephine and Stanley Albanowski simply wasn't acceptable.

—8—

AT 2:00 A.M., MARCH 3, I sat alone in the gray, spirit-sapping homicide room, its floor littered with paper and other debris, the ghosts of murderers past almost a palpable taunting presence. The homicide room when deserted appears to have been ransacked, the men who work this grim detail being the least fastidious of people about their surroundings, though not their clothing (Mutz requires coat and tie). Desks and walls display posters and cartoons, sometimes wry, often negative, and it's impossible not to sense the prevailing mood: graveyard-humor despair over the human condition. Of course, a homicide cop views the world through a distorted lens, associating on a regular basis with assorted maniacs, misfits, and morons who also happen to be killers. Nothing better captures the dark, sanity-saving humor of a homicide detective than the black "gimme" caps a number of us wear. Emblazoned across the crown are a vulture perched atop a tombstone at the entrance to a graveyard, the single word "HOMICIDE," and the unit's unofficial slogan, "Our day begins when yours ends."

My desk's chaotic clutter made the messy floor seem a model of decorum, and compared to my mood, my most sour-thinking compatriot viewed his existence with rosy optimism. My desk hadn't started out this way. Six hours earlier, at 8:00 P.M. on March 2, the big room abuzz with locker-room jocularity, talks about planned family outings, informal chatter about which watering hole to hit at shift's end, and even an occasional reference to a case being investigated, I'd cleared off the desk, wiping it clean with a wet rag, and placed every scrap of information I'd garnered on the Albanowski case in neat, orderly stacks.

An impressive collection of paperwork: notebooks; scraps of paper; correspondence with other police agencies; typed, signed statements; copies of insurance policies; coroner's report; traffic accident report; credit card receipts; retail credit reports; crime lab reports; photographs; memos to Mutz; and dozens of photostats of documents, such as Giesick's marriage license and Corey's criminal arrest record.

Counting scraps, there had to be several hundred sheets of paper, and I intended to study each one. Drinking at Miracle Mile hadn't helped. Rather than being struck by lightning bolts of inspiration, I'd alarmed Diane and succeeded in getting straight-arrow Fred Dantagnan concerned about my well-being. "I don't think you're going to find the break you're looking for in the Mile," he at first suggested, and when this didn't work: "Don't mess up life with your family. The job will be here tomorrow, but your family might not."

But the hours that night droned by, the room slowly cleared to a few lost souls and then emptied entirely. My eyes blurred and my mind slowed. I'd told myself a good detective, when stymied, returned to review the information he'd already acquired, a notion probably obtained from watching TV mystery dramas, and convinced myself, because I needed convincing, that the solution of the case lay hidden in information previously obtained. But shuffling that mind-numbing mountain of paperwork, pausing, trying to think, to read between the lines, to see something I had missed, I succeeded in bringing on a headache and an infinitely worse backache. Sitting tense, hunched motionless over those damnable papers, the spine rebelled and twisted itself into a painful corkscrew.

I groaned aloud in the ghost-filled chamber, and thought *fuck all this and this goddam job too, what am I doing in this hellhole working for a shit system that makes murder a game and rewards asshole killers like slick-face Giesick and crap-belly Corey, any airheaded piss-brained idiot could see those two did it.*

The saner part of my personality pulled me out of this morass of no-win thinking and spotlighted the blame where it belonged, not on a system of justice but on my own shortcomings. So far I hadn't been skilled and enterprising enough to crack the case; that was where the fault lay. And the solution, if one existed, likely lay hidden in one of those unappetizing mounds of paper. I went back to them, knowing I couldn't face the alternative, admitting defeat to the Albanowskis, not now or ever.

I don't know what it was, maybe the ghosts of loved ones who'd mourned for victims in this room and now cheered me on, just as the killers hissed and hoped I'd fail, but something—about 4:00 A.M.—forced my hand to pick up the papers containing Ramada Inn desk clerk Fay Keller's statement, and then, forcing again, made my tired mind work.

There it was, in Fay Keller's own words: "I saw Dr. Giesick and a fat man loading clothes into a white-over-maroon car." *White-over-maroon.*

The car Giesick had bought Patricia was a blue Monte Carlo, and the vehicle Corey had driven to New Orleans was a black 1973 Buick. Giesick's car had been eliminated in the murder-vehicle sweepstakes by the San Antonio crime lab check and the FBI report. The Monte Carlo might indeed have been used to kill Patricia, but if so I had a problem I didn't want to think about: I'd never be able to prove the Monte Carlo was the murder weapon.

One slight hope I'd clung to after the FBI's negative report was that Corey's Buick might have run down Patricia. On such a slender thread did I hope to keep the investigation open. Although I didn't have, according to Volz, probable cause to impound the vehicle, I suspected

Corey qualified as an excellent candidate to be arrested, and his Buick could be checked over then.

But somehow I never believed the Buick was the murder weapon. Steven Lamartiniere, the security guard at Methodist Hospital, spotted Corey in the big black car, and I didn't think the preacher would risk such a foreseeable occurrence if he'd used the automobile to murder Patricia. Brazen nerve the massage parlor operator had, but did it extend to driving the car he'd used for murder to the scene where Giesick waited for his wife to die? I didn't think so.

The potential importance of Fay Keller's information gave me new momentum. It also lifted a heavy weight from my shoulders, knowing I'd received a reprieve from having to deliver crushing news to the Albanowskis.

Where to look for that white-over-maroon car? I could think of three possibilities: a third party was involved, the vehicle had been stolen, or it was a rental automobile. The last seemed the most likely. I'd been unable to uncover any information to indicate a third party, and the stolen-vehicle thesis didn't ring true to me. During the entire period surrounding the time of Patricia's death, both Corey and Giesick continually used credit cards (I had records of numerous purchases and transactions), and these pieces of plastic were usually needed to rent a car. If this third automobile had been rented, it was with a different card from those used for motel charges and gasoline, meal and airline ticket purchases.

I wondered what hours car rental agencies kept. I wanted to start a canvass right away. But it was 4:30 A.M., and I might appear a lunatic to some graveyard-shift worker if I began asking questions at this hour. I decided to catch up on the paperwork on other cases (by necessity, most of the hours I'd spent on the Albanowski investigation had been on my own time), and begin the search at the start of regular business hours, 9:00 A.M.

Hertz's advertising claims of being Number One refers to its volume of business, so that seemed the logical place to start. Promptly at eight-thirty I headed for the Hertz office downtown, figuring to be first in line at the counter (I hate flashing a badge, pulling rank, and forcing customers to wait), but luck intervened. On Canal Street, on my way downtown, I spotted an Avis sign, and thought why not? I would eventually have gotten to Avis, but I welcomed the time saved.

The Avis office manager's name was Pam St. Romaine. She ran the names of Giesick and Corey through a computer to determine if one of them had signed a rental agreement in January, and drew a blank. Okay. I'd never for a moment thought I'd hit paydirt on the first try. I was almost out the door when I remembered to ask her to check the name Guilliam.

Dr. Charles Guilliam, on January 14, at 3:36 P.M., rented a blue 1974 Chevrolet Monte Carlo. He used an Avis credit card, and gave his address as 8602 Tuxford, San Antonio.

I must have looked thunderstruck to Pam St. Romaine, and she had to wonder what she'd said to leave me dumbfounded. Actually, the information was too much to digest all at once, and my brain short-circuited trying to sort it out.

A blue Monte Carlo? I was looking for a white-over-maroon. But a blue Monte Carlo was the vehicle Giesick had bought for Patricia's honeymoon present. If he had rented a murder weapon, as I suspected, why get one nearly identical to his own? Wouldn't he choose a car radically different?

Giesick checked his own car into Bob McKinnon Chevrolet at 2:00 P.M. on January 14, so he must have come straight over to the Avis office. And he didn't pick up his own car until 5:22 P.M. on the fifteenth. The bogus psychologist would need a lot of fancy footwork to explain why he didn't tell Patricia about the rental car, why in fact she'd walked her legs off believing they were without transportation.

But why a blue 1974 Monte Carlo? That's what my mind couldn't comprehend. Again I was on my way out the door of the Avis office, to find a cup of coffee and get my head together, when Pam St. Romaine called me back.

"What I don't understand," she said, "is why Dr. Guilliam returned a different car. The car he brought back was a red-and-white Monte Carlo, also a 1974 model."

Red and white? I stopped dead in my tracks. *Red is maroon,* I thought, not very brilliantly. "Run that by me again," I said.

"The computer shows Dr. Guilliam turned in a red-and-white Monte Carlo to our New Orleans International Airport office at 2:07 P.M. on January sixteenth."

About two hours and forty minutes after Patricia died. "He must have exchanged one Monte Carlo for the other," I said. "Do you have any record of this?"

"Let me check." She tap-tap-tapped into a terminal, and in a few minutes obtained a printout. Reading data as it appeared, Ms. St. Romaine said, "Here's what you want. Dr. Guilliam exchanged the blue Monte Carlo for the red-and-white one at two A.M. on January fifteenth at International Airport."

Ten-and-a-half hours after he'd picked up the first rental. Twenty-four hours and twenty-two minutes before Patricia was run down. Dates and times seemed important.

"Why did he exchange cars?" I asked.

"I don't have that information. You should talk to the person on duty at the airport when the blue Monte Carlo was returned."

"Could you call and find out who that was?"

It was Louis Malain. He was at work at that very moment. I told him I'd see him in forty-five minutes.

"Dr. Guilliam," Malain said, "turned in the blue Monte Carlo claiming that it drove 'rough.' I said I'd go out and test it, but he said 'don't bother,' he wanted something else."

"So you gave him the white-over-maroon Monte Carlo?"

"Right."

"Did you check out the blue Monte Carlo?"

"As soon as he left. Ran like a top, far as I could tell. I sure couldn't find anything wrong with the car."

"Is two A.M. an unusual time to be exchanging cars?"

"Sure is. I can't remember it ever happening before. This place is a cemetery at that time. We're only open to cater to the occasional passenger who arrives on an off-hours flight."

"Was Dr. Guilliam alone when he exchanged cars?"

"No. A man was with him."

"This man?" I showed Corey's picture.

"That's him. I couldn't pick Dr. Guilliam out for you on a bet, but this fellow I remember."

Maybe Giesick and Corey realized the first rental car too closely resembled Patricia's car. You can never be sure there won't be an eyewitness to a hit-and-run, and how would it look if someone identified the murder vehicle as a blue Monte Carlo? That would immediately tip the investigating officer to check Patricia's car, and even if it was clean (the possibility exists that a vehicle would be free of telltale signs of the crime), a jury might still decide it was the offending automobile. Anyway, that seemed the most likely reason the one Monte Carlo was traded for the other. It wasn't possible at this time to know the true purpose, one as bizarre and grotesque as its inventors.

"Do you know where that white-over-maroon is right now?" I asked. Finding that vehicle suddenly reduced every other aspect of the case to insignificance. Something about that car, the devious manner in which it was obtained, the fact that Patricia knew nothing about it, the need of the perpetrators for a car difficult to trace, *something* seemed right about it. Or wrong, looked at in another way.

Malain tap-tapped his computer, waited, shrugged his shoulders. "I'm afraid I can't help you," he said. "I only have information on cars in Louisiana. This automobile is in another state, which means you need to go through our corporate headquarters."

Corporate headquarters for Avis is Garden City, New York, and I talked to regional vice president Ethan Welborn. He put me on hold while he found the computer records on the suspect car, then asked the purpose of my call.

"This vehicle," I said, "is needed in an investigation here in New Orleans. Do you know where the car is?"

"Not exactly. It will take some time to find out."

"I need to know. And I need the car. I want to know how many times it's been rented since Dr. Guilliam had it in New Orleans. And when you can get the automobile here for us to check it."

"I can do all those things. I just don't know how long it will take."

"As soon as you can, please." I rode the heady but fickle crest of momentum and didn't want it slowed.

"We always do our best to cooperate with the police."

"Also, I'd like to know if the car has been repaired since January sixteenth. Specifically, any body damage or undercarriage damage."

"I can tell you that right now. The automobile hasn't been damaged. We check carefully each time it's returned to us—have to, you know, have to stay competitive—and this car hasn't required repairs of any kind."

I didn't want to hear this unwelcome news. Traffic officers told me that ninety-nine percent of the time a car involved in a fatal hit-and-run accident would sustain some kind of body damage. Maybe just a broken headlight, but something. There was always the chance Avis had missed the telltale markings of an accident, been careless in this instance, but Welborn's self-assured telephone manner rendered the prospect unlikely.

I couldn't let the absence of repairs dampen my new-found optimism. The alternatives were giving up, desultorily handling the case, thus letting it die, or returning to the Mile with its depression and despair. "Get that car for me," I told Welborn, and put down the receiver. I persuaded myself no other explanation washed—besides murder—to explain renting the automobile. And surely an eyeball check by an Avis employee couldn't compare to the microscopic examination given by a crime lab.

For six more days, the Albanowski matter always on the fringes of my mind, I handled the daily fare of cases assigned to me, ably but certainly with no Holmesian flair. I called Welborn a couple of times, hoping to speed up the process, but he sounded less definite each time we spoke. I imagined the corporate bureaucracy had taken over, that Welborn had delegated finding the car to a lower chain of command, and no way short of raising a ruckus with bigger shots would make the Avis machinery move quicker. I didn't want to raise that ruckus. Caution represented the best policy, since the thought occurred to me that maybe I, not Volz or Mutz, heard the drummer wrong and marched out of step. What seemed obvious to me—being able to prove the guilt of Corey and Giesick—elicited a different judgment from others. Another reason for not pushing: hope lingered while the white-over-maroon Monte Carlo remained at large. But where would I find myself if it turned out not to be the murder vehicle?

Still, I didn't think it possible that the Monte Carlo could be pushed almost entirely out of my mind, but it happened on March 9 when I received a call from Sergeant Bob Ellis of the San Antonio Intelligence Division. "I understand," he said, "you're investigating the death of Patricia Giesick."

"Right," I said.

"I've got something you should know. On March eighth Sam Corey was administered a polygraph examination by a William Carlton, who is vice president of an outfit called Truth Verification, Inc. From what I know, it's a respectable firm. Carlton holds a polygraph examiner's license. He graduated from the Federal Polygraph School at Fort Gordon, Georgia, and has qualified as an expert witness in military courts and U.S. district courts. In any event, this guy Corey, whose name I understand is connected with your case, went to see Carlton. He said he was getting heat from New Orleans about a hit-and-run accident he had nothing to do with and wanted to put himself on the polygraph to clear his name."

"Remarkable," I said. Again my own failure to view this case from all sides surprised me. I'd operated on the assumption Corey was in the catbird's seat, all the high cards in his hand, he could sit smugly secure figuring I'd never tie him to the murder, when in reality he was as frightened as anybody else who knew Louisiana had a death penalty and an electric chair waiting for him. I'd feared never being able to try him; he believed that it could happen.

"What's that?" Ellis asked.

"Nothing. I'm just thinking. Do you know if Corey passed or failed the polygraph exam?"

"Failed. At least the way I see it. Carlton says Corey was possibly involved in the death of Patricia Giesick, and positively had knowledge her life was in danger."

"Possibly? Positively? What does that mean?"

"Just the way it sounds. These guys think of themselves as scientists, and use very precise language. *Possibly* Corey was involved with killing the girl. If you believe in the validity of polygraph examinations, which I do: that is, if the guy administering the test is competent, and I understand Carlton is. *Positively* Corey had knowledge before the fact that the girl's life was in danger."

"Will this guy Carlton talk with me?"

"More than that. He's willing to testify in court if you get that far."

"How did you find out about this? Why did Carlton contact you?"

"At first he wasn't aware of all the ramifications. But the more time he spent with Corey, the more he worried about getting mixed up in a murder case. He decided to contact the chairman of the State Board of Polygraph Examiners, who told him his dealings with Corey weren't privileged. He was advised to contact the police."

"So Corey thought he could beat the box," I speculated.

"That'd be my guess. A lot of people figure that way. It doesn't usually work out, does it?"

"Anything else you can tell me?"

"You'll like this: as soon as Corey found out he flunked the test, he called Carlton and insisted the results not be communicated to the New Orleans Police Department."

"What did Carlton say to that?"

"Wouldn't commit himself. Corey called four different times telling him to keep quiet."

The fact that Corey had information he didn't want the police to know—positively had had information that Patricia's life had been in danger—absolutely demanded, it seemed to me, another trip to San Antonio. If I could obtain a statement from Carlton, I'd then confront Corey. Corey could tell the truth, which advanced my goals; or lie, which would put him in a bigger pickle, combined with the other lies; or refuse to talk, which would feature him in the worst possible light: from the lie detector test it was clear he had knowledge of Patricia's death, and if innocent of any culpability, what possible justification (except his own guilt) could exist for not sharing his information with the police?

I went into Mutz's office, bristling, armed with arguments, prepared to do battle if he objected to another trip to Texas. I resembled an angry employee, ready to go to the mat with his boss over a raise, sure the man possessed countless cunning arguments to deny justice, only to become surprised the boss agreed with him.

"I need to go to Texas," I concluded, after relating the news about the polygraph exam.

"I concur."

Huh?

"I told you before you could go when you had good cause," he continued. Suddenly I felt so good toward Mutz I almost complimented him on his checkerboard jacket and polka-dot tie.

"I don't want you leaving," Mutz said, "until nothing is left hanging with your present caseload. It would be hard for Corey to disappear.'' He allowed himself a chuckle. ''I don't want you going alone.'' He hesitated, I suppose for emphasis. ''I understand Corey is given to threats.'' A longer pause. ''You never know. Why not take Dantagnan along?''

9

"MY HEART!" Reverend Sam Corey moaned, clutching his chest with his right hand, while lifting his left toward the heavens. He reeled back in his chair, mouth agape, face contorted in agony. "My heart! Geesus, it's my heart! I'm having a heart attack!" Corey's eyes squeezed shut and his left hand sought purchase from the air. "I'm dying!" he groaned. "My God, can't anyone call an ambulance?"

Not Fred Dantagnan. He looked at me and sneered.

"Oh, God, the pain!" Corey floundered about in his big chair, a white, overweight Fred Sanford having "the big one."

Fred and I stood over his desk. Neither of us moved. It was quite a show, and we wanted to remember so we could tell our kids.

"Please! I beg you! I'm dying! I'm pleading with you, in God's name, get help!"

Fred didn't budge. I certainly wasn't going to. The biggest danger would be his tumbling out of his chair, so violent were his contortions, and cracking a collarbone. That would be something to see, too.

But this was the Tokyo House, Corey's private office, and two of his masseuses were present for the show. One of them, Tonie Rogers, seemed as fascinated by the heart attack as we were, but she worked for Corey and I guessed she supposed she should do something. Ms. Rogers walked hesitatingly to the phone and dialed the emergency police number.

"I don't think I'll make it!" Corey gurgled. His right hand went limp and slid down his bosom. The left hand waved feebly in the air.

"Let's leave," Fred said disgustedly.

"You don't want to watch any more?" I said.

"Nah."

"Oh, Christ! Knives are in my heart!"

"I don't either," I said.

"I'll talk to you guys tomorow," Corey said weakly. "If I'm able. But I'm afraid it's the end." His left hand fell to his side. "Argggghh! Oh, God, save me!"

"Save *me*," Fred mumbled.

"Arggggghhh!" Corey said.

Fred and I shuffled out of the office, through the reception room, and out to the parking lot. Corey was ludicrous. On the other hand, given the series of events that had transpired since Fred and I arrived in San Antonio, a phony heart attack might have been his best move.

Two weeks had passed after the talk with Mutz before Fred and I could get ourselves clear to come to San Antonio. We arrived on a late-night flight, thought it a bad omen when the airline lost our luggage (actually, sent it out to Los Angeles), and visited William Carlton the next morning.

"Sam Corey," Carlton said, "came to me with a list of fifteen questions he wanted me to ask."

"He'd written out the questions himself?"

"Yes. As soon as I read them over I knew they related to someone's death. I told Mr. Corey that different questions would be more appropriate, and he agreed to let me make changes."

"When did you give the examination?"

"The next day. March eighth. Here in my office. I must say I went through some soul-searching before administering the test. I wondered about the legality. What if Mr. Corey flunked the test? I'd be right in the middle, which is where I am now. I didn't want to violate a client's privileged relationship, but I couldn't see withholding information about a possible crime, either."

"Did Corey actually fail the test? I'm not sure I know exactly what's involved in polygraph examinations."

"I ran three separate tests. From reading the three charts I determined that deception and/or guilt was indicated in two of Corey's negative answers."

"What were those two questions?"

"I'll read the questions to you. 'Do you know who killed Patricia Giesick?' and 'Do you know who was driving the car that struck Patricia Giesick?' "

"Did Corey know you recognized his lies?"

"I confronted him with them. I asked him if he really believed he could deceive me when he did indeed have knowledge of the girl's death."

"What did Corey say?"

"He got flustered. Paced around. Then he said he was in Dallas when he learned that Patricia Giesick's husband, Jim Giesick, planned to kill his wife on their honeymoon trip to New Orleans. Corey said he called Jim Giesick in New Orleans and tried to talk him out of committing the murder. When he was unsuccessful, he flew back to San Antonio, picked up his car, and hurried to New Orleans where he contacted Giesick. He said he talked to Giesick for several hours and convinced him he should not kill his wife. Her subsequent death, claimed Corey, was merely an accident and a coincidence."

"Right," Fred snorted. This man of action hadn't liked Corey from the beginning, and hadn't forgotten—would never forget—the threat against my children. Fred itched to inform Corey he was charged with murder, read him his rights, and then slap on the cuffs.

I had a more subdued reaction. I knew enough about Corey that I didn't think anything he said would surprise me. His story to Carlton, of course, was pure fiction.

Through credit card receipts I'd traced most of his movements, and he couldn't have called Giesick in New Orleans from Dallas, taken a plane to San Antonio, and then
driven to Louisiana.

As often happens in murder investigations, the perpetrator's own deeds started to turn things sour for him. I'd
been stymied, forced to hope the white-over-maroon Monte
Carlo (despite no visible body damage) would yield the
needed physical evidence. I still hoped for that, though the
car hadn't been located yet and returned to New Orleans.
But Corey didn't know I was stymied. He'd taken matters
in his own hands, thinking he could beat the lie detector,
and hurt himself. Just how much I didn't know.

As for Patricia's death being a coincidence after the
heroic preacher saved the girl's life, well, it was indeed a
coincidence so fantastic I didn't think the world champion
of gullibility would buy it.

"Corey's explanation of events," I said, "doesn't explain the lie—or whatever you call it—of his not knowing
who drove the murder vehicle."

"I'm not a policeman. I was nervous about this from the
beginning, and I didn't interrogate him on that point. I
figured that job belonged to the police. What I do know is
his negative answer to the question of whether he knew
who drove the vehicle showed guilt and/or knowledge."

"Knowledge?"

"Yes. I asked if he knew who drove the car. His answer
indicated he did."

"Did you ask if he drove the car?"

"I only asked the questions previously agreed upon."

"Let me ask you this, Mr. Carlton. You ran three
separate tests on Sam Corey. In your professional opinion,
was Sam Corey involved in Patricia Giesick's death?"

"Based on the results of the tests and his subsequent
explanation and especially his behavior, I formed the definite impression that Corey was involved in the girl's death,
or at least had knowledge of Jim Giesick's involvement."

"What do you mean by 'his behavior'?"

"Mr. Corey has called me numerous times since I gave him the results of the tests. He's been extremely anxious that the results not be communicated to the New Orleans authorities."

Carlton accompanied Fred and me to San Antonio police headquarters where we took his statement. I wondered how much of it mattered at this point. A lie detector test would be admissible in front of a grand jury, but not a jury. Also admissible to a grand jury was Corey's bizarre explanation of going to New Orleans to talk Giesick out of committing murder; whether this could be told to a jury was questionable, but possible: another example of the criminal's being better off doing nothing—a judge might rule Carlton could testify to what Corey told him.

Polygraph examinations, generally, are not admissible in front of a jury, and perhaps rightly so. Personally I consider them quite valuable, and so do most detectives I know. The famed defense lawyer F. Lee Bailey routinely requires his clients to undergo such a test. But the tests are only as good as the individual giving them, and there's the rub. There are good truck drivers and unsafe ones, brilliant medical doctors and quacks. How can you be sure of the type you're dealing with on polygraph exams, when a man's life might be at stake? From all I'd learned about Carlton, he ranked in the top echelon, but this wouldn't matter where a jury was concerned. Whatever. I did appreciate Carlton's help, told him so and thanked him. Few people in his position would have gotten themselves involved.

I obtained a complete list of the questions Carlton had asked Corey. The preacher may have been foolish to take the test in the first place, but there was method in his madness. He thought ahead. Two of the questions were: (1) Did any police officer ever advise you that a criminal matter was under investigation when you spoke with Detective Dillmann? and (2) Were deceit and subterfuge used to get you to speak with Detective Dillmann at San Antonio police headquarters?

Corey thought ahead, all right, all the way into the future and his own possible murder trial. Corey knew his signed, notarized statement could show up to haunt him. By taking the polygraph exam, he tried to prove I had violated his rights: he hadn't been advised of his rights, and he'd been tricked into giving the statement by Detective Koby's call (not mentioning me) bringing him to San Antonio police headquarters.

I didn't worry, but I should have. I hadn't advised Corey of his rights because at the time he wasn't a suspect in a criminal investigation. The reason Corey had been interviewed was his connection to Giesick, who'd been refusing to answer my phone calls. I'd been desperate to talk to anyone with information about the pseudo psychologist. As a matter of fact, no criminal investigation existed at the time. The investigation's "open" classification meant we hadn't determined that a crime had been committed. Still, I didn't stop to think, as I should have, that a high-powered defense attorney could turn this into a nice question of law.

As far as using deceit and subterfuge to get him to talk to me, I suppose that was true enough. But I didn't think anything illegal was involved. Besides, once he'd seen me, he could have left. No one held a gun to his head to keep him there.

Listening to Fred, a person might have thought Corey's first name was cocksucking. The tough homicide detective, so gentle with his family, exuded anger at the mention of the preacher's name. His mood toward Corey hadn't been warmed by the news from Mick Hanson of Mutual of Omaha that the accident the preacher and Giesick had in their cars was probably deliberately staged so injury claims could be filed. In addition, Giesick, whom Fred contended was probably activated by Corey's strings, had recently filed several claims contending his house had been burglarized.

We headed straight for the Tokyo House after arming ourselves with Carlton's statement. The Massage Parlor

King would be confronted with those three alternatives—tell the truth, lie, or refuse to talk.

The preacher wasn't there, but two of his masseuses were: Tonie Rogers and Linda Stordahl. Where had I heard the name Tonie Rogers before? I searched my mind and it didn't take long to come.

Tonie Rogers had witnessed Patricia's marriage to Jim Giesick. Corey had told me she was Patricia's friend. I asked Ms. Rogers if she'd step into Corey's office (I'd interviewed Giesick there while my motel room got burglarized) and talk with me.

"Tonie," I said when we were alone, "I understand you were a friend of Patricia Giesick."

"I'm afraid you're mistaken. I didn't know Mrs. Giesick." I saw fear in her eyes. She didn't want to go on, but even less did she want to involve herself with lying to the police.

"Do you know James Giesick?"

"Yes. I know Jim. Sam introduced me to him."

"Didn't you witness the marriage of Jim and Patricia Giesick in Dallas?"

Her face tensed. Her eyes darted. "Look, man, I didn't witness nothing. I don't want to get involved in this shit. Sam brought that marriage license in here and told me to sign it. He said it wasn't illegal for me to sign. I took his word for that. Does that make me a criminal?"

"When did he bring the license to you?"

"I don't remember exactly, some time right after the New Year."

"You signed it here at the Tokyo House? You didn't sign it in Dallas?"

"Right here in this room. Look, man, I just did what Sam told me. He said it was okay."

"How about C. R. Lee?" I'd remembered the name of the second witness to the marriage. "Who is C. R. Lee?"

"I don't know. I swear I don't. Maybe she's one of Sam's girls at one of his other places."

Just then I heard a thud in the reception room—an

elephant taking a step?—and Sam Corey was framed in the doorway of his office. He had a beet-red face and his eyes blazed. I could see Fred standing behind him.

"What the hell is going on here?" the preacher shouted. "What the hell are you doing talking to my people?"

His voice thundered. I caught a glimpse of Fred's malicious smile. He ached for Corey's verbal violence to turn physical. "Do my people know you're cops? You showed your identification? I bet you brought guns into my place of business! You got guns? Get the hell out of here if you've got guns!"

I'd been sitting in front of Corey's desk, Tonie Rogers behind it, but as he rumbled into the room she got up and he took her place. Fred stood next to my right shoulder. Corey was filled with bluster, steaming mad, but I knew Fred, still smiling, was by far the more dangerous of the two, a bundle of compressed fury.

"Look, you big fat sack of shit," was Fred's way of starting the interview, "you don't tell us where to go or what we have to do."

"Sam," I said loudly, rising halfway out of the chair, more menace in my voice than I ever thought I could muster, "we're here on an official police investigation. We came to talk to you and you're acting like an asshole. If you want to talk, fine. If not, fuck you! We'll handle this another way, and you won't like it."

At least his mind worked (had the anger been an act? ours wasn't), and I could see him bringing himself under control. He maintained his defiance, but since bullying hadn't worked he'd try sullen cooperation. "I don't know why you guys are harassing me," he said in a martyred voice. "I've done nothing wrong and I have nothing to hide."

"That's good," I said. "Sam, I'd like you to come back to New Orleans with us. We'll pay all expenses."

"New Orleans? For what?"

"I want you to give me a statement in New Orleans. I

want to know about your knowledge of Jim Giesick's plan to kill his wife.''

"Are you crazy?"

"You better hope so, Sam."

"I don't have any such knowledge. What you're saying is insane."

"Don't bullshit me, Sam. I'm looking down your throat. Your best bet is to come clean with me."

"I don't know what you're talking about. You're wasting my time. You're persecuting me."

"Sam, you've taken three separate polygraph tests and flunked each one miserably. Bill Carlton has made all of the results available. There's no doubt on this green planet that you have guilty knowledge. Now cut the crap and open up with us."

Corey's mouth dropped open and, just as during my first interview with him, the sweat literally popped out of his face. What I remember most, however, were his eyes. They filled with anger and hatred. He picked up the phone and dialed a number.

When William Carlton answered, Corey said, "Bill, I've got a couple of New Orleans detectives in my office. They tell me you've given them the results of that privileged polygraph exam." Corey listened to the answer, his face growing darker. "Goddam!" he screamed into the receiver. "You goddam are in a lot of trouble! What you've done is illegal and unethical!" The phone being slammed down sounded like the report of a rifle. Corey's eyes were those of a desperate madman. I didn't know what to expect. Then . . .

"My heart!"

Fred and I didn't expect much when we returned to the Tokyo House the next morning, and weren't surprised. The masseuse on duty told us that Corey had suffered a stroke and that if we required any additional information we should contact his lawyer, one William Miller. We spent the rest of the morning and part of the afternoon trying to reach Miller and then caught a flight home.

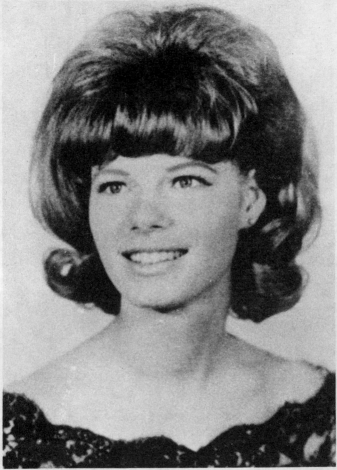

Yearbook photo of Patricia Ann Albanowski, the beautiful New Jerseyan who came to Texas for love and found instead a con man and a preacher, and ultimately death on a lonely Louisiana road.

Sam Corey, 300-pound preacher, San Antonio mayoral candidate, massage parlor operator, and murderer. Corey drove the vehicle in the phony hit-and-run and intended to collect the lion's share of insurance money.

James Giesick (*left*) posed as a psychologist to marry Patricia so he could kill her.

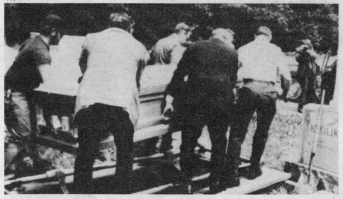

Exhuming the body of Patricia Albanowski Giesick. Hair taken from the victim matched that recovered from the underside of the car rented by Giesick.

John Dillmann (*right*) walking Corey (*left*) from the courthouse to police headquarters to book him for first-degree murder. Second-degree charges had been dropped moments before. Also shown is Irwin Dymond, one of Louisiana's premier defense attorneys.

Homicide commander Robert Mutz, who, like Dillmann, first thought a simple hit-and-run had taken place. Mutz provided support and encouragement throughout the long, difficult investigation.

Homicide detective Fred Dantagnan, Dillmann's closest friend, disliked Corey before he ever met him, even more after.

Ralph Whalen, one of the first to believe the case might be won, was the dynamic D.A. who prosecuted Corey for murder. Today he has a successful private practice.

Corey, shown here shortly after his conviction, still resides in the Louisiana State Penitentiary in Angola.

The bridge where Patricia stood just before being run down; the car (*background*) stands where Corey's rental car waited in the dark for Giesick's signal to speed ahead.

One of Patricia's last sights: the ducks on Michoud Bayou near Chef Menteur Highway.

Patricia A. Giesick's headstone.

—10—

I BELIEVED COREY'S failed lie detector test brought us considerably closer to a grand jury presentation, and other things happened to advance the case, though not at the speed I desired. At least during my frequent talks with the Albanowskis I detected more confidence in my voice. I think they did, too. No more did I phrase everything with a "maybe" or a "we hope," and occasionally I even indulged myself with a "when." I thought Patricia's parents placed an almost childlike trust in me and my ability to see justice accomplished, and this made up one side of the double-edged sword that kept prodding—the other was disgust for Corey and Giesick.

Matters stayed pretty much at a standstill during April, a month when Watergate dominated international headlines. In my own world, Avis seemed incredibly slow getting that white-over-maroon Monte Carlo back to New Orleans.

But in April I kept in mind the lessons learned earlier: the fact that I was getting nowhere wasn't apparent to the suspects, and one or both of them might take action in a manner counterproductive to their best interests.

It happened on May 4, a Saturday. I'd just managed to wrestle "my" desk away from a graveyard-shift detective working overtime, and the first call came from Bernard Koby in San Antonio.

"You won't believe," he said, "who I met with yesterday."

I dislike phone conversations that begin this way. "Who was it?" I asked.

"None other than the famous Dr. Giesick."

"What happened?"

"He confessed. Sort of."

"What does that mean, Koby?"

"You're going to love the bullshit story he's got. Sam must be putting the pressure on. Anyway, you shouldn't have to listen to it twice, so why not get it straight from Giesick?"

"I understand you want to talk with me," I said, when I had Giesick on the line. "But before you say a word, remember that anything you tell me can be used against you in a court of law. You need not say anything until you've consulted an attorney. If you can't . . ."

"Detective Dillmann, I've already contacted several attorneys in San Antonio, but they want too much money. I'd like to come to New Orleans and have a court-appointed lawyer represent me. Once I've been given an attorney, I'll furnish your department with a confession pertaining to a conspiracy that I was involved in to kill my wife, Patricia. I'm currently seeing a psychiatrist because of my habitual lying, and I believe my condition is improving. Because of my emotional condition, there's no way I can serve a prison term of any length that may result from a murder indictment. I'm willing to come to New Orleans to plead guilty to criminal conspiracy if you will guarantee my receiving a short sentence."

Amazing, I thought. And later, when I knew what was going on in Giesick's mind, I thought it even more amazing. Giesick knew the law better than I did. He wanted to plead guilty to criminal conspiracy to commit murder (he would say the murder was never carried out), a misdemeanor, and by seeing a psychiatrist hoped to beat even that charge on an insanity plea.

"Jim," I said, "Sam must be putting a lot of heat on you."

"You don't understand. Sam's the hero. He stopped this whole thing."

"He did a great job. Patricia is dead."

"But I didn't kill her. You have to understand what happened. You have to hear the truth."

"I'm listening." I leaned back in my chair, wadded up a sheet of paper, and tossed a bull's eye to the back of Fred Dantagnan's head.

"Me and a guy named Ronnie planned to kill Trish for over three hundred thousand dollars of life insurance. Ronnie and I were to divide the money equally, after we made the death look like an accident. I planned to bring Patricia to New Orleans, where early one morning I'd beat her on the head with a rock, lay her on the ground, and have Ronnie run over her with a truck. After we got to New Orleans I had second thoughts, and called my best friend, Sam Corey. Sam talked me out of killing Patricia, and early that morning Trish and I took a walk. I had guilt feelings, and told Trish all about the terrible plans I had for her. I begged her forgiveness. Instead she started to cry and became hysterical. Because of her hysterics, she ran out into the street and that's when the hit-and-run vehicle came along and struck her. I guess this was God's way of punishing me [punishing *him?*] for planning evil deeds. Believe me, Detective Dillmann, I planned to kill her, and this has haunted me ever since, but I didn't kill her, as the Lord is my witness. It was an accident. A horrible, freaky coincidence. The truth can be stranger than fiction. But I didn't kill Trish."

Would anyone on earth believe this story? I tossed another wad of paper at Dantagnan—"Do that again and I'll knock the shit out of you," he said—and asked Giesick: "Who is this guy Ronnie?" I didn't care, Ronnie didn't exist, but I was paid to do a job.

"He's a guy I met in one of Sam's massage parlors. We plotted the murder together."

"How do I know Ronnie didn't run over Patricia?"

"He couldn't have. He was waiting in Dallas for word from me to come to New Orleans."

"How can I contact Ronnie?" I knew Giesick's answer before he gave it.

"I don't know where he is. I haven't talked to him since before the accident."

"What's his last name?"

"I don't know it. He was just a guy who looked like he might go for a big score."

"Well," I said. I couldn't really think of what to say. "That's some story."

"It's the truth. And don't forget, Sam Corey had nothing to do with this. He stopped it. It was me and Ronnie."

Right.

I wondered if Corey stood at his elbow. I'd have bet on it. I yawned and wondered if I could risk another missile at Dantagnan's head.

"What about the deal?" Giesick asked.

"What deal?"

"If I come to New Orleans, sign a statement to what I've told you today, will you guarantee the charge will be criminal conspiracy?"

I didn't know at this time even how the criminal conspiracy statute read (though I suspected Giesick did), but it didn't matter, I had no interest in any charge that didn't frequently contain the phrase, "Murder—First Degree."

"I don't have the authority to make a deal," I told Giesick. "I'll talk to the district attorney and get back to you. This is Saturday, so you won't hear from me till Monday."

"I'll be waiting for your call."

Later that morning I took Fred to lunch at Central Grocery on Decatur Street in the French Quarter right on the Mississippi River. Central Grocery is famous for its muffulatta sandwiches, a combination of choice ham, salami, imported cheese, and olive salad. The Italian bread is stuffed three inches thick.

I talked while Fred munched. It was a gorgeous spring New Orleans early afternoon, the Crescent City at its most beautiful, even the muddy Mississippi sparkled in the crisp sunlight. Fred pretended to be watching the paddle boats, their ancestors as old as New Orleans itself, but I knew he heard every word.

"It looks to me," he said, dabbing his lips with a napkin, "like both of those scumbags are cracking. Keep applying the heat. It may not be long now."

When I arrived at headquarters Monday morning, May 6, I intended to get my paperwork in order and pay a visit to John Volz. I had plenty to tell him: he still didn't know about Corey's failed lie detector test or the bizarre tale spun by Giesick. But before I had time to sit down my phone rang, with Giesick on the other end. I detected fear in his voice, even with the first few words.

"Have you been able to work out that deal yet?" he asked.

"I just got here," I said. "I was . . ."

"Great! I was afraid you'd already settled something. What I told you the other day wasn't true."

"Really?" Maybe the Number One fan of his con was himself. Did he really think *anyone* would buy that story?

"Well, you've got to know the truth now. My own life is in danger. Someone tried to kill me yesterday, and I think it was Sam."

"What happened?"

"I don't want to go into it. I could have been killed. I need protection."

"Tell me whatever you want. But remember what I said Saturday. Anything you say can be used against you in a court of law."

"Can it. I know my rights. Here's what I'll do: I'll come to New Orleans and testify in front of a grand jury. In exchange I need your promise that I won't be arrested and that later I'll be able to plead guilty to a lesser charge than murder."

"I don't make the deals around here," I said. "But

right now I don't even know what you're talking about. If you want to tell me another story, and propose an arrangement, I'll carry it over to the district attorney.''

"Well, I need to know something, and I need to know it quick. I'm not just afraid for myself, but also for Kathy and the kids.''

Now *you* know how it feels.

"I can't tell you anything. If you want me to go to the D.A. to see what I can do, you'll have to inform me of what you know. Nobody will make a deal if they don't know what the deal is. Use your head.''

"Okay, here it is. Trish's death wasn't an accident, it was murder, and Sam Corey killed her. He ran her down. We planned it together for the insurance money, but he killed her.''

"What about Ronnie?''

"Forget Ronnie. There isn't any Ronnie. Corey and I made him up.''

"You had nothing to do with Patricia's actual death?''

"Only that I was there and saw what happened. If you want the rest, you better agree to what I want.''

"I'll get back to you.''

So the murderers had had a falling-out. I imagined it had to be that way, and I didn't doubt Corey had put the fear of God into Giesick. Corey figured Giesick had become the weak link in the operation, and with him out of the way the crime could never be pinned absolutely on the preacher himself. I had to admit Corey might have a point, a fact Giesick clearly recognized also. I had much more evidence incriminating Giesick than I did linking Corey to the crime.

John Volz listened carefully to the presentation of what I'd learned since our last meeting. But he leaned over his desk this time, no laid-back elegance greeted the information, and when I concluded he said matter-of-factly, "I imagine we should talk to our friend Giesick, as he suggests.''

Volz did the interviewing—over a speaker phone—and Giesick was apprised of my presence.

"I understand," said Volz, "you think you have something we should know."

"Yes. A lot. But do we have a deal?"

"Repeat that deal to me."

"I'll come to New Orleans and testify. I'll name Sam Corey as the individual who drove the car that killed my wife. You promise that I won't be arrested when I come to New Orleans, and when I am charged, it will be for something less than murder. I'm only guilty of conspiracy, so it should be that."

"That's your judgment. You change your story on a daily basis. You need to come to New Orleans and tell us the truth. Let us judge what you're guilty of. If it's conspiracy, then that's what the charge will be."

"What you're telling me is maybe."

"Exactly. We won't make any promises until we hear precisely what you have to say."

"That's no deal at all."

"It's all you've got."

"Will I be arrested?"

"Yes."

"For what?"

"Murder."

"Jesus Christ! What am I doing talking to you?"

"I understand you called us. Look, Mr. Giesick, if you come to New Orleans on your own volition and cooperate fully with us and if your testimony can be corroborated, then your cooperation will be taken into consideration at a later date."

"That's a bunch of vague bullshit."

"No, it's not. We don't know what you're going to say. How can we make a deal with you before we know? Your record for honesty isn't outstanding. A sane person, which I consider myself, would insist on corroboration. Think on it, Mr. Giesick. What juror would believe you?"

I couldn't see down the line, but this issue would end up being the rub.

"You're not offering me anything," Giesick decided.

"Mr. Giesick, you're not thinking clearly. We're offering—except for the no-arrest business, which if I agreed to would make me the laughingstock of the legal profession—exactly what you say you want. You claim Sam Corey is the murderer and you are guilty only of conspiracy. If that's the truth, Corey will be tried for murder, and you on a much lesser charge of conspiracy."

"I can't trust you. I need an agreement in advance."

"*You* can't trust *us?* Mr. Giesick, you're a notorious con man, currently under indictment for bigamy, living under the phony name Guilliam, undoubtedly involved in numerous scams, which only a matter of time separates us from uncovering, and you act offended because we dare to want to corroborate your story."

"I know you're not giving me anything."

"Except for one point, we're offering what you ask."

"It ain't nothing!" Giesick's voice escalated to a scream. "Not a damn thing! I try to help and you want to lock me up forever. I'd rather take my chances with Corey than you guys."

The sound of Giesick slamming down his receiver rang through Volz's office. I wasn't sure, if the choice was between Corey and us, that Giesick's selection made sense.

Corey could be a tough character, as witnessed by the gang war he fought, or at least the people he did business with were tough. And clearly Giesick threatened him: he'd just volunteered to finger the preacher for murder.

I agreed with Volz's not giving in to Giesick's demands. Events moved fast now, always a time to slow down. When a case stands still, that's the time for flurries of activity, to get things rolling. I still had that car—when would the trying-harder Avis ever deliver it?—to inspect. Regardless of what it revealed, Volz intended to head for the grand jury when we had the results.

The case would be no cinch winner, Volz emphasized,

but we'd have a chance. Along with the strong circumstantial case, now he added inculpatory statements from both Corey and Giesick: Corey's lie detector fiasco with Carlton (admissible in front of the grand jury, iffy during an actual trial), and Giesick's statement to us. I could tell Volz yearned for just one piece of physical evidence. "Maybe the car," I said, and convinced myself it had to be the car. Patricia had been run down—no doubt about that—and what other automobile made sense?

Volz intended to indict Corey and Giesick for murder, not a difficult task, and then initiate extradition proceedings against them, which could present a problem. Once the grand jury handed down the indictments, Corey and Giesick could voluntarily return or fight the extradition. I didn't have any doubt which path they'd choose. We would then have to obtain a warrant from the governor of Louisiana who would forward it to the governor of Texas. The Texas authorities would have to determine the warrant's validity, which meant a hearing, probably several hearings, and miles of red tape and quarreling and, possibly, if one of the defense lawyers was good enough, or, surely not, if the governor of Texas didn't like the governor of Louisiana, the Lone Star authorities might not act on the indictment at all.

All this was highly unlikely. The extradition request would probably be duly granted. The key word was "duly." A long period of time could elapse if Corey and Giesick chose to go that route.

Two days later, on May 8, Giesick's attorney, newly hired if Giesick was to be believed, one Robert Spicer from San Antonio, showed up completely unexpectedly at police headquarters and asked if I could arrange a meeting for him with John Volz. I said I could. Spicer worked for a prestigious San Antonio law firm, and I wondered how Giesick could afford his services.

The meeting, which I attended, took place late in the afternoon in Volz's office. Basically Spicer wanted to know whether the district attorney's office, in exchange for Giesick's cooperation, would accept a conspiracy plea. I believe Spicer knew there was next to no chance of this occurring, but what did he have to lose? He also seemed interested in our plans (when were we going to the grand jury? how much did we know?). Before the meeting broke up he wondered if we'd accept a plea of manslaughter. Again, Volz answered, that would depend on the extent of Giesick's involvement, and how could a decision be made before he opened up? Volz said that he wouldn't believe Giesick if he were knee-deep in Bibles and that independent corroboration would be required.

Spicer returned to San Antonio, and just as we still faced an uphill pull, so also I imagined did he. I could only guess at what had transpired between Spicer and Giesick. Probably Giesick went to the lawyer and said he and Corey plotted the murder of Patricia, but Corey drove the murder vehicle, therefore only Corey was guilty of murder. Spicer would have coughed upon hearing this interpretation of the law, perhaps even had a coughing spell, and then proceeded to set the con man straight. Giesick, so good at understanding the law when it favored him, would not be unusual among criminals in not grasping the factors weighing against him.

Of course, Spicer would have told him in no uncertain terms that unless he had dropped out of the conspiracy *and* actively tried to prevent Corey from carrying out the killing, he was as guilty as the preacher. I didn't believe it had happened that way, especially with Corey and Giesick, locked in each other's arms, performing that little dance.

There were no sure Gibraltar-solid precedents I could hang my badge on and say, This case is solved; justice will be done. Corey and Giesick, with sharp lawyers, a less-than-perfect legal system, and a spirited defense, might yet get away with murder. But the odds had shortened considerably.

—11—

THE 1974 WHITE-OVER-MAROON Monte Carlo was finally returned to New Orleans International Airport on May 12, and the next morning a pair of detectives drove it to what we call the Crime Lab Cage. This walled-off area in the police headquarters building is kept immaculate, brightly lit, and when not in use, under lock and key. It is used primarily to process (check for evidence) automobiles, but it has housed bicycles and motorcycles also, and I suppose it could handle a tank.

I watched as criminalist John Palm went over the Monte Carlo with the figurative fine-tooth comb. If the car had ever been so much as nicked, even the Michelangelo of automobile retouching wouldn't be able to hide the damage from Palm.

But there wasn't anything; the car might just have come off an assembly line. Well, Avis had said the automobile was clean. Still, with damage occurring in the majority of hit-and-runs, I didn't think I'd been overoptimistic to hope the eagle-eyed Palm's microscopic examination would uncover something. Now that it hadn't, I wanted to groan. A murder conviction would be more difficult if we couldn't produce the weapon.

We moved the car some fifty feet to a grease rack and hoisted it up. A powerful drop light illuminated the Monte

Carlo's undercarriage as brightly as a surgeon's operating arena. I drew a deep breath. A failure here and I was back to square one with the murder weapon. No, worse than square one. I'd have eliminated the two most likely cars, this one and the one used as Patricia's honeymoon present. Hunching over, I followed Palm underneath the vehicle.

The criminalist traced with his index finger an approximately eight-inch scrape mark on the oil pan.

"What you got?" I asked.

"The car ran over something."

"Any way of telling what?"

"No. Oil pan's the lowest part of a car. It's not unusual for it to show damage. Now if we could find something to go with this . . ."

He found the something just moments after he photographed the scrape. On the A-frame near the left front tire Palm discovered a tiny patch of cloth, no more than a thread. He removed the thread with tweezers and placed the fiber in a petri dish. "We've got the Giesick girl's clothing in the evidence section. Maybe we can get a match."

The odds opposed what happened next. I felt like a fish out of water, with the neophyte's fear that the car might come crashing down and crush us, while Palm was as much in his element as Andy Granatelli, yet *I found the hairs.* It seemed they could be important, but I didn't fully grasp their grave and long-lasting significance.

The hairs, two of them, one eight-and-one-half inches long, the other thirteen inches long, were wrapped loosely around the tie rod and imbedded in grease. The grease held them firmly.

I called Palm over to look, and he whistled, photographed them, carefully wiped grease aside, and with infinite care unwound the two precious hairs. These he placed in a petri dish.

We stayed under the Monte Carlo another hour, but it yielded no more secrets. Next we headed for the crime lab, where Palm compared the fiber we had to the sweater

Patricia had been wearing, and the two hairs to a hair of hers we'd found on her sweater. The bottom line: Palm just didn't have the equipment required to make positive matches. What he could determine was that the hairs were "similar," and so were the fibers; for something positive, unshakable in a court of law, we needed help from the FBI.

I've never lost anything sending it to the FBI, but I'm always nervous. I wished a courier could be used, but I supposed that would be a budget-buster, what with police departments all over the country, each thinking *their* evidence the most important, deluging Washington, D.C., with messengers. Regardless, as we dropped our two packets in the U.S. mail (stamped everywhere with the words "evidence," "fragile," and "handle with care"—maybe someone would pay attention), I knew I wouldn't rest until I had the findings in hand.

The suspense lasted eight days, until May 21, when at the 10:00 A.M. mail call I checked my pigeonhole and found the official-looking packet from the FBI. I walked out into a corridor, temporarily deserted, and tore open the envelope. Better to get the news alone than in the madness of the homicide room:

> Microscopic analysis determined that the textile fibers submitted, those located on the rental vehicle, were not like the fibers removed from the victim's sweater.

> Microscopic analysis proved that the two hair specimens which were removed from the tie rod of the rented vehicle consisted of light-colored head hairs of Caucasian origin. Both hairs had been crushed and forcibly removed from the scalp. These hairs showed some similarities with the submitted hair from the victim's sweater. However, there is not a sufficient amount of hair to adequately constitute a comparison. This evidence has been retained in our laboratory for possible future comparisons.

*   *   *

I read the message over and over, but it always came out the same. I didn't have the final nail to drive into the joint coffin of Corey and Giesick. So much evidence, so much certitude, yet the clincher still eluded me. The physical evidence. The irrefutable, unassailable physical evidence needed to seat these two cold-blooded killers in the electric chair.

Back at my desk I called Washington, D.C., to speak to FBI Special Agent John Hicks, the laboratory criminalist who'd sent me the analysis of the hairs and thread.

"You indicate," I said after identifying myself, "there are 'similarities' between the hairs we submitted. What exactly does this mean?"

"Similarities were found between the two hairs taken off the vehicle and the hair removed from the sweater. However, there is not a sufficient amount of hair to adequately constitute a comparison."

He could have been reading from the report he'd sent me. Hicks sounded articulate and professional, just what you'd expect an FBI man to be, someone who knew of what he spoke, but I hadn't called him so he could paraphrase what he'd already written.

I supposed I hadn't asked the question correctly, but my second effort was just as clumsy. "How 'similar' is similar? What precisely could you testify?"

"Human head hairs do not possess a sufficient number of unique individual characteristics to allow us to determine positively that they come from any one individual."

"Wonderful. So we can never match these hairs."

"I didn't say that."

An image came to mind of Special Agent Hicks: my high school physics teacher. Couldn't layman's language explain complicated physical phenomena?

"What do you mean?" I said.

"There are fifteen similarities associated with hair, such as color, texture, oil, scales, etc. My problem is I don't have enough hair to identify possible similarities under microscopic analysis."

"You need more hair."

"Correct."

"But what good would that do? I understood you to say human hairs lack the necessary 'unique individual characteristics' to prove they come from a specific person."

"You're forgetting those fifteen similarities. If I had an adequate hair sample, I might be able to match all fifteen."

"Yet you couldn't state positively the hair from the car came from the victim."

"That's right. I could testify, however, that all fifteen similarities were present."

My head spun. I pictured myself back in physics class. "What are the chances, if all fifteen characteristics match, that the hair came from someone else besides the victim?"

"I'd say there was no chance."

"You couldn't say the hair came from the victim, but you could say there isn't any chance it came from somewhere else?"

"You've got it."

I didn't think so.

"Let me attack this from another angle. Let's say you do match all fifteen similarities. How much weight would a court give this?"

"From my experience, a lot. I've qualified as an expert witness in twenty-six states and the District of Columbia, and the identification of hair samples is considered almost as reliable as fingerprints."

I told Special Agent Hicks I hoped I hadn't heard the last of him, and decided I could use a cup of coffee. In a restaurant a block from headquarters I spotted Dr. Franklin Minyard, New Orleans' Dr. Jazz, seated at a table with one of his pathologists. I welcomed his invitation to join them.

Chatting with Minyard was always a pleasure. He knew all the great New Orleans jazz musicians. This day he talked about his friend Al Hirt, the nonpareil trumpet

player, and the time an idiot tossed a brick at the Mardi
Gras float upon which he rode and struck him in the face.
Hirt, Minyard believed, still ranked as the best of the best,
but was not what he once had been.

When I had the chance—a person didn't want to interrupt Minyard, he was a storyteller to listen to and enjoy—I
asked if his doctor friends in Texas had provided any
information on Claudius Giesick. Minyard had said he
would check, which meant he had.

"The Albanowski case, eh? I've wondered how you
were doing. But to answer your question, no, none had
heard of him."

"I'm sure they run in different circles," I said. "Giesick's
not a doctor."

"Yes?"

I caught him up, briefly, on the progress of the investigation. Then I asked, "What are the possibilities of
retrieving a usable hair sample from a person buried more
than four months ago?"

"They're excellent. Hair, teeth, and fingernails are among
the last things on a body to deteriorate. Four months is no
time at all."

I went straight from the coffee shop to the district
attorney's office in the Criminal Courts Building and talked
to Ralph Whalen, who had replaced John Volz (Volz now
was a U.S. attorney). Whalen believed the earlier news of
Corey's failed lie detector test brought us considerably
closer to a success. "Not quite there yet," he'd said. "But
you're making progress. I think we might come out all
right on this."

This represented the first time I'd actually heard a peer,
or in Whalen's case someone in authority, suggest this
investigation might end up as anything other than frustration and disappointment. It meant a lot coming from Whalen,
a man I liked and respected.

A graduate of Tulane University, Whalen joined the
D.A.'s office right out of law school, not really thinking
he would be much of a success because he had empathy

for many of the unfortunates charged with crime. But certain types of criminals, chiefly murderers he'd closely studied, elicited a profound negative reaction from him. A hard worker, Whalen found plenty to do, especially on homicides, of which there were nearly one a day in New Orleans. In the three years he'd been a district attorney, he had the best record in the office (won-lost records, like baseball pennant-race standings, were actually displayed prominently on a wall), and his superiors—duly impressed—steadily promoted Whalen from a lowly trial assistant to Volz's former position, first assistant district attorney.

The newspapers took notice, also. Five feet ten and slender, always well-prepared and aggressive (I'd buy a ticket if necessary to see him cross-examine Corey), Whalen had earned the nickname "The Whacker" because he relentlessly beat aside his opposition. His colorful personality plus his excellent success record explained the media attention. He'd get right into a defendant's face, waving the photograph of a mutilated victim, and dramatically proclaim that here was the monster responsible.

Whalen, who was my age, probably would have gone to the grand jury after the news about the lie detector test if it came down to the choice of letting Corey and Giesick walk. But Whalen believed it was only a matter of time before the case became stronger. The news I related now from the FBI lab didn't alter his opinion.

"What are the legalities for having Patricia's body exhumed?" I asked.

"I can tell you about Louisiana, but I don't know about New Jersey. You need to get in touch with the Trenton prosecutor's office. You should realize this is a very unusual request. Courts don't often permit a body to be exhumed. You need a very strong argument, which I think you have, and even then a dozen other things can trip you up. There's a strong feeling in this country about the sanctity of the grave."

I couldn't hook up with John Noon, chief investigator for the Mercer County prosecutor's office in Trenton, until the next day, May 22. Whalen had already talked with Noon, which must have been interesting, because Noon's reaction to what I had in mind was a low, warning whistle. "I'm not betting you'll succeed," he said.

"Just tell me what I need to do."

"Bring your entire case file. I hope it's strong. Damn strong. You're going to have to convince a judge, who's not going to want a grave violated just because you *hope* it might clear up a murder investigation. You'll have to be very well prepared. This is like a trial before a trial, and you need to be extremely persuasive. One other thing, without which you have nothing: the victim's parents have to agree to the exhumation. If they say no, you're out in the cold."

"They'll agree."

Actually, I had no idea whether they would. It would be a terribly traumatic event for the Albanowskis. I knew they had deep religious convictions, and I couldn't be certain how they would react. I'd have to deal with that when the moment came. I did believe I could convince them that our goals were identical—justice for Patricia—and that this was the best way.

Well, I'd do what I could, with both the Albanowskis and the judge. I couldn't help remembering my session with John Volz, and how easily he'd waved away what I thought to be ironclad arguments. I comforted myself by reasoning that the case was stronger now, and I felt I knew it backward and forward.

I telephoned the Albanowskis and told them I'd be coming to New Jersey, without telling them why. Thinking about my purpose, what I'd have to ask of them, the confidence I'd exhibited to John Noon turned to dread.

—12—

I KNEW ABOUT these things happening, always to somebody else, a visiting celebrity, usually, but nothing in my past prepared me for the greeting that awaited on May 29 when I stepped off the Delta flight to Philadelphia International Airport. There must have been a dozen reporters on hand, representing the wire services AP and UPI and newspapers from as far away as New York City. I found myself bombarded with questions I didn't want to answer. At least no radio or television reporters were present. It turned out they would make their appearance the next day, in formidable numbers.

What had happened was that an enterprising New Orleans *Times-Picayune* reporter named Walt Philbin discovered that the grand jury proceedings against Corey and Giesick had been postponed, and some digging on his part uncovered what seemed an engrossing investigation. Philbin learned we aimed for an exhumation of Patricia's body, and did a story in the *Times-Picayune*. The wire services picked up the article, discovered it piqued the interest of readers, particularly in areas like Texas where Corey was well known, New Jersey, home of the victim, and New York City, which could be counted on to appreciate a good yarn: beautiful girl struck down on her honeymoon; wealthy (or was he?) child psychologist living two lives; preacher/

massage parlor owner/erstwhile mayoral candidate/murder suspect; grieving parents; and of course the young southern detective come north to dig up the dead.

I tried to sidestep all questions. Commander Mutz instructed us to be cordial with the media, ''but never say anything that can compromise your case.'' Often this means revealing the progress of an investigation in a manner that tips off the suspects. It had happened several times over the years in New Orleans.

John Noon came to Philadelphia International Airport to meet me, and when we shook free of the reporters we drove to the Mercer County prosecutor's office in Trenton. A big, husky man with a conservative approach to his job, Noon was a veteran policeman who guarded against hurt by not expecting too much. He didn't offer encouragement that the exhumation order would be granted.

I sat at Noon's desk while he went through my case file. If I'd expected him to ask questions, or believed he wanted to hear how brilliantly I'd conducted the investigation, it became clear I'd be disappointed. I wanted to tell him some of the items weren't important, go on to something else, but he had his own pace and wouldn't be pushed. I stared at him, a man frozen in place, a picture of superslow motion going ponderously from note to note, statement to statement, report to report. Occasionally he grunted, a noncommittal sound. I'd arrived in Philadelphia at 11:00 A.M., it hadn't taken us *that* long to get away from the reporters, but I could tell from the shadows outside that the sun's last light had begun to fade. Noon plodded on.

At last he reached the end. He put the last piece of paper down and stared at me.

''Well?'' I said. He didn't seem a man you wanted to say a lot to.

The heart of the hardest cop would have melted when he finally spoke. ''I've been in law enforcement a long time, and this is the most thorough, professional investigation I've ever seen.''

Once Noon began talking, he couldn't quit. He spoke

about Corey and Giesick in tones dripping with disgust. He said how sorry he felt for Patricia, getting married, thinking a whole happy life stretched out in front of her, killed by these "filthbags." Noon went over the entire investigation, starting that first morning in Mutz's office— "Bet those two thought they were in good shape then" —right up to the present, Giesick's falling-out with Corey and the proposed exhumation.

Noon had already arranged for the exhumation hearing to be conducted the next morning, and I'd expected to make the arguments. Noon said he would like to make the presentation; it would be a pleasure to argue something so "airtight." I told him of course, go ahead.

Still pending was the all-important task of obtaining permission from the Albanowskis. No matter that Noon thought the case airtight, nothing could take place unless the parents agreed. I couldn't remember anything I'd less wanted to do than go to the Albanowski home and explain what I wanted.

I rented a car, phoned ahead, and drove to their home in Mammoth Junction, a suburb of Trenton. When I'd first told them I'd be coming, they'd said I should stay as an overnight guest, but a motel seemed a wiser choice. I'd never met them. There had only been all those phone calls.

The house was small and immaculate. I'd seen just one other place to match its cleanliness: Patricia's apartment in Richardson, Texas. The neat lawn might have been cut with scissors, and the house itself, warm and cozy, could have come off a Norman Rockwell *Saturday Evening Post* cover. A nice place to call home.

The Albanowskis welcomed me like family, and seemed more like grandparents than parents. I suspected they had aged considerably since their daughter's death. Patricia, after all, had been a contemporary of mine.

"Detective Dillmann," Mrs. Albanowski said, "we've so looked forward to meeting you."

"Please. Call me John."

"Of course. Could we fix you a soft drink, Detective Dillmann? A cup of coffee?"

Good people.

I'd scarcely settled on the couch when they produced the family album, and they sat, one on each side of me, to look at pictures. A family album it might be called, but virtually every photograph featured Patricia: Patricia as a baby, Patricia as a little girl, in grade school, high school, college, Patricia as a young woman. They explained each photo, and all the happy stories made us sad, summoning the most tragic of images, what might have been.

That Norman Rockwell home became a terribly depressing place for me. The air itself seemed charged with the gloom of a funeral parlor, the chill of the graveyard. Everywhere, on tables and walls and mantles, were pictures of the only child.

Josephine Albanowski, some ten years younger than Stanley, did most of the talking. You couldn't help seeing that Patricia had been Josephine's daughter. The mother was tall with the same red hair. She would still have been beautiful just a few months before.

Stanley Albanowski stood well over six feet tall, strong, wiry, big hands, good character lines written all over his face. If he made a promise, you could go to the bank with it. What you saw with Mr. Albanowski was what you got: honesty, candor, trust of his fellow man.

They were qualities Patricia possessed in the extreme. Especially trust. Patricia, like her father, had been down-to-earth, a truth teller, and believed others were also. In a better world this trust would be a valued quality. In our world it killed.

Slowly what the Albanowskis knew about their daughter's whirlwind courtship by Giesick came out. "Mommy," she had told Josephine, "I like him, and I'll learn to love him." Family counted a lot to Patricia. She wanted nothing more from life than her mother had, an honorable husband and a good home where she could raise children and be happy. Giesick, of course, promised more, a royal existence filled with yachts and mansions. Trish believed.

One of Patricia's teachers had understood: "Sometimes very religious people are too trusting and too naive about the kind of people who exist in this world. I think Trish was the kind of girl who could be fooled by someone."

Patricia's upbringing, strict Catholic, had indeed been religious. And her family had been very close-knit. Josephine and Stanley simply didn't make plans involving themselves, for instance a weekend outing or even a movie, that didn't include Patricia. The sun rose and set on their beautiful daughter.

Despite press coverage of the purpose of my trip, the Albanowskis had no idea of why I'd chosen this time to visit. Nor did they ask. They seemed content to reminisce about Patricia.

I feared telling them all I knew, the part about bigamy, the dance in the restaurant when Corey and Giesick knew Patricia was dead, and so much more that made even veteran John Noon sick. Forget these were parents whose world revolved around their daughter. It had to be done. They needed to know so they could understand how important it was to violate Patricia's remains.

I talked and they listened, though I couldn't be sure how much they understood. They didn't interrupt. Stanley nodded a great deal, as if something was being confirmed for him; Josephine's face could have been carved from stone, a monumental effort, I guessed, needed to keep it that way. It occurred to me that they really didn't understand at all the legal niceties—hearsay, circumstantial, corroboration, physical evidence—but that they trusted me.

The cozily eerie little living room lay quiet when I finished. Finished except for the most important part, and I'd rehearsed a dozen lines to deliver. When the moment came, I couldn't remember one.

"I have to obtain samples of Patricia's hair," I said. "To obtain them we need permission to exhume Patricia's body."

The room became totally still, now that I'd stopped. I could hear myself breathe.

"If that's the only way," Stanley said. It was about the only thing he'd said all evening. "If that's the only way, I guess you better do it."

"When will this take place?" Josephine asked.

"Tomorrow afternoon."

Again, a long silence.

"What time should I be there?" Stanley said.

"Mr. Albanowski, you and your wife, God knows, have been through enough suffering. It's not necessary for you to attend the exhumation. I can take care of everything."

"I want to be there."

"Mr. Albanowski . . ."

"I'm going to be there."

The casket came out of the ground at 2:00 P.M. on May 30, Memorial Day weekend. The reporters outnumbered police, and TV cameras recorded the bizarre ceremony.

A black hearse transported the casket to the Winowica Funeral Home on Adeline Street in Trenton. I followed behind in Noon's car, and the TV crews followed us. Trenton police carried the casket to the basement embalming room, where it was opened by Dr. David Fluck, the Mercer County medical examiner. I stood right over the casket, Stanley Albanowski just inches behind at my right shoulder. "You don't have to stay for this," I whispered, but he wouldn't budge.

I guess we saw what remained of Patricia at the same time. For me, going through this for the first time, it wasn't as bad as I had thought it would be. She wore a pretty satin dress, and the chief sign of deterioration was a spider-web configuration, very intricate, traced all across her face. She might have been one hundred years old.

Everybody took a little step backward when the casket opened, out of respect, I suppose, and Mr. Albanowski came forward. He looked at his daughter, his face blank, but so much emotion and love there, and then he leaned down and over and hugged her one last time.

Dr. Fluck asked how many hair samples I needed (a hair sample consists of a patch of hair—perhaps twenty strands—and scalp), and I said at least three. The M.E. ended up taking four, placing each carefully into its own individual vial, which he taped shut, initialed, and gave to me to initial.

I walked with Mr. Albanowski out to his car, telling him how sorry I was that this had to take place.

"It was one of the few times she didn't listen to me," he said.

"Patricia?"

"I told her Giesick was no good. I never met him before the marriage, but I knew from what she said. He was in too big of a hurry."

I flew to Washington, D.C., that night, called the FBI from National Airport, and asked which hotel was nearest to their crime lab. The agent on the other end said it was the Watergate.

"Pretty expensive place, isn't it?" I asked.

"It's not too steep."

"I keep reading it's expensive." Mutz no longer worried about austerity programs with this case—it had become a heater—but I saw no sense in annoying him.

"Look," the FBI man said. "I know some people over there. I'll call and get you a special rate."

So I stayed at the Watergate.

I asked for John Hicks when I got to the FBI lab early the next morning. I'd phoned a few days before, and he'd agreed to run the tests on a same-day basis. I gave him the vials containing the hair patches, and he said I could come back in three hours.

The time got well spent at the nearby Smithsonian. I promised myself I'd bring Diane someday, to see the Hope Diamond, the dinosaurs, Lindbergh's *Spirit of St. Louis*, so much history. I refused to think about what an unfavorable report from Hicks would mean.

"Well, Agent Hicks," I asked, when the three hours elapsed and I'd returned to the lab, "how did we do?" Hicks wore a white lab smock with the FBI logo emblazoned on it, and black wing-tip shoes.

"Fifteen out of fifteen. We couldn't do any better."

I let this sink in. I wanted to jump in the air and click my heels. Physical evidence. I'd heard those words until they made me sick. Here was their goddam physical evidence. I felt like I'd won an Olympic Gold Medal.

"Fifteen out of fifteen," I said, needing to hear it again.

"That's it."

"And that means . . ."

"We can't say the hairs came from Patricia Albanowski, but . . ."

"They couldn't have come from anyone else."

"You've got it."

Yes, I did! Not what Hicks meant, but something much more important.

We'd had a powerful circumstantial case: one I thought we'd win. But now we possessed the physical evidence, which *everyone* agreed was what we needed to win. How could hairs found on the undercarriage of a car Giesick rented, match fifteen out of fifteen characteristics of Patricia's own hair (couldn't have come from anywhere else, said Hicks), if that car hadn't run her down?

My excitement ran so high I don't remember much about the return flight to New Orleans. Just that I wanted to get back and tell Diane what happened, then spend the whole blessed night waking up Mutz, Volz, Whalen, Dantagnan, Saladino, everyone I could think of who'd touched this case.

—13—

ON JUNE 6, a D day of sorts for us, Ralph Whalen introduced me to the grand jury, said I'd be presenting a murder case, and retired to a chair a discreet distance away. Stomach churning, bone-deep tired (I'd been awake all night, actually rehearsing), I stood at one end of the long table, the foreman of the grand jury at its head. The eleven other members of the blue-ribbon panel were arrayed along each side: a cross-section of New Orleans—women, men, blacks, whites, even a Cajun.

Whalen aimed for a second-degree murder indictment, conviction for which carried a sentence of life in prison. We'd wanted to go for first-degree, the electric chair, but Whalen didn't feel the crime fit first-degree murder as defined under Louisiana Revised Statutes 14:30, which read as follows: "First degree murder is the killing of a human being: (1) When the offender has a specific intent to kill or to inflict great bodily harm and is engaged in the perpetration or attempted perpetration of aggravated kidnapping, aggravated rape or armed robbery; or (2) When the offender has a specific intent to kill, or to inflict great bodily harm upon, a fireman or a peace officer who was engaged in the performance of his lawful duties; or (3) Where the offender has a specific intent to kill or to inflict great bodily harm and has previously been convicted of an unrelated murder or is serving a life sentence; or (4) When the offender has a specific intent to kill or to inflict great bodily harm upon more than one person; or (5) When the offender has specific intent to commit murder and has been offered or has received anything of value for committing the murder.''

Premeditation, talked about so much on television police dramas, and cold-bloodedness didn't figure in determining first-degree murder. I thought the police dramas depicted what the law *should* be. Certainly few murders had been planned as thoroughly as this one.

I talked to the grand jury for four hours. Adrenaline took over and I rode its heady high through a mass of evidence. None of what I presented, taken alone, could justify a murder indictment, but seen as a whole it comprised a convincing case. Of course, persuading a grand jury to indict is much easier than getting a jury to convict. An indictment does not indicate guilt, only that enough evidence has been presented to warrant a trial. More important, the grand jury hears only one side.

The grand jury could have asked tough questions. For instance, Who drove the murder vehicle? "Corey, I think," I would have answered because that's what Giesick told me, but a fuss could have been made.

Instead, when I finished and apologized for "such a long and confusing presentation," no questions came forth. I stared at what seemed to be blank faces. Finally, the grand jury foreman spoke up, and it was as though I were listening to John Noon again: "Detective Dillmann, this grand jury has been sitting for many weeks, and this is the most thorough presentation we've heard."

Thirty seconds later, Ralph Whalen, who was in an adjoining room about to pour a cup of coffee, was called back by the grand jury. They wanted him to know the indictments were being issued. Whalen couldn't tell me this—I'd have to wait until evening for a judge to make the announcement—but when he came out of the grand jury room and shook my hand, I knew.

The news media got the results that night, and I started receiving calls from all over the country. What meant the most, however, were the congratulations I received from fellow homicide detectives. I was becoming one of them, after all.

But this case hadn't been half won. We had much stronger evidence against Giesick than Corey. The murder vehicle itself had been rented by Giesick. Giesick was the beneficiary of the insurance. We could place Giesick at the scene of the crime, but Corey only in the vicinity. Giesick had made inculpatory statements. Corey hadn't.

Because both of the accused men lived out of state, fugitive warrants were issued. The widespread media coverage guaranteed speedy action.

Corey and Giesick turned themselves in. William Miller, considered an elite San Antonio defense attorney, represented Corey; the preacher returned to New Orleans voluntarily, was arrested, arraigned, and pled not guilty. Corey gave the impression of a man deeply wronged but eager to clear his name. Whalen asked for $250,000 bail, but the judge set the figure at $100,000, an amount Corey evidently had no trouble posting. We wondered if this meant the judge believed our case a weak one.

David Evans, a former influential state legislator, very well connected politically, represented Giesick. The high-powered Evans was considered one of the best defense lawyers in Texas. Neither Corey nor Giesick intended to entrust his fate to someone appointed by the court.

Evans proposed a deal to Whalen within a matter of days. Giesick, Evans said, could fight extradition "for years." Moreover, Evans didn't think we had much of a case against Corey. Giesick would be willing to turn state's evidence if Whalen would reduce the charge against Giesick to manslaughter. To say I didn't like this deal is putting it mildly. I hated it, and so did Whalen.

I flew to San Antonio on June 29, 1974, the fifth-month anniversary of Mutz's having given me the case. My purpose was to meet with Evans and Giesick to learn what the phony psychologist would say and relay the information to Whalen. Before this took place, however, I met in the San Antonio district attorney's office with a sixteen-year-old girl named Patrice Clor, who had read about the case in the newspaper and come forward voluntarily. Patrice said she had been in Giesick's Tuxford Drive home on January 2, the day of Patricia's marriage. Not only was Claudius Giesick, whom she knew as Guilliam, in the house, but so too was Sam Corey. Later, this would become an important piece of information.

I met with David Evans in his office, which could only be described as luxurious. Evans, in his early fifties, quite distinguished in a four-hundred-dollar suit, had an engaging manner and a quick mind. A person would like him right away, a potential disadvantage for the individual if he or she forgot about business.

Immediately we had problems. Evans wanted Whalen to agree to a manslaughter charge, then Giesick would talk. The first assistant district attorney's scenario for justice envisioned Giesick confessing, at which time Whalen would consider a deal.

For a time it seemed an insurmountable barrier, but lawyers have their ways. Whalen said Evans should make a "proffer," that is, Evans himself should relate what Giesick would say (this could not be used in court), and from this a decision would be made, assuming Giesick did indeed confess to what his attorney promised.

I sat open-mouthed as Evans ran the case down for me.

The deal was Whalen's to make, but he wanted my agreement. It would not be an exaggeration to say I've never had a tougher decision. Whalen said the same applied for him. We'd known Giesick was no boy scout, but hadn't been prepared for the depravity we'd just heard. It chilled the blood. Just listening to Evans turned my fingers icy cold, and he'd been trying to put the best face on the murderer. Hideous, evil, grotesque, all were words lacking the adequacy to describe this killer.

To let Giesick off with twenty-one years for manslaugh-

ter represented an abomination of justice. Evans' account
of the crime echoed in my mind, my stomach knotted, and
I wanted to smash something, anything.

Whalen and I hemmed and hawed. Neither wanted to
make a recommendation.

"I'm not sure we can convict Corey," Whalen finally
said.

"But—Geesus!" I swam in a freezing sea of frustration.

"Maybe it boils down to this," Whalen said, as I feared
he had to. "Who's worse? Corey or Giesick?"

"What kind of question is that?" But I knew what kind
of question. Now that I understood the case, most of it, the
thought of Giesick and twenty-one years made me sick.

"Tell me. Who's worse?"

"I have to think about it."

"Then think!"

And I did. The entire case flashed through my mind,
like it's said a drowning man sees his own life. My voice
contained no confidence at all when it said, "Corey. I
guess."

"Then we'd better make that deal with Evans."

Brain reeling, hating what life had become, I went to
the defense attorney and told him to go ahead, to bring
Giesick into the office. I think Evans knew how miserable
I felt. I knew this decision would haunt Whalen and me
forever.

Even Evans, who'd heard it before, became freshly
shocked by Giesick's account, not just by what he said but
how he said it. Without a trace of remorse. Pitiless. *I got
caught*, his attitude screamed, *so I'll lessen the damage.
Wish I had gotten away with it. A damn good plan we had.
But the time's come to minimize the harm to myself.*

What follows is the confession of Claudius James Giesick, which I took, given with the understanding that if it
was not true, murder charges would be reinstituted against
him:

*   *   *

DILLMANN: Mr. Giesick, for the record would you please state your correct name, date of birth, social security number, and place of employment?

GIESICK: My correct name is Claudius James Giesick, Jr.—G-i-e-s-i-c-k. I was born October 11, 1947. I am twenty-six years old. My social security number is 454-74-0361. My place of employment is with the San Antonio New Residence Buyers Directory in San Antonio as a salesman.

DILLMANN: Mr. Giesick, have you ever used an alias prior to this statement?

GIESICK: Yes, I went by the name of Charles J. Guilliam, G-u-i-l-l-i-a-m.

DILLMANN: Did you obtain any identification in the name of Charles J. Guilliam?

GIESICK: Yes. A driver's license. And then several credit cards at a later date.

DILLMANN: Relative to the death of your wife, Patricia Ann Giesick, who was killed in New Orleans on January 16, 1974, on Michoud Boulevard approximately 764 feet from its intersection with Chef Menteur Highway, this death was first reported to our department as a hit-and-run accident. Did your wife's death result from a hit-and-run accident?

GIESICK: It was a hit-and-run, but it was not an accident.

DILLMANN: Would you please relate exactly what happened on that night and the circumstances leading to what you have just stated was not an accident?

GIESICK: My wife Katherine and I moved back to San Antonio on November 5, 1973, with the hope I could work with Mr. Corey on a franchise with a credit card company, and also with the idea of helping him franchise his massage parlors. And we discussed a little bit of salary and what I could make with him, and at this time my wife and I felt we could afford a house on Tuxford in San Antonio. We signed the papers for intent to buy it, and in discussions with Mr. Corey, we decided not to get the credit card franchise. We actually decided to do the franchising of the massage parlors, my not knowing at the time of his financial status, and him thinking that would be a fast source of revenue.

At some point between November fifth and approximately the first of December, Mr. Corey discovered my real name was not Guilliam, and he learned I had a warrant for my arrest for check fraud in Bexar County, Texas. He said if I helped him my secret was his secret and Kathy need never know he knew the truth. I asked him what he had in mind, and he mentioned a simple car accident. We proceeded around the fourth of December to Ardmore, Oklahoma, to obtain an Oklahoma driver's license under the name of Giesick, came back to San Antonio, and he paid me $500 to engage in a rear-end collision with his 1973 Buick on December 7, 1973. During the accident, there were no occupants in his vehicle. After I crashed into the back of his vehicle, he, his wife, a young lady named Deborah White, and Edie Hernandez all claimed injuries and collected insurance money from Allstate Insurance Company in the collision.

At that point Mr. Corey invited me out to eat one afternoon at Sir George's Royal Buffet, and he hit me with the idea of using my identification in the name Giesick, marrying a young lady from Dallas, taking out a short insurance policy on her, and on a seventy-five–twenty-five basis take the girl's life. I told him it sounded good, but asked why was he interested in the money, and he explained to me his financial status. He not only explained it to me, when he took me back to his office, he showed it to me. His financial status was really down. Then I knew I had no earthly way of making any money with Mr. Corey. He brought up the check situation again. At this time, the idea of going to jail was a motivation to continue working with Mr. Corey. I told Mr. Corey I would work with him provided I did not have to see the accident, that I could be totally someplace else. Originally he said it would be set up with me in El Paso, and she would be driving to El Paso, have a two-car collision, and I would get the news in the midst of a group of people in El Paso. Well, this was fine with me as long as I didn't have to actually participate in it.

At some point later, before we discussed choosing the girl, he mentioned an alternative of using a rental car. If we used a rental car, most rental car companies had a $50,000 policy on the actual person who drove the car in an accidental death. And I told him no, because under the name of Giesick I had no credit cards, I had no way of getting a rent-a-car with that type of insurance coverage. Your good rental companies require credit. So we abandoned the idea, and set forth to find a girl.

Originally, I was to join a lonely hearts club and pick a girl out of the names given to me by this club. I met one girl in person, and the rest I talked to briefly on the telephone. It was the very next day at the Marriott Hotel that Mr. Corey and I met with Mr. Jim Floyd in the coffee shop. Mr. Floyd had a young lady with him that worked for him whose name was Ann—I believe her last name was Turner. Ann made a comment to Mr. Floyd that if I wanted a massage, being a friend of Mr. Corey's, they would arrange for it at their Geisha House in Irving, Texas. I was agreeable. They called and told me they had a strawberry blonde over there, and her name was Trish. I went over with the intent of getting a massage. The young lady cried, I talked to her for a while and became sympathetic with her. Later I explained to Mr. Corey what had happened. Trish had given me her home phone number and I talked with her on the phone the next day and had subsequent calls to her, I guess Christmas Day, and actually between Christmas and New Year's Katherine and I had a falling-out. Christmas Eve I had a big fight with Katherine's mother to the point that I would not allow the two children to go. And I went on to Dallas.

I came back between Christmas and New Year's and Kathy presented me with my suitcases and told me to go my happy way. So I did. I went back to Dallas and dated Trish a couple of times, and she came to San Antonio a couple of times. This was between Christmas and New Year's.

Trish talked about a young man she followed to Dallas and she broke up with him. After several talks with Trish, between me and her, and between her and Mr. Corey, Mr. Corey decided we should pursue Patricia.

I pursued by discussing the idea of marrying her. She was under the impression I made a lot of money, that I had a lot of nice things, it was the beginning of a good future for her. We tried to get married before January first. We could not, so we tried to get married January second. I was supposed to fly to Dallas early in the morning; we were to get our blood tests in Dallas. I called her because Mr. Corey didn't want me to go up that early in the morning. I told her I'd get my blood test in San Antonio, which I did do, for her to get hers in Dallas, and we would go to the Dallas County Courthouse and get a marriage license, which we did do. That evening after unsuccessful attempts to find a justice of the peace to marry us, we called Mr. Corey to come up to Dallas. Mr. Corey performed the ceremony in Dallas. There were no witnesses to the ceremony.

I left the next day on what I explained to Trish was "business" and returned two days later. The marriage license came back to us three days later. It had on it witnesses. When I presented this to Mr. Corey, it was explained to me that Tonie Byas, who is his manager at the Tokyo House in San Antonio, had signed the certificate "T. Rogers." There was another signature, I forgot the first initial, the last name was Lee, but it was signed by Edie Hernandez. And I believe her name is Edith Lee Hernandez. I asked why this was done, and he said to make it look more formal. It being his first wedding ceremony, that's what he wanted.

Mr. Corey and I made a couple of trips to Dallas that Trish did not know about. On one of these trips, we stopped at the Mutual of Omaha insurance counter in San Antonio and picked up a brochure on trip insurance. On reading the brochure on the airplane, we found out it had a coverage A, B, and C. Coverage C, in fact, covered automobile accidents, including hit-and-run. We stopped at the Mutual of Omaha counter at Dallas' Love Field that very same day. We asked to see a copy of the policy and read it and verified that it did cover hit-and-run and automobile accidents. We asked to speak to someone who knew more about the policy than the young lady there. About that time, her manager came in and explained to us exactly what the policy covered. A statement was made to the effect that a friend of mine had been killed by a car hit-and-run, and I do not remember the name of the country we mentioned. And in this other country, we said, the insurance companies did not pay off, and we wanted to know would this, in this case, pay off. I don't remember if I directed the question or if Mr. Corey did. I know I was prompted on several questions by Mr. Corey. That was not the final visit we had to Mutual of Omaha. We made one other visit inquiring about the insurance policy.

Then around the sixth or seventh of January, after Mr. Corey and myself had planted into Patricia's head that we needed family life insurance protection, we contacted several agents. I set up appointments to take out a regular life insurance policy. Mr. Corey brought to our attention that Farmers had what is known as a nonsmokers insurance policy with accidental death benefit, not double indemnity but triple indemnity. So he and I together talked her into making an appointment with a Farmers insurance agent. We met at a coffee shop right outside of Love

Field on Mockingbird Lane. I set up with the agent an appointment for him to come to the apartment to take an insurance application. We also arranged with him to bring a nurse so we could have our physicals on the spot. He made the appointment at the apartment; we bought the insurance policies. The natural sales pitch was to increase them; the original idea was to have a small policy between $30,000 and $50,000. We took out a $50,000 policy on each of us. We each took accidental death benefit, triple indemnity on the nonsmokers policy. Mr. Corey gave me the money to put into my checking account at the Harlandale State Bank in San Antonio. The amount of money he gave covered the accidental death policy which was purchased later. And he gave me money to pay the rent on the apartment, he gave me money Trish needed to pay a couple of bills, and I wrote her a couple of checks. I wrote two and stopped payment on one. And also to pay for the insurance policies on her and myself.

After we took the physicals and bought the insurance, I returned to San Antonio and explained everything to Mr. Corey. We took her car down and traded it in on a 1974 Chevy Monte Carlo. We did this at Johnson Chevrolet in Dallas.

I believe that same day I drove the car to San Antonio, and Trish flew down the next day and picked the car up and drove it back to Dallas. While in San Antonio, she contacted Mr. Corey's wife, Rita, and spoke to her. It was a surprise to Mrs. Corey; she knew nothing of what was going on.

It really was not on schedule, because we originally weren't going to set any accident up until after March. But Mr. Corey got in the mail about the tenth four judgments against him, and the Internal Revenue Service contacted him in reference to some money he owed and were threatening to take his businesses away from him. He said we were going to have to rush things, we were going to have to speed things up. We proceeded to pick a city. We chose New Orleans.

We proceeded to the Dallas–Fort Worth Regional Airport January thirteenth, their grand opening day. We went there specifically to purchase the travel insurance from Tele-Trip, which is Mutual of Omaha. We purchased the insurance. We dropped it from $300,000 to $200,000 because we found that the extra $100,000 only covered commercial carriers. So we went back to the $200,000 figure. Mr. Corey deposited $294 in my checking account to cover the $300,000 figure, and we only used $234 to cover the $200,000 figure.

Patricia and I left that evening, after first stopping and answering an ad in the paper to buy a Saint Bernard dog. It was raining very heavily, and we were going slow, so it took us a while to get to Houston. We were both so tired we couldn't proceed any further, so we stopped in Houston on Interstate 45 and stayed at the Ramada Inn. We proceeded on to New Orleans the next morning. We got to New Orleans at approximately one P.M. We tried to check in at the Ramada at the Pontchartrain Causeway and the Interstate there; we could not, and proceeded to the Ramada Inn on the Chef Menteur Highway. Originally, Mr. Corey had told me it was the first one as you come into town on old Highway 90, and coming into town, I came in on

Interstate 10, and the first one I came to was the high-rise. I went to the Ramada Inn on the Chef Menteur Highway and checked in, left Patricia, and took the Monte Carlo to the shop to get it fixed. I gave a long list of items to be fixed, but the only thing wrong was the cruise control, which I had jimmied. Now, on leaving the car there, I called Trish and told her they were going to keep the car and that I would hitchhike back.

In the meantime, I called the downtown Avis Rent A Car. They picked me up in a Plymouth. They were going to give me the Plymouth and I asked for a Monte Carlo instead. I got a light-blue Monte Carlo and took it over to the Holiday Inn. By that time I'd learned Mr. Corey was checked in at the Holiday Inn at Pontchartrain Causeway. I went to the Holiday Inn, and I took everything I had with me that had Guilliam on it with the exception of my Exxon credit card and gave it in a locked briefcase to Mr. Corey. Now, also in that locked briefcase was a copy of the Tele-Trip insurance policy, which he had not seen, and the receipts I had from Farmers, which he had not seen either. And I showed him both of these because he wanted verification there was insurance. I told him where we were staying. He drove over to that area to find out where it was and came back, and I met him later that night, and used the excuse to Patricia that I wanted to get out by myself for a little while; and this was very early in the morning. Trish and I had been walking that night. She knew nothing of the rental car. I left it parked at the Exxon station at the corner of Michoud and Chef Menteur Highway.

That night when Trish and I were walking, I saw several of your patrol cars spotlight the rental car. They walked around and took a look at it. As a signal to Mr. Corey, I was to leave the white Avis Rent A Car litter bag on the window of the car, and the keys would be on top of the tire on the driver's front side. When I noticed the police checking the car out, I panicked a little and put on the "it's getting cool" bit and took Trish back to the hotel. I got back to the hotel and took a shower. After I got out of the shower I told her I really felt great and wanted to just go for a walk and just, you know, really go over things.

I went out of the hotel, and Mr. Corey was driving around at this time in a 1974 Buick that we stole from Dallas' Love Field in December. I got into the car with Mr. Corey, and we discussed what happened as far as the car being spotlighted by the patrol cars. I told him we had to return that car and get another car. He asked what would we use as an excuse to Avis, and I told him, well, wait a minute, and I took the transmission linkage and spread it a little bit to cause it to shift rough, and I took the car back to them and gave them the excuse the car wasn't running right.

We took the car back to Avis Rent A Car at the airport. I'd forgotten my driver's license and my Avis credit card, and the man was hesitant to give us another car. But he went ahead and took a chance, and gave us a maroon 1974 Chevy Monte Carlo. I dropped Mr. Corey off at the Holiday Inn. He checked out of that Holiday Inn and checked into the Quality Motor Court right next door to the

Ramada where we were staying, with a room facing our room. He parked his Buick behind the hotel, and I gave him the rental-car keys. Now, where he parked it, I don't know. He had the only set of keys to that rental car.

He and I discussed what was to take place. He said he had driven around the area and had seen three places that looked good to carry the death out at. And we decided on the Michoud Bayou area mainly because it was coming out of a residential section.

The very next afternoon, I took the Monte Carlo out of the shop and back to the hotel after hitchhiking to the Chevy dealership to get it. On hitchhiking to the Chevy dealership, I caught a ride a little ways down. Trish was watching me hitchhike and I had to thumb a ride. So I actually caught a ride. I got him to let me out a few blocks down the road, and Mr. Corey picked me up and took me to the Chevrolet dealership in the Buick. Again, we confirmed everything that was to take place that night.

Later Trish and I went to a pizza parlor on Chef Menteur Highway and came back to the hotel. By that time it was getting dark and foggy. As the night proceeded on, it became more foggy, which made a good excuse not to go out that night. At that point, Mr. Corey and I had not picked a specific time. When the fog came on, I pardoned myself for a little while. I wanted to go next door and get something to drink. At the time Trish had something in the room, a present for me, and she pulled it out. "Surprise! surprise!" she said, and I had to dig up more excuses. I got over to the motel next door, and went into Mr. Corey's room. He was smiling and laughing and said, "It's foggy, it's tonight, it's perfect, we're going to do it tonight." About eleven-thirty or twelve o'clock, he says.

I don't know exactly what time we went over there. I do know Trish had fallen asleep and I had to wake her up. I woke her and said, "Come on, it's real foggy, and it's a real neat night. Let's go walking." So we did. We went walking over to the bayou. It got busy around the area for quite some time, and then it started dropping off. I had seen Mr. Corey make several trips around the area in the Buick. And I guess there was about a fifteen- or twenty-minute period of time that I did not see him at all. When in position, he would signal by flashing his parking lights. He was to be parked down the street in front of this house. I saw the parking light flash. I knew he was there. I knew everything was ready. My signal to him was with a flashlight. I was to flash a flashlight, you know, just wave it back and forth. When he gave me the signal that he was there, when I was ready, I waved the flashlight. When I flashed the flashlight, he flashed the parking lights back that he was coming. His lights were off, completely off. I waited about four or five seconds to give him enough time to get started. I tripped her into the road, and he came by and hit her. It was him, he was driving the car, and I did see him. Seconds later the police were there because a guy came by and called the police. Then Mr. Corey came back in the Monte Carlo, just drove on by.

DILLMANN: Mr. Giesick, what were your reasons for becoming involved in this conspiracy with Sam Corey?

GIESICK: When I found out Mr. Corey's financial status, having signed the papers for a house I did not have the down payment on, I found it necessary to come up with enough money for the down payment. Mr. Corey told me that if I didn't cooperate with him, he would go to Detective Koby and tell Detective Koby who I really was, so I could go to jail on my check charge; and it was a felony check charge, so it would have been an extremely serious matter.

DILLMANN: Mr. Giesick, you mentioned a meeting between yourself, Mr. Corey, and one Jim Floyd. At the time of this meeting, what exactly was the relationship between Mr. Corey and Mr. Floyd, and do you believe this meeting was held strictly for the purpose of introducing you to Patricia Albanowski who, in fact, worked for Jim Floyd at the Geisha House in Irving, Texas?

GIESICK: I don't think it was set up for that particular reason—why they picked that particular girl, I don't know, but they did have a girl in mind for me to get a massage from—the two of them together did, even though Sam was without any knowledge of this girl prior to that time.

DILLMANN: At this meeting, did you get the impression from Corey that Patricia would be used for the plan you and he had conspired?

GIESICK: No, sir. Originally, I was supposed to go to the massage parlor by myself, and then suddenly I went with Mr. Corey, and then somebody came back and told me Mr. Corey and Mr. Floyd had left for a while, to take our time. And Patricia and I were there probably three or four hours. For some reason she kept coming up with things to talk about. We were there a long time.

DILLMANN: In your opinion, what made Sam Corey pick Patricia Albanowski as the victim to be used in this hit-and-run accident?

GIESICK: Several things. In his opinion she maintained hardly any intelligence at all. She was emotionally upset and shaken because of breaking up with Mr. Foley. She was—well, she was lonesome, nobody was asking her out—it was just an ideal situation. Mr. Corey counseled her several times before he said, "She's the one."

DILLMANN: Prior to this decision by Mr. Corey, had you and he discussed using anyone else?

GIESICK: Well, the reason for joining the lonely hearts club was to find someone. We had discussed only one other girl, and Mr. Corey couldn't stand being around her. He said he would blow her head off before we even had a chance to buy insurance, the way she was.

DILLMANN: Who was this girl?

GIESICK: Sheila Creeden, C-r-e-e-d-e-n. She's a girl Sam and I met at Victoria Station in Dallas. She and I hit it off. She has an extremely brilliant mind, and she and I hit it off.

DILLMANN: Mr. Giesick, to your knowledge, is Sam Corey actually an ordained minister?

GIESICK: He carried all the credentials and all the certificates. I know he wrote a thesis, because I helped pick out some of the passages for his thesis.

DILLMANN: Do you know his reasons for being ordained a minister, and, if so, did these reasons have anything to do with the ceremony between you and Patricia?

GIESICK: The reason for him becoming a minister was to separate church from state. He operated a massage parlor, and as an ordained minister, by converting the girls, his masseuses, into sisters of his order and turning his massage parlor into a massage temple, he could separate church and state. His full purpose was making the church separate so the police could not come in and raid him and so he could write things off of the tax rolls.

DILLMANN: So, in fact, his becoming an ordained minister had nothing to do with your marriage to Patricia?

GIESICK: Well, if he had not been ordained, we would not have gotten married January second; but he did not become a minister specifically for that purpose.

DILLMANN: Did either you or Mr. Corey when you inquired about insurance specify that you were only interested in hit-and-run insurance? And at this point, were you planning on collecting on a hit-and-run accident?

GIESICK: Yes, sir. At that point we were.

DILLMANN: To your knowledge, what made Patricia want to buy an insurance policy on her and yourself after the marriage?

GIESICK: Well, to build the family relationship. Part of the getting-married bit was promising her a family, and the security of insurance gives the security of family, and she was definitely in favor of the family insurance policy for college purposes at a later date.

DILLMANN: Did either you or Mr. Corey have anything to do with her feelings toward this?

GIESICK: Yes, sir. Very definitely.

DILLMANN: And what were the reasons behind this?

GIESICK: Well, the reasons behind it were to convince her that the insurance was necessary so we could make the contacts to get the insurance.

DILLMANN: Mr. Giesick, you mentioned that the premiums paid on the insurance policies were paid by you, but in fact the money was given to you by Sam Corey, is that correct?

GIESICK: Yes, sir.

DILLMANN: Mr. Giesick, did your wife Kathy have any idea of what was taking place?

GIESICK: No, no. She had suspicions of other things, but not of this, no.

DILLMANN: Mr. Giesick, when you married Patricia Albanowski on January 2, 1974, were you legally married to Katherine Kaiser?

GIESICK: Yes, I was.

DILLMANN: So your only purpose for marrying Patricia Albanowski was to obtain these insurance policies on her and obtain the money from her death, is that correct?

GIESICK: Yes, sir.

DILLMANN: At the time of her death, exactly how much insurance had been taken out on her life?

GIESICK: In regular insurance $50,000, and regular and counting accidental death, $350,000.

DILLMANN: Could you explain to me why you picked New Orleans?

GIESICK: Well, New Orleans—Number One, it's on the way to Disney World, which makes a good excuse for stopping off. And Number Two, it's a honeymoon city, and it just seemed like a natural place to go.

DILLMANN: Prior to arriving in New Orleans with Patricia, had you and Mr. Corey actually picked a location in New Orleans where this accident was to take place?

GIESICK: No, sir.

DILLMANN: How were you to contact Mr. Corey once you arrived in New Orleans?

GIESICK: Well, I was supposed to check into the first Ramada Inn on Old Highway 90 as you come into town, and the one he was speaking of was on the opposite side of town. And I didn't know this. It was a big misunderstanding. I then proceeded to call, or to make attempts to call him, and was unable to. He had called Katherine and told her he was in New Orleans and where he was at, and that he knew I was here, and that if I happened to call and see how everybody was, to tell me where he was.

DILLMANN: Mr. Giesick, when did you first contact Mr. Corey upon your arrival in New Orleans on January fourteenth?

GIESICK: From the Chevrolet dealership where I left my car.

DILLMANN: Did you call him at the Holiday Inn?

GIESICK: Yes, sir.

DILLMANN: And this is the Holiday on I-10 at Causeway?

GIESICK: Yes, sir.

DILLMANN: And you had made prior arrangements with Mr. Corey that he would be staying at this motel, and this is where you could contact him, is that correct?

GIESICK: Well, he was supposed to stay at the Holiday Inn closest to the Ramada where I was staying.

DILLMANN: What was the reason for putting your 1974 blue Monte Carlo in the shop here in New Orleans?

GIESICK: To have an excuse to get a rental car. A rental car for Mr. Corey to drive. The other reason was so Patricia would not know we had a car, and therefore we would have to walk wherever we went, and that particular Ramada Inn did not have a restaurant in the evenings.

DILLMANN: What means of transportation did Mr. Corey use to get to New Orleans on January fourteenth?

GIESICK: The 1974 Buick that was taken from Dallas' Love Field.

DILLMANN: Mr. Giesick, would you elaborate on this

1974 stolen Buick that Mr. Corey came to New Orleans in on January fourteenth?

GIESICK: We stole it, as I said, from Dallas' Love Field. We drove it to San Antonio. The idea was, a stolen car involved in a hit-and-run could have been driven by anyone.

DILLMANN: So, in fact, this car was stolen by yourself and Mr. Corey for the express purpose of bringing the vehicle to New Orleans to kill Patricia Giesick, is that correct?

GIESICK: That's correct.

DILLMANN: To your knowledge, where is this vehicle located at this time?

GIESICK: At this time it's in Houston; it's being used by the husband of Tonie Byas.

DILLMANN: Has this vehicle been altered in any way since it was returned from New Orleans?

GIESICK: Yes, sir, it very definitely has. Even the vinyl roof has been cut back to a half vinyl roof, and the car has been repainted to an off-brown color.

DILLMANN: To your knowledge, when Mr. Corey departed from San Antonio en route to New Orleans to meet you, did he do anything to this vehicle so as not to draw suspicion that it was a stolen vehicle?

GIESICK: The license plates that were on the car when he drove to New Orleans were the duplicate set of license plates Mr. Corey had obtained from Orsinger Buick Leasing Company in order to replace the license plates on the seventy-three Buick he had leased from Orsinger.

DILLMANN: Were any plans made to put the stolen plates back on the car once it was in New Orleans?

GIESICK: Not only made, but it occurred.

DILLMANN: Was this vehicle to be used in the actual commission of the crime, or was it in fact to be used as Mr. Corey's getaway?

GIESICK: The vehicle originally was to be used as Mr. Corey's getaway.

DILLMANN: At any time, did Patricia have any knowledge that Sam Corey was in town?

GIESICK: No, sir.

DILLMANN: Were any pains taken by either you or Mr. Corey to keep him concealed so Patricia would not know he was in town?

GIESICK: He would call our motel room, and if she answered he would hang up.

DILLMANN: At the time Mr. Corey checked into the Quality Inn, which would be January 15, 1974, after you swapped cars at the airport, exactly where was the rental vehicle, the seventy-four maroon Monte Carlo?

GIESICK: It was in his possession. I don't know where he put the car, but he had it, and the only set of keys.

DILLMANN: And the seventy-four stolen Buick, was that also in Mr. Corey's possession?

GIESICK: Yes, sir.

DILLMANN: So at this point you were under the impression that the stolen vehicle would be used in the accident, is that correct?

GIESICK: Yes, sir.

DILLMANN: Did you and Mr. Corey discuss how the girl would be placed in front of the car and be hit?

GIESICK: I had to put her there.

DILLMANN: And you made prior arrangements as far as signals go?

GIESICK: Yes, sir.

DILLMANN: With a flashlight, as you previously stated, and the blinking of his parking lights? Correct?

GIESICK: Yes, sir.

DILLMANN: Mr. Giesick, after giving Mr. Corey the signal, you tripped Patricia into the street, is that correct?

GIESICK: Yes, sir.

DILLMANN: Was she lying on the ground at that time?

GIESICK: She was in a semiprone position; she was attempting to get up, part of her body was facing up trying to get up.

DILLMANN: In exactly what position was her body when she was struck by the vehicle?

GIESICK: She was laying sort of diagonally with her head heading north in the center where the stripes are of that southbound lane.

DILLMANN: But she was on the ground?

GIESICK: She was on the ground, yes, sir.

DILLMANN: Did the vehicle roll over your wife, Mr. Giesick?

GIESICK: Yes, sir.

DILLMANN: And what would you estimate the speed that Mr. Corey was driving the car at that time?

GIESICK: Between twenty and thirty.

DILLMANN: Can you positively identify Samuel Corey behind that wheel?

GIESICK: Yes, sir.

DILLMANN: And for the record, would you again state exactly what car he was driving?

GIESICK: He was driving the 1974 maroon Monte Carlo rented from Avis Rent A Car at New Orleans International Airport.

DILLMANN: Did you question Mr. Corey as to why he didn't use the Buick?

GIESICK: No, sir.

DILLMANN: At the moment of impact, was Patricia lying flat on the ground, or was she on her hands and knees, or what?

GIESICK: Well, she was on her hands trying to get back up again, but she was facing up. As she was trying to get up, she had sandals on, and she was slipping. She couldn't get up.

DILLMANN: Did Patricia fall on her back or fall on her stomach?

GIESICK: She fell on her back. When I tripped her, I hit her leg, and she fell over.

DILLMANN: So her face would have been pointing up and her back would have been to the road, is that correct?

GIESICK: Yes. There was a double thud. It very distinctly hit her twice.

DILLMANN: Was her head above or below the bumper of the car?

GIESICK: I really don't know.

DILLMANN: Her hips, were they above or below the bumper?

GIESICK: Again, I don't know.

DILLMANN: Do you know if she was struck by the bumper of the car?

GIESICK: No, I don't. I don't know at all. I know she was down. Mr. Corey said she was down and didn't do any damage to the car, and we were home free.

DILLMANN: Did the driver's side or the passenger's side of the automobile pass over her head?

GIESICK: I don't know because I don't know if it spun her, or if it just went over her, because when she fell, she didn't fall the way she was laying, she fell almost straight across the road, and yet, when the car was gone she was laying diagonally. It could have spun her, so I don't know.

DILLMANN: But from the original position that she fell, it would have been the passenger's side of the vehicle that would have passed over the area where her head was?

GIESICK: No, from the original way she fell, it would have been the driver's side.

DILLMANN: Mr. Giesick, after the accident occurred and you proceeded to Methodist Hospital, did Mr. Corey at any time contact you while at the hospital?

GIESICK: No, sir, I contacted him to come to the hospital.

DILLMANN: And what was your reason for contacting him?

GIESICK: I was scared to death.

DILLMANN: Did he, in fact, contact you at the hospital?

GIESICK: Yes, sir.

DILLMANN: What was the discussion between you and Mr. Corey when he came to Methodist Hospital?

GIESICK: Mr. Corey was extremely scared that Patricia might live and be able to identify him and me both.

DILLMANN: When did you learn your wife had expired?

GIESICK: We were back at the Ramada Inn, Sam and I both, when we got a call from the hospital, and we were asked to come back to the hospital. And Sam jumped up and touched his fists together and said, ''She's dead. We're okay.'' We went back to the hospital, and as soon as the doctors told me, we went outside for a few minutes, and his whole talk was of how the money was going to get spent and we needed to get the insurance papers filed immediately because he needed the money as soon as possible.

DILLMANN: Did you and Mr. Corey depart New Orleans together?

GIESICK: Yes, sir.

DILLMANN: And what means of transportation did you use to go back to Texas?

GIESICK: We used the airlines. I think Delta from here to Houston; from Houston we used Braniff commuter passes to San Antonio.

DILLMANN: When you and Mr. Corey left New Orleans, where did you leave the seventy-four maroon Monte Carlo used to kill Patricia and also the stolen car that was brought in originally?

GIESICK: The stolen car was left at the Ramada Inn on the Chef Menteur Highway with the stolen license plates on it. The rental vehicle was turned in to the downtown Avis office, and then Mr. Corey and myself proceeded out to the airport in my Monte Carlo.

DILLMANN: Where did you leave this seventy-four Monte Carlo, your own personal car?

GIESICK: I think they call it Park and Fly.

DILLMANN: Did either you or Mr. Corey return to New Orleans after this to retrieve the vehicles?

GIESICK: Yes, sir. Myself, Katherine, the two girls, Mr. Corey, and Tonie Byas. We put the good license plates back on the Buick.

DILLMANN: Then it's my understanding that you, your wife Kathy, your two children, Sam Corey, and Tonie Rogers Byas returned to New Orleans after the death of Patricia for the express purpose of picking up the stolen vehicle which had been brought to New Orleans to commit the murder, is that correct?

GIESICK: That's correct.

DILLMANN: Mr. Giesick, did you and Mr. Corey fly to Trenton, New Jersey, to attend the funeral of Patricia?

GIESICK: Yes, sir.

DILLMANN: In what capacity did Mr. Corey accompany you to the funeral?

GIESICK: As a minister. He was wearing Catholic-priest clothes and was paid by the Albanowski family as a priest; he accepted several donations.

DILLMANN: What specifically were these donations given to Mr. Corey for?

GIESICK: I believe they were for prayers for Patricia.

—14—

THE TRIAL. WHICH began on April 22, 1975, brought them all together for the first time: the witnesses, each with a small parcel of information to add; FBI Agent Hicks; people who worked for insurance companies, auto rental agencies, motels; policemen like San Antonio's Koby and New Orleans' Fayard; hospital personnel; medical doctors; young Patrice Clor (the girl who had seen Giesick and Corey together on January 2, 1974, in "Guilliam's" home); and plenty of witnesses for Corey himself—they'd been put up by the defense in a nearby hotel, and everyone wondered what they would say. Did Corey have a rabbit to pull out of his hat?

Set to play their roles were the major attractions: the State's star witness, Claudius Giesick, who'd tell the jury the entire plot; the Albanowskis, one or both of whom would testify, looking old as the macabre and bizarre drama approached its climax; Kathy Giesick, who the day before had relayed explosive information to prosecutor Ralph Whalen, information perhaps too melodramatic even for Perry Mason (I didn't know what Kathy would say, only that it excited Whalen, and scared him); and Sam Corey himself, outwardly composed, a man supremely confident of vindication—if he testified, everyone agreed, with The Whacker interrogating, it would be theater of the first rank.

Texas Monthly magazine described what the prosecutor had to overcome: "Whalen found himself matched against a lawyer whose reputation was as old and established as Whalen's was new and promising. Irvin Dymond, the most famous criminal lawyer in New Orleans, the man who had defended Clay Shaw, had taken Corey's case. While Whalen was short, trim, neatly dressed, and aggressive and intent in the courtroom, Dymond had a calmer style, slower, and, in appearance at least, not at all flamboyant. About thirty years older than Whalen, Dymond had not only the benefit of longer experience in the courts but also a marvelous deep voice and a talent for a sonorous and compelling oratory that is seldom found outside of the South. William Miller, Corey's San Antonio lawyer, also helped with his defense. . . . Dymond's responsibilities were to try the case, while Miller's were research and investigation."

Irvin Dymond had demolished Jim Garrison in the Kennedy assassination conspiracy trial, and he'd won many other headline trials over the decades. It was said he'd never lost a case, which didn't seem possible, even Clarence Darrow lost cases, but no one came forth with an example. From the confidence I'd observed in pretrial hearings, Dymond didn't expect to lose this one.

Not a great number of events took place between the taking of Giesick's confession and the opening day of the trial, but those that did weighed heavily on prosecution and defense alike. After my meeting with Giesick in San Antonio, he was brought to New Orleans, repeated his confession to Whalen, and was told he could plead guilty to manslaughter after he testified. The killer con man was held in jail without bond. Giesick wanted to be free until the trial, but Whalen wouldn't hear of it. The prosecutor feared Corey might try to kill him. Just as important, Whalen felt ill, as I did, every time we thought of the deal

made with Giesick, and didn't intend him to be loosed on
the citizenry.

Letting Giesick go with manslaughter preyed on my
mind. Flashes of his confession kept assailing me. Patricia
giving him a present that night, while he schemed to meet
with Corey to finalize plans for her death. Giesick virtually
auditioning young women to find the best one to kill.
Giesick playing on the human desire of a would-be mother
to provide for her children's education, getting her to
purchase life insurance. So much more.

I didn't think I could feel worse about the deal we'd
made, but this was before I received the call from Wade
Renfro in the San Antonio prosecutor's office. "I want to
pass on some information," Renfro said.

"Yes?" I said.

"Your guy Giesick and his wife, Kathy. Looks like
they'll lose those two adopted children of theirs."

Giesick had somehow convinced the state of Texas that
he was a child psychologist, eager to adopt unfortunate
children and provide them the benefits of a loving, warm,
prosperous home. These were the kids I'd seen playing
and hugging Kathy Giesick on my first visit to the Tuxford
Drive residence.

"I should hope they'd lose them," I said.

"No," said Renfro. "You don't understand. Giesick
tried to take out large life insurance policies on those kids.
With himself as beneficiary."

Why would someone take out large life insurance policies on preschool children?

I thanked Renfro for his call, and wondered if any of the
effort on this case had been worthwhile. Giesick, tripping
his wife underneath the vehicle driven by the grotesque
Corey, would get twenty-one years. The preacher, judging
from his demeanor and that of his attorney, might not get
anything. Looking around for someone to blame, I focused
on Ralph Whalen, but he tortured himself as much as I
did. And we *had* made the decision together.

Originally the trial was set for September 1974, but

Irvin Dymond obtained a continuance. Evidently William Miller, the lawyer in charge of research and investigation, was still busy lining up those witnesses we feared.

The trial was reset for November 6, and Whalen called me into his office a few days before to drop a bombshell. "You won't believe what I plan to do," he said.

"What?"

"I'm going to drop charges against Sam Corey."

"What!" Whalen's words rang in my ears. It had to be a joke, but Whalen wasn't smiling.

"We're due for trial next week, and this time *I'm* not ready. Some of our important witnesses have moved. This is the biggest trial in New Orleans since Clay Shaw, and I'd look like a fool without those witnesses in the courtroom. I don't intend to look like a fool."

"I don't care how you look," I said hotly. "Get a continuance until you can find the witnesses."

"Dymond won't give me one."

"You gave him a continuance."

"He says that's too bad. He's a tough old bird."

I think Ralph wanted to play his game a little longer, but could see I might start throwing furniture. So he said, "Calm down," and in a tone almost conspiratorial, told me what he really had in mind. He planned quite a show, and it turned out to be everything he hoped for. It all happened very quickly.

"I'd like to ask for a continuance," Whalen told Judge Rudolph Becker on November 6. The courtroom was packed.

"We object to a continuance," said Irvin Dymond.

"I want to drop charges," said Ralph Whalen.

Judge Becker wasn't sure he'd heard correctly. Dymond seemed thunderstruck. The first to react was Corey. He broke into an ear-to-ear grin. He gave Dymond a little pat on the shoulder. Then the audience in the courtroom realized what had happened, and emitted an audible collective gasp. It was just incredible, after all the buildup in the press, that the case would simply never be tried.

"I want to drop the charges," said Whalen, when the courtroom quieted, "because we intend to indict Mr. Corey for *first*-degree murder."

Again the big vaultlike chamber buzzed, chiefly with confusion. A few reporters hurried to telephones. Others sensed the drama had not been entirely played out. Judge Becker gaveled the arena to order and proceeded to grant Whalen's request.

Corey, still thinking himself a winner, a broad smile on his face, came bustling through the double doors of the courtroom into the corridor where I waited. Dymond walked right at his side.

"Mr. Corey," I said, "you're under arrest."

"For what?" Dymond asked.

"First-degree murder. I'm putting the cuffs on you. Taking you over to be booked."

"Can't we wait to see if he's indicted?"

"No."

"Hold off on the handcuffs, will you?"

I thought this over. I thought of Patricia.

"No," I said. "We're going to do this right."

I cuffed him in front. I would have cuffed him in back, but he was so fat his hands wouldn't reach.

We had to go two blocks to get to headquarters, an elating walk for me down what detectives jokingly call Hollywood Walk, and TV cameras ground away the entire journey. Corey looked shocked. Dymond seethed. He didn't think this a proper way to treat a client of his. An innocent client, he believed.

The next day, November 7, I appeared again in front of the grand jury, which promptly issued an indictment for first-degree murder. The key was Giesick's confession, specifically the part where he said Corey paid the insurance premiums. This made the case murder-for-hire, which is what Part 5 of Louisiana Revised Statutes 14:30 intended as first-degree. The preacher could now be sentenced to the electric chair. It took a little of the sour taste away from the bad arrangement we had with Giesick.

Corey spent overnight in jail, and the next day Dymond argued for bond. It seemed Corey had an excessive fear of jail, especially the Orleans Parish Prison, admittedly an undesirable and dangerous facility. So great was Corey's fear that he appeared willing to take any risk: he insisted on testifying at the bond hearing, which made Whalen ecstatic. He questioned Corey about the murder, which he said "locked" the preacher into certain positions he later might regret. Corey got his bail, but Whalen believed it to be an expensive victory.

The courtroom was packed on April 22, even for jury selection, which lasted well into the afternoon. Some two hundred people could fit into the impressive chamber, with its thirty-foot-high vaulted ceiling, and when one left the room there were twenty waiting to take his or her place.

Judge Becker's courtroom differed from most. Since he liked to smoke, he allowed the jurors, prosecutors, and defense to smoke. Becker used cigarettes. Sam Corey puffed on a pipe.

Rudolph Becker didn't look his forty-one years. Youthful and trim, with jet-black hair, his reputation was one of firm impartiality: the facts would speak for themselves. I felt we couldn't ask for more. I didn't think breaks were needed to win this case, just a fair judge and an intelligent jury. The jury needed to grasp a mass of evidence.

Diane and I had had dinner with the Albanowskis the night before, and I had arranged for their hotel room. I believe I was more on edge than they. This represented by far my most important case. I'd been the one who pushed it, became obsessed with it. I'd forged ahead when others indicated it might best be forgotten. In a real sense I thought I was on trial. At the very least my work was.

When the Albanowskis asked if I thought Corey would be convicted, I said yes. That seemed good enough for them. They trusted me. I said yes, but I felt *maybe*.

What worried me was Dymond's air of supreme confidence. Was it just a show? I wondered about those witnesses he had.

Diane didn't come to the opening day of the trial. I'd told her it would be mostly jury selection. I didn't know that Judge Becker, faced with a crowded court docket, would allow each court session to run late into the night.

John Dillmann, Sr., my grandfather, didn't miss a single day. His father, my great-grandfather, had been a New Orleans detective from 1904 to 1944.

Ralph Whalen's opening statement to the jury consisted of a low-key telling of what the State intended to prove. A great deal of testimony needed to be digested, and Whalen wanted to alert the jurors, prepare them. Not until the end of his closing arguments did Whalen become emotional:

WHALEN: What all of this testimony and all of this evidence will add up to, ladies and gentlemen, is that Jim Giesick and Sam Corey killed Patricia Albanowski Giesick.

You're going to hear from Jim Giesick. You're going to hear from an avowed killer. You will hear the testimony of a man who will tell you that he pushed the girl into the street so somebody else could run her over. That makes him a killer.

But I will not ask you, ladies and gentlemen, to find this defendant guilty simply on the basis of the testimony of a killer who has been allowed to plead to manslaughter. I will ask you at the conclusion of this trial to find the defendant guilty based on the testimony of Jim Giesick because you will believe him when you hear him, and based on the corroboration—on the backup testimony you will hear from several other witnesses that will establish that in fact what he tells you is true.

It's not a situation I want to be in, ladies and gentlemen. It's not something I want to

do: make a deal with a killer. But were it not
for the testimony of Jim Giesick, we might
not be able to get the man that was behind
the wheel, the man who was the brains behind this operation, the man who crushed that
girl's skull with that automobile.

Again I tell you that it will not be on his
testimony alone that I'm going to ask you to
convict, but on the extensive corroboration of
the other witnesses: witnesses who, along with
the testimony of Jim Giesick, will prove to
you beyond a reasonable doubt that a brutal,
cold-blooded, premeditated, calculated, cold
and greed-driven murder was committed by
two people who came from out of town to do
it. Testimony that will leave you convinced
at the conclusion of this trial that in order to
be true to your conscience and in order to be
true to the oath you have given the Court,
you must return a verdict of guilty as charged
against Sam Corey.

Thank you.

One side, I thought, our side, of the picture had been
admirably painted. I couldn't have felt more confident.
Now came Irvin Dymond, and district attorneys and defense lawyers in other courtrooms found excuses for re-
cesses and tried to get into Judge Becker's court to hear
the old spellbinder. Dymond didn't disappoint. He gave a
shining performance, though what he said bore no resemblance to the Sam Corey I'd investigated:

DYMOND: May it please Your Honor and ladies and
           gentlemen of the jury. We intend to give you
           some background on this man Sam Corey
           whom the State has tried to paint as a fiend.

           We will show you that Sam Corey studied
           to become a Catholic brother. He became a

Catholic brother. He was a Catholic brother
and teacher. After leaving the Catholic order
he went into business. He is now forty-one
years of age and has never been convicted of
any crime in his life. That is the type of
individual upon whom you will be asked to
pass judgment.

The State has gotten up here and said they
will not ask you to convict Sam Corey on the
testimony of their murderer, Claudius Giesick,
but in the next breath they tell you that without his testimony they probably wouldn't have
a case against Sam Corey. I submit that adds
up to their case being dependent upon this
admitted murderer they're going to give you
as a witness.

We will also present some evidence pertaining to Giesick. We will show you that throughout his mature life he has been nothing but a
con man. He has made his living ripping off
insurance companies. He and his wife together—not the dead girl, his legal wife.

We will show you with respect to the bigamous marriage Mr. Whalen said Sam Corey
performed that this marriage was, in fact,
performed by Corey who was an ordained
minister, but that his reason for performing
it, once again, was based on the lie of Giesick.
Giesick told him he had been divorced. On
the strength of that lie, Giesick got a marriage license and presented the marriage license to Sam Corey, asking to be married.

We will show that Claudius Giesick has
literally lied his way through life. Right up
until the time he was arrested in this case, he
was posing as a psychologist—Dr. Charles
Guilliam. We will show you that Giesick was
actually performing the services of a psychol-

ogist and collecting fees for it. As a matter of
fact, he did some work for Sam Corey as a
psychologist under a phony name. We will
show you that with some of his "patients"—I
put the word "patients" in quotes because he
was not a doctor of anything—this man was
taking advantage of his female patients as a
psychologist by telling them the most appropriate treatment for them was frequent intercourse with him. This is the kind of a man
the State is going to put before you.

Now, ladies and gentlemen, we will give
you also evidence from disinterested witnesses
to the effect that Claudius Giesick told them
before this killing that he had a plan by which
he was going to hook Sam Corey into a
murder charge here in New Orleans, which is
precisely what he has done. We will present
for you, ladies and gentlemen, the testimony
not of a civilian, but a San Antonio, Texas,
police officer, to whom Claudius Giesick first
made a confession saying, yes, he had conspired to kill his wife and had killed her, but
that he had conspired with another man by
the name of Johnny Cue.

We will show you many contradictory stories. This is the last one he's come up with
that he was able to make a deal. He can save
his own neck at someone else's expense and
that's why he's doing it.

I submit that the State has left out many
details of the evidence in this case. In the
opening statement, Mr. Whalen seemed to
make capital of the fact that human hair was
found on a vehicle rented by Giesick and that
the FBI lab had identified this as closely as it
can be identified as the hair of Patricia. Ladies and gentlemen, we have no quarrel with

that at all. It very probably was her hair. It very probably was that automobile that killed Patricia. We merely tell you, and tell you in all sincerity, that this man, Sam Corey, was not the driver of that automobile. Certainly, Patricia's dead. Certainly, she was hit by an automobile, but the question is who was in with Giesick on this job, and we will show you that it was not this defendant, Sam Corey.

Now, when I pointed out to you his record which consists of no criminal activity, I don't mean to say by that a man with a clean record can't commit a crime. But it is something to be considered by you as jurors for the simple reason that it's unlikely at age forty-one a man will change from a law-abiding citizen to a cold-blooded, calculated, hit man—a murderer for hire.

Now, there is the matter of massage parlors being operated by Sam Corey. That sounds a little horrifying when you realize he was a Catholic brother and is now an ordained minister, but a San Antonio policeman will tell you they never had any evidence of prostitution or illegal activities being conducted in any of Sam Corey's massage parlors.

We will give you evidence that Claudius Giesick, Dr. Jim Guilliam, whatever you want to call him, stated to more than one person in San Antonio that it looked like he was in trouble on this thing in New Orleans and he had a plan to hook Sam Corey into it. Now, I'll show you just how that plan fell into place. As you know, Sam Corey performed this marriage between Patricia and Giesick. On January the thirteenth, 1974, Sam Corey was in San Antonio and Giesick and his new wife, his bigamous wife, I might say, were in

Dallas. Giesick phoned Sam Corey. He had previously told Corey that he and Patricia were going to drive to New Orleans and on to Miami and take a Caribbean cruise. So on the thirteenth of January, he called Sam Corey in San Antonio and told him that he and Patricia had been fighting and that he was mad enough to throw Patricia over the rail of the ship into the Caribbean. Sam Corey became quite excited. He tried to talk sense into the man on the telephone. After not being successful, Corey said, "Where will you be staying in New Orleans? I'll come over to talk to you both." Perhaps this was some of his Catholic training coming out from the brotherhood. I don't know. Giesick said he was going to stay at the first Ramada Inn coming into New Orleans, and Corey said, "All right. I'll drive over and see you there."

Corey had a premonition there might be some danger, and before leaving San Antonio he took out an insurance policy on his own life. Now, Sam Corey had back trouble at the time and he asked a female employee to drive him to New Orleans, but he ended up driving himself. That young lady will be produced as a witness here. The reason I say that is important, ladies and gentlemen: if a man is coming over here to commit a murder, is he going to go out of his way to bring another witness with him? To bring someone else who knows he's coming to New Orleans and coming to see Giesick? Plain common horse sense answers that—no.

So Corey took off in his automobile for New Orleans, stopped at Lafayette, and registered in a motel under what name? Under the name Sam Corey. His correct name. He drove into New Orleans from the west by way of Baton Rouge. Obviously, Giesick had come in from the east and had stopped at the Ramada Inn out on the Chef [Menteur] Highway. Corey came in from the west and saw a Ramada Inn with a Holiday Inn across the street. He had a credit card for the Holiday Inn, so he checked into the Holiday Inn in Metairie, way out past Causeway Boulevard. Does this sound like a man following through on a plan to meet with another killer to kill that man's wife? Can you believe the plan would have been so shoddy that Giesick would have been on the Chef Highway and Corey on the Causeway? He registered in the name of what? Under the name of Sam Corey, San Antonio, Texas. Covering up nothing. Having nothing to cover up. He checked in and called across the street to the Ramada Inn and learned no Giesick was registered there. He then tried the other Ramada Inns and finally located Giesick at the Ramada Inn on Chef Highway and told Giesick he would be out as soon as he cleaned up.

Later that day, Corey drove out to the Ramada where Giesick and his wife were staying, and that evening the three of them had dinner at the Congress Inn near the motel. This would be on the evening of January fourteenth, the early night of January fourteenth. They spent that evening together, and at about ten o'clock Corey decided to check into the Quality Inn right next door on the Chef Highway, which he did, once again under the name Sam Corey. He went in and went to bed. In the meantime, he had learned that Giesick and his bigamous wife had driven to New Orleans in a brand new Chevrolet owned by them. And on the trip here—according to what Giesick told him—the cruise control on the Chevrolet had given them trouble, so Giesick put the car into the shop and rented an automobile from Avis Rent A Car.

So the night of the fourteenth, after Sam Corey had retired in the early morning hours of the fifteenth, Giesick came pounding on Corey's door and said the rental car was not running properly and he wanted to take it to the airport and exchange it. I am certain this will all be borne out by the man from Avis at the airport.

Giesick, either accidentally or very conveniently, I don't know which—if fingerprints show up it will be obvious it was very convenient—left his wallet in his motel room when he came to get Corey to drive the rental car back with him to the airport to exchange it. When they got to the airport, Giesick had none of his papers with him to identify himself. Consequently, the man at Avis was reluctant to turn over another rental automobile. Giesick said Sam Corey could identify him. The man said, "I don't know Sam Corey."

At that point, and this is very significant, Giesick tried to get Sam Corey to put this second rental car in Corey's name. Wouldn't that have been a great deal better for the murder automobile to have been in Corey's name? I would say so. But Corey didn't do that. He said, "No. I'm not renting a car." Finally the man at Avis consented to let Giesick take the car. They looked at the contract, had him sign on another piece of paper, were convinced he was the same individual and let him take the automobile.

Corey drove back to Chef Menteur High-

way with Giesick in this second rental automobile, which was probably the murder
automobile. I do not know whether there will
be evidence of fingerprints. I doubt it or it
would have been mentioned, but there could
be. Now, there's no doubt but that Sam
Corey's fingerprints would be on the steering
wheel of the automobile. Probably on the
rearview mirror, too, which is a classic place.
I'd be surprised if they were not. They drove
back to their respective motels.

Corey went to bed and did not awaken
until around noon on the fifteenth of January.
He had been up very late. Corey tried to get
breakfast at the Quality Inn, but it was too
late. So he went to a diner on Chef Highway.
After breakfast he went back, saw Giesick
and his wife at the motel, and told them he
wanted to drive around New Orleans. He told
them he wanted to check on some massage
parlor operations and see the city. As a matter of fact, he had a massage at the Magic
Touch Massage Parlor on Canal Street.

Then something occurred which I'm not
proud to tell you, and I'm sure Sam Corey
isn't proud either. Sam Corey was hustled by
a young prostitute named Linda in front of
the massage parlor on Canal Street, made a
date to take her out that night, and, in fact,
took her to dinner, and then took her back to
the motel with him. They were in bed when a
telephone call was received from the night
supervisor at Methodist Hospital out in Gentilly
telling Corey of the accident in which Giesick's
wife had been involved and that Giesick
wanted him to come over there immediately
since he was the only friend he had in the

area. Corey woke Linda up and told her he had to leave.

Ladies and gentlemen, I will tell you that I cannot produce Linda as a witness. We will produce evidence that we have made every effort to locate her. I ran ads in the *Times-Picayune* and got no response. There was literally no way of tracking this young girl down.

So Corey went to Methodist Hospital and stayed there with Giesick. Finally, at about eight o'clock, he told the people at the hospital he had to go back to the motel, but would return shortly. He went back, told Linda what the situation was, and offered to take her any place she wanted to get transportation. After dropping her off, Corey stayed with Giesick until Giesick received word that his wife had died.

Sam Corey assisted in arranging for clerical help. They wanted a Catholic priest. He assisted in arranging for the funeral. He advised Giesick to go to New Jersey for the wake and Giesick said, "No. I couldn't face her parents." Finally, Giesick did go up for the funeral. He asked Corey to go with him and paid Corey's way there.

Now, this thing started out as an insurance investigation, or so everybody thought. Detective Dillmann went from New Orleans to San Antonio in the course of this investigation. He posed as an insurance investigator and interviewed Sam Corey. Sam Corey gave him a statement in which he denied having been in New Orleans at that time. Strangely, he wrote at the bottom, "Subject to my changing my mind." You'll see that statement in evidence.

Ladies and gentlemen, I do not like the reason for his having to give a false statement like that. By seeing fit to do so. But the evidence will show these were his reasons. He thought this was an insurance investigation. He had no idea a murder was involved. But he had been in the motel room over here with a girl when he was a married man, and, consequently, denied that he had been in New Orleans. However, within a very few days, he confessed to his wife what he had done.

Ladies and gentlemen, no matter how you cook it or look at it, you will have to accept Giesick's testimony in order to accept the State's theory of this case.

I submit that when you hear the evidence in this case, you will be able to do nothing other than go back in that jury room, take your vote, and come out here and announce a verdict of not guilty as to Sam Corey.

Thank you.

From Dymond's opening statement it was clear Giesick would be his chief target, Giesick would be the one on trial. Corey, according to Dymond, played the role of good guy, coming all the way to New Orleans to try to *prevent* a murder. Corey lied in his statement because he didn't want his wife to know he'd spent the night with a prostitute, and, besides, I'd posed as an insurance adjuster. I hadn't told him about a homicide.

The point would loom large later. If I'd suspected Corey at the time, I would have been required to read him his rights. But I didn't suspect Corey. He knew Giesick, and I'd wanted to find the bogus psychologist. I did believe a homicide had been committed, and so did the Albanowskis, but few others concurred. The investigation itself was classified as "open."

Whether putting on a performance or not, Dymond *seemed*

a man completely convinced of his client's innocence. The defense lawyer would never be persuaded Corey wasn't a suspect when he gave that statement.

Corey himself sat through Dymond's opening looking relaxed and confident. Puffing on his pipe, he might have been a college professor listening to a colleague explain the intricacies of logic or physics to a class of new students. But people I talked to in the courtroom didn't think he suited the part. He had short hair, looked big and tough. "He radiates an air of menace," said an assistant district attorney.

The jury, wide awake as we'd hoped (I've heard countless stories of jurors sleeping during a trial), featured several members openly showing distaste when Dymond mentioned the prostitute—a point in the prosecution's favor. But all the jurors, if facial expressions are determining factors, came clearly prepared to dislike and disbelieve Giesick—a point we knew would be in the defense's favor. The jury didn't like Giesick when Whalen spoke. Dymond, doing his job, turned dislike into abhorrence.

One important witness (I wished the Albanowskis didn't have to hear him) needed to testify before court could adjourn and everyone could get a night's sleep in preparation for Claudius Giesick. The witness was Dr. Ronald A. Welsh, who had performed Patricia's autopsy, and without a trace of emotion he gave a chilling account of the injuries that had killed her.

Dr. Welsh said there was a "long list" of injuries, and in a matter-of-fact monologue began to chronicle them. His testimony had to be terribly traumatic for the Albanowskis. Listening to the injuries he described was like having a knife plunged into their hearts.

He began by describing a bruise over Patricia's left eye. Next he talked about abrasions, "a big, broad area," over the left side of her face extending down onto her neck. The car had run over her head.

Patricia suffered injuries to her shoulder, her right el-

bow, and her right hip; hemorrhages in her right eye; and
"a very large fracture" of her pelvis.

Neither of Patricia's legs was fractured!

There was considerable hemorrhaging in the front of
Patricia's skull, extensive hemorrhaging in the covering of
the brain, and hemorrhaging in the membrane of the brain.
Her lungs were very bloody and filled with fluid.

Dr. Welsh also testified: "Almost always with moving
pedestrians who are struck by an automobile, they will
have a fracture or serious injury to the knees or somewhere
below the knees. Most of the time someone who suffers a
fatal injury will have fractures of one or both legs where
the bumper of the automobile strikes them."

This, of course, fit exactly what Giesick would testify,
that he tripped Patricia into the street and she was nearly
prone when Corey ran over her.

Irvin Dymond took a different tack during his cross-
examination:

DYMOND: Doctor, would these injuries be consistent
           with a person punching this woman and then
           beating her head on the sidewalk?
WELSH: They would be consistent with someone hav-
           ing struck the side of her face. The abrasions,
           not so much. The abrasions look more like
           the whole body moved against the ground
           and picked up this whole area.
DYMOND: Taking all these injuries together, would they
           be consistent or inconsistent with a person
           knocking that girl unconscious, hitting her
           head on the sidewalk, and then running her
           over with an automobile?
WELSH: There could be nothing inconsistent with that.
DYMOND: So that could be the case, is that correct?
WELSH: It could be. Yes, sir.

Was Dymond going to say Giesick committed the crime
all by his lonesome? Probably not. Enough that he plant in

the jury's mind that it could have happened. Reasonable doubt.

I told myself there would be plenty of time for stress later, and that night I tried to put the case out of my mind. But it wasn't possible. What went on now represented the worst time. At least before, the outcome had depended largely on what I did, I could stay busy following a hundred leads, but now it would be decided by others, and I could only stand idly by and wait. I fervently hoped that what appeared so obvious to me would not be lost upon the jury by Dymond's obfuscations and cleverness.

I didn't look forward to being questioned by Dymond. He had a lifetime of experience working for him. "He chews up cops and spits them out," I'd been told. His opening statement, saying I'd posed as an insurance adjuster, had left no doubt; he'd go after me.

But this would surely come on Day Three. Giesick would be up first the next morning, Day Two, and I shuddered when I thought of what Dymond would do to him.

—15—

CLAUDIUS GIESICK, LOOKING clean-cut and modern in a sport coat and tie, round baby face framed by tinted glasses, left the shocked jury with mouths open and heads shaking. His matter-of-fact delivery, no remorse or feeling at all, came across as glacial. The con man wanted to be believed, and I guess he figured ice to be stronger than warmth, a foreign emotion for him, anyway. Even my family, and they were all there (Diane, my mother and father and grandfather, Diane's sister and brother-in-law), knowing the importance of his testimony in my first heater case, felt he made a totally negative impression.

Understanding what Giesick was, I could have nothing but regrets about his testimony. Often the prosecution is forced to use the sleaziest of witnesses (who else usually knows the actual mechanics of a crime?), but I've never become accustomed to it.

Still, what can the State do? Mother Teresa is not likely to have relevant information on a New Orleans murder case. Whatever. Giesick was no "clean hands" witness, and the jury couldn't help but know it.

And this occurred in basically what amounted to a run-through of his confession, with Whalen doing the questioning. Dymond, dripping disgust with every gesture, rose to cross-examine. The prosecution held its breath. They knew

Dymond's investigative team, headed by William Miller, had done a crack job, an outstanding probe into Giesick's background. Dymond had a dead-duck target, and he made the most of it.

DYMOND: In what capacity were you employed by Mr. Corey?

GIESICK: Mr. Corey wanted me to interview girls that would be prospective masseuses for him.

DYMOND: At that time, were you posing as a consulting psychologist?

GIESICK: Yes, sir.

DYMOND: So, actually, you were doing the work of a psychologist when you were not, is that correct?

GIESICK: That's correct.

Having established that Giesick would practice psychology without a whit of accreditation, Dymond proceeded to other matters.

DYMOND: Are you presently under bigamy charges in Texas?

GIESICK: Yes, sir, I am.

DYMOND: How about hot-check charges? Are you presently under hot-check charges out there?

GIESICK: Yes, sir.

DYMOND: And you murdered this girl because you were afraid of hot-check charges? That, and the fact that you needed money?

GIESICK: That's correct.

DYMOND: Do you know what the penalty is for a hot-check charge in Texas?

GIESICK: Well, under the new penal code that would become effective after January first, they were talking severe penalties of ten to twenty years.

DYMOND: You ever hear of anybody getting ten to twenty years on a hot-check charge?

GIESICK: Well, I had spent the last year in Arizona. I was not familiar with the kind of time being issued.

DYMOND: So then in order to save yourself from the possibility of going to jail on a hot-check charge, you were willing to kill somebody, is that correct?

GIESICK: Yes, sir.

Listening to Dymond carve up Giesick was torture. And it had just begun.

DYMOND: You said you had a lot to talk about with Trish, and that's the reason you wanted to take her walking, is that correct?

GIESICK: Yes, sir.

DYMOND: What did you have to talk about just before you planned to murder her?

GIESICK: Well, newlyweds usually talk about what they want to do with the rest of their lives, and this is what we were discussing.

DYMOND: Is that what you wanted to talk about with her when you went out walking?

GIESICK: Well, it seemed the logical thing to talk about at the time.

DYMOND: What she was going to do with the rest of her life was the logical thing to talk about?

GIESICK: Well, it gave her the sense of knowing there was going to be a longer time than just a few minutes.

Listening to this had to be excruciating for the Albanowskis. Their daughter had married a monster. Been killed by him. Now in the coldest terms they heard her murderer explain how he'd lied to her to the very end.

But Dymond did an excellent job of showing the jury it would be folly to believe Giesick. As the con man continued to be demolished by the master lawyer, I had to hope

Whalen's own strategy would succeed: proving the jury didn't *have* to believe Giesick, everything he testified to would be corroborated.

Next Giesick revealed that he and Corey had concocted a scheme whereby the con man told Detective Koby he planned to kill his wife with the assistance of a third party (Johnny Cue), but the plan got shelved and—coincidence! —Patricia died in a genuine hit-and-run. Dymond, of course, as any sharp lawyer would, made certain the jury wondered if the mysterious Johnny Cue drove the murder vehicle. However, over and above this (and the earlier inference that Giesick might have beaten Patricia to death, then run over her), Dymond aimed to make the jury concentrate so much on the unsavory con man that Corey became the forgotten figure. I imagine Whalen, had he been on the other side, would have employed an identical strategy. Whatever, Dymond wasn't about to let up.

DYMOND:	Did you ever attempt to take out an insurance policy on your two adopted children?
GIESICK:	Yes, sir.
DYMOND:	What was this, another accident policy?
GIESICK:	No, sir. It was a straight life policy on me, my wife Katherine, and the two kids. We could not proceed with the policy because Mr. Swift of State Farm wasn't sure we could take out coverage on kids who weren't completely adopted. He also had an argument with me about a claim I had on a loss at my home. State Farm was refusing to pay.
DYMOND:	Was that a fraudulent claim?
GIESICK:	It was partially fraudulent and it was partially real. The house was broken into, but not everything on my list was stolen.
DYMOND:	In other words, you were trying to cheat the insurance company again, is that right?
GIESICK:	That's correct.
DYMOND:	Did the policy you wanted for the children

	have a provision in it for double indemnity for accidental death?
GIESICK:	At this time, I don't know. I never saw the policy.
DYMOND:	Is it not a fact, Mr. Giesick, that applying for this policy on these children was one of the reasons the children were taken away from you?
GIESICK:	That was one of the reasons. Yes.
DYMOND:	They were afraid you'd kill the children for the insurance money, is that right?
GIESICK:	That's what it said in the newspapers.
WHALEN:	Objection, Your Honor. The witness has no way of knowing what someone else was afraid of.
BECKER:	The question has already been answered.

Several jury members had been shaking their heads. Fortunately, in everyday life you don't run into many Claudius Giesicks. But that's the thing about murderers, and it's what often adversely affects a cop. People like Giesick, or watered-down versions, become everyday realities. A police officer can forget how to behave in decent company. He can forget such a thing exists.

DYMOND:	Now, this same video equipment with which you ripped off State Farm, didn't you also claim that was stolen on a Braniff airlines trip?
GIESICK:	No, sir.
DYMOND:	You never made any claim to Braniff airlines on that equipment?
GIESICK:	I did on video equipment, but not the same equipment I claimed was stolen in the house theft.
DYMOND:	Oh, this was different video equipment?
GIESICK:	Yes, sir. It was portable video equipment that was taken from Braniff airlines.

DYMOND: You say that was a legitimate claim?

GIESICK: No, sir.

DYMOND: Oh, it was illegitimate, then?

GIESICK: Yes, sir.

DYMOND: Now, Mr. Giesick, I've refreshed your mind on several insurance company ripoffs. I'm going to ask if you can name some more fraudulent claims that you lodged and collected, or tried to collect. Think carefully.

GIESICK: I probably could if I had plenty of time to think about it. But at the moment I can't think of any more that were fraudulent.

DYMOND: Given time, you think you could, right?

GIESICK: No. I can think of one.

DYMOND: Oh, you've thought of another one?

GIESICK: I can think of one. I pulled an engine out of a car. The insurance paid for the engine, and I put the car back together.

DYMOND: Think a while longer and see if you can come up with another one.

GIESICK: That's all that comes to my mind, Mr. Dymond.

DYMOND: How about a set of tires for this Monte Carlo automobile that you had? Was there a ripoff in connection with those?

GIESICK: Yes, sir, there was.

I figured Dymond had neared the end. He'd already decimated Giesick. Made mincemeat of him. If a running score were kept, the defense had the early lead. But we'd expected that. The corroborating witnesses would not be so easy for Mr. Dymond to shake.

DYMOND: Did you ever suggest to Carol Wheeler an insurance ripoff in connection with her automobile?

GIESICK: Not with her automobile, no, sir.

DYMOND: With what?

GIESICK: With the Tokyo House massage parlor.

DYMOND: I see.

GIESICK: With it changed over into her name, I told her how we could take the television and other stuff out. I told her the claim would be covered by her property insurance.

DYMOND: Now, do you know how many instances of cheating insurance companies and other people you have told this jury about while you've been on the witness stand?

GIESICK: I haven't kept count. No, sir.

DYMOND: Are you able to approximate?

GIESICK: Probably seven or eight or nine.

DYMOND: Seven or eight or nine? How many lies have you told them about?

GIESICK: I could not put that in a number figure, Mr. Dymond.

DYMOND: Would it be more or less than the instances of cheating?

GIESICK: It would be a larger number.

DYMOND: So you have seven or eight instances of cheating people. A larger number of instances of lying to people, is that correct?

GIESICK: Yes, sir.

DYMOND: And the reason that you're testifying here is to try to save your own skin, isn't it?

GIESICK: And to turn over a new leaf in life—telling the truth.

Dymond, the sophisticated southern gentleman, backed away from Giesick as if the con man had a disease you could catch. The lawyer had done his job: he'd portrayed Giesick as contemptible, and who could argue with that? Giesick's talk about turning over a new leaf seemed unlikely to be believed by anyone.

I didn't know it at the time, but Dymond hadn't finished with Giesick. He had information from witnesses he would later call that would make insurance company ripoffs seem like playful diversions. Giesick was a far more rotten apple than Whalen and I had imagined.

After Giesick's testimony, the court took a one-hour recess until 4:20 P.M. Judge Becker meant business when he said the trial would remain in session late into the night.

I introduced members of my family to the Albanowskis, and talked to Patricia's parents about the trial's progress. We had the right defendant, I assured them, and a top-notch prosecutor in Ralph Whalen. By the time the trial ended, the jury wouldn't have any doubts about Sam Corey's guilt. I was relieved that the Albanowskis didn't deluge me with questions about the deal we'd made with Giesick.

The first witness after the recess was Kathy Giesick, and what she'd testify to gripped Whalen with apprehension. A scene occurring only on television melodramas appeared likely. Certainly a New Orleans courtroom had never witnessed its like.

The night before Whalen had gone over Kathy's testimony with her. Whalen had records of phone calls made to the Tuxford Drive address, records I'd obtained from the phone company, during the time Corey and Giesick were in New Orleans. I'd suspected the phone calls could add up to only one thing. Whalen, brandishing threats of prosecution, persuaded Kathy to confess the truth. Now she'd tell the jury, and no one could predict the outcome.

The packed courtroom had no inkling of the dramatic testimony about to be given. Kathy had been called, spectators thought, because she could verify how well Giesick knew Corey. The witness herself wore a skirt and blouse, stockings, high heels. Kathy was in her mid-twenties, five feet six inches and slim, an attractive woman with clear features and long blond hair.

WHALEN: Mrs. Giesick, are you presently married to
            Claudius James Giesick?
KATHY: I am.

WHALEN:	Is any change in your marital status pending at this time?
KATHY:	I filed for divorce last month.
WHALEN:	Mrs. Giesick, do you know the defendant, Sam Corey?
KATHY:	Yes, I do.
WHALEN:	For how long have you known him?
KATHY:	I first met him in October of 1973.
WHALEN:	Mrs. Giesick, do you know anything of a plot to kill a young lady named Patricia Albanowski?
KATHY:	Yes, I do.
WHALEN:	When did you first hear of this plot?
KATHY:	Several weeks before it was supposed to happen.

Several barely audible cries arose in the courtroom. People leaned forward to hear. Had their ears betrayed them? Had she really said what they thought?

WHALEN:	How did you learn of the plot?
KATHY:	My husband told me.
WHALEN:	What did he tell you?
KATHY:	He informed me they had this plan. He and Mr. Corey were going to kill this girl for insurance money, and—he didn't explain all the details to me. He said they were taking out insurance on a girl and planning on killing her for this insurance money.
WHALEN:	Did he tell you he was going to marry the girl?
KATHY:	No, he did not.
WHALEN:	Did you eventually find out that he had, in fact, married the girl?
KATHY:	I found out when he was arrested for bigamy.
WHALEN:	Did you play some part in this plot to kill the girl?

*   *   *

Judge Becker, having been apprised of what Kathy Giesick would say, had addressed her in open court before she testified. He told her she might be prosecuted. He made it clear she had the constitutional right to remain silent. She had the right to a lawyer. Now, with the key question having been asked, everyone waited for her answer.

KATHY: When they came to New Orleans, I stayed at home as a go-between for them, as far as answering the phone to let each one know where the other was.

WHALEN: Were you, in fact, called by both of them?

KATHY: Yes, I was.

WHALEN: Were you called by Sam Corey?

KATHY: Yes, I was.

WHALEN: Do you remember on what days you were called by Sam Corey?

KATHY: I talked to him on the fourteenth.

WHALEN: What was the subject of that conversation?

KATHY: He told me where he was and asked if I had heard from Jim.

WHALEN: Where was Corey?

KATHY: I said, yes, I'd heard from Jim, and Jim was in Houston. Corey said, "Fine. I'm on my way. Tell Jim I'll call you later."

WHALEN: When was the second time Corey called you?

KATHY: I don't remember if it was the same day or the next day. When he got to New Orleans, he called and told me he was in New Orleans and where he was staying.

So Kathy had served as coordinator between Corey and Giesick. That explained how the motel mix-up—Giesick's going to the wrong place—had been remedied. When I'd learned through long-distance records that Corey called the Tuxford Drive address several times, I suspected the reason, but Whalen deserved the credit for bringing it into the open.

It was clear to everyone in the courtroom how much this testimony damaged Corey. What made the testimony extraordinary, however, was the harm it did to the witness herself.

WHALEN: Did Corey call you again?

KATHY: He called me the morning of the sixteenth, shortly after the accident.

WHALEN: Do you recall what time that was?

KATHY: It was about three A.M. It was the middle of the night. I was asleep and the phone woke me up.

WHALEN: What was the subject of this conversation?

KATHY: He said everything was over. I asked him what he meant, and he said: "You know what I mean. Everything's fine and everything came off great. I'm going to be home early in the morning. Jim will call you to pick him up, or I'll pick him up at the airport later in the afternoon."

Twice now, first from Giesick and then from his wife, the jury had heard how marvelous Corey thought his accomplishment to be. I think jury members also were shocked by the type of crime, which struck at the very foundations of civilized behavior. Could this happen to one of them? Might they not give their trust and love to someone whose motives were absolutely sinister? Corey and Giesick had played on a beautiful emotion—love—to commit the most heinous of crimes, murder.

WHALEN: Did you and your husband spend very much time with Sam Corey?

KATHY: Yes.

WHALEN: When did you begin to spend time with Sam Corey?

KATHY: Well, after my husband quit the company he was working for in Arizona, he and Sam were supposedly going into business together, and we spent a lot of time at his massage parlor in San Antonio; with his family at his home; and at our home.

WHALEN: Approximately how many times a week do you think you and your husband saw Sam Corey around the first of the year of 1974 and the end of that year, 1973?

KATHY: Almost daily.

WHALEN: How long did you and your husband continue to see Sam Corey on this daily basis?

KATHY: When the investigation started, we didn't see each other hardly at all. It was strictly telephone conversations then.

Darkness had set outside, and it seemed to be descending for Sam Corey, also. Next Whalen showed that the charge should indeed be first-degree murder.

WHALEN: Mrs. Giesick, I'm going to show you what I've marked S-9 for purposes of identification, and ask if you can tell me what this document is?

KATHY: It's a deposit slip for my husband's special account.

WHALEN: Have you seen this document before?

KATHY: Yes, I have.

WHALEN: Where did you first see it?

KATHY: I picked it up at the Tokyo House from Mr. Corey.

WHALEN: What happened at that time?

KATHY: Mr. Corey told me I needed to take it to the bank immediately, that Jim was in Dallas writing a check for some insurance and that money had to cover it.

WHALEN: Who filled out this form?

KATHY: Mr. Corey did.

WHALEN: In your presence?

KATHY: Yes.

WHALEN: Did he give you anything to go with the form?

KATHY: He gave me a check and cash.

WHALEN: In the amounts reflected on this form?

KATHY: Yes.

WHALEN: And what did you do with the check and the cash?

KATHY: I went to Harlandale Bank and deposited it.

WHALEN: Were you aware that sometime prior to the date this happened that your husband and Sam Corey intended to kill Patricia Giesick?

KATHY: Yes.

Through all of this Corey remained relatively impassive, hands folded across his ample belly. Occasionally he leaned forward to whisper something to Dymond. By now he had to know the worst of Kathy's testimony was yet to come.

WHALEN: At any time after the hit-and-run did you have occasion to discuss Patricia's death with Sam Corey?

KATHY: Yes, I did.

WHALEN: Would you tell these ladies and gentlemen of the jury about that occasion?

KATHY: My husband, Mr. Corey, and myself were on a plane going to Dallas. They were sitting together. I was sitting across the row from them. Jim handed me some documents that were from the doctor describing the injuries to the girl, and asked me to read them. I started to read them, but gave them back. It upset me. I didn't want to have anything to do with it and told him just to drop it. Jim got up to get a drink and Sam asked me to come sit with him. So I went over and sat with him, and he said, "I want to tell you something. Jim did not kill that girl. I was

driving the car. I killed her.'' I asked if that
was supposed to make me feel better, and he
said he hoped it did a little bit, but he wanted
me to know Jim did not kill her.

When Dymond's turn came to cross-examine, he went
after Kathy Giesick as he had her husband, but with less
success. Dymond established, if such needed to be done,
that here testified an individual of less-than-sterling character. Kathy knew her husband's primary income derived
from cheating insurance companies. Kathy, while married,
went out on a date arranged by her husband with another
man. Kathy knew a murder would be committed and did
nothing to stop it: in fact, by serving as go-between, she
facilitated the killing. Dymond summoned up every parti-
cle of his considerable contempt for Kathy Giesick when
he asked the question that rattled around in everyone's
mind.

DYMOND: Have you ever been arrested or charged with
           anything in connection with this case?
KATHY: No, sir.
DYMOND: Do you mean to tell me that you have stated
           to the district attorney's office that you par-
           ticipated in this plot, and just nothing has
           been done?
KATHY: No, sir.
DYMOND: Why? Do you know?
KATHY: No, sir, I do not.
DYMOND: Did you expect to go to jail when you . . .
KATHY: I didn't know what to expect.

She found out soon enough, in a truth-is-stranger-than-
fiction scenario. Judge Becker asked the jury to step out of
the courtroom, had Kathy Giesick, trembling now, stand
in front of the bench, and addressed her directly.

BECKER: Mrs. Giesick, it's my duty to inform you that

I'm placing you under arrest for the offense of criminal conspiracy to commit murder. I'm issuing an arrest order for you. I'll set bail—Mr. Whalen?

WHALEN: Could I have an explanation of what's happening?

BECKER: Yes, sir. I'm placing her under arrest.

WHALEN: The court's placing her under arrest?

BECKER: For conspiracy. Have you granted her immunity, Mr. Whalen?

WHALEN: No, I haven't, Your Honor.

BECKER: I'm placing her under arrest. It has come to my attention, from her own testimony, that she's involved with the commission of a felony in the State of Louisiana. She will be informed of her rights. I'm ordering her arrested and placed in the Central Lockup, Sheriff, to be transported to the Magistrate Court so she can be informed of her rights and bail set.

WHALEN: Do you want a recommendation from the State as to bail?

BECKER: I think the magistrate will take that recommendation.

WHALEN: I would recommend that the subject be released on her own recognizance.

BECKER: All right, Mr. Whalen. Sheriff, I'll need a matron to take Mrs. Giesick to Central Lockup. I want her booked under Louisiana Revised Statutes 14:46, conspiracy. Mrs. Giesick, follow the sheriff. I'll set bail at this time, Mr. Whalen, at $10,000. If the magistrate desires a recognizance bond or the district attorney desires a recognizance bond, they can do so. Mrs. Giesick, you'll be transported to Central Lockup to be booked. You'll then be brought over to Magistrate Court to be informed of

	your rights and bail will be set. Do you understand?
KATHY:	Yes.
BECKER:	Do you have a lawyer representing you?
KATHY:	No, I don't.
BECKER:	Do you desire a lawyer to represent you?
KATHY:	Yes.
BECKER:	I want Mr. Numa Bertel—I'll call for Mr. Bertel and appoint him to represent Mrs. Giesick at the hearing. I want Mr. Bertel personally to represent her. I might say this, Mrs. Giesick, this has nothing to do with either the truth or falsity of your testimony, but only the fact that you testified, under oath, that you knew and aided and abetted in the commission of a felony, to wit: murder. I have no other choice, Mr. Whalen and Mr. Dymond. As an officer of this court, I have no other choice.

Reporters scurried for telephones. They had a sensational story: Witness Arrested Off Stand.

No more bombshells developed this second day of the trial. Officers Fayard and Henderson related their roles at the hit-and-run scene, and later at Methodist Hospital. Good Samaritan Ricky Mock told how Giesick had waved him down and asked him to call for help.

But the sensationalism didn't subside. It simply rested overnight. What awaited on Day Three made everything beforehand seem tame.

—16—

I OPENED DAY THREE on the witness stand, facing a friendly Ralph Whalen. He led me through the entire investigation. I did, of course, despite a fusillade of objections from Irvin Dymond, provide corroboration for much of what the Giesicks had said. The phone records, the rental cars, the visits to purchase insurance, evidence of Corey's activities in New Orleans, these and more, it seemed to me, increasingly pointed the finger of blame at the preacher.

Dymond's cross-examination was anything but friendly. He represented me as an overzealous detective reading things into the case to promote my own career. I hadn't just investigated the case; I'd pushed it to prosecution. Impressive as Dymond was to spectators, he loomed even more formidable and awesome when you faced him on the stand. Sweat poured all the way through my shirt to stain my coat.

Much of my nervousness stemmed from not wanting to appear ludicrous in front of my family. Dymond excelled at making just such a portrayal. No one who saw the way he had demolished Jim Garrison in the Clay Shaw trial would ever forget it.

What at least partially saved me was how well I knew this case. I'd immersed myself in it. I figured I couldn't get in too much hot water if I stuck with what I'd found out. Dymond could score debating points, I thought, I provided no match for him, but facts were facts.

It turned out what upset Dymond most was that statement I'd taken from Corey in San Antonio. A major, full-scale debate erupted between prosecution and defense over this critical portion of evidence:

DYMOND: Did you ever advise him that he had a right to have an attorney present?

DILLMANN: No, sir, I didn't.

DYMOND: And that anything he said might be used against him?

DILLMANN: No, sir.

DYMOND: If the Court please, I respectfully submit that from the evidence given by Detective Dillmann, it is abundantly obvious that Sam Corey was a suspect. Mr. Dillmann has admitted he suspected foul play. He had information that with the Giesicks here in New Orleans at a time surrounding the time of the murder, there was a man fitting Mr. Corey's description, and here he is questioning Corey about the last time he saw Giesick and when was the last time he was in New Orleans. All things pertinent in a case of this kind. There are no Miranda warnings given. No compliance with Escobedo. The man had a lawyer, and the lawyer wasn't there. He was not advised of his rights, and I respectfully submit that this statement is inadmissible.

BECKER: I don't know that the gentleman had a lawyer at that point, Mr. Dymond.

DYMOND: I'll be happy to put evidence on the stand for the restricted purpose of showing that.

WHALEN: Your Honor, I'm willing to stipulate that the defendant had a lawyer at that time if I'm allowed another question to Detective Dillmann.

BECKER:	Go ahead.
WHALEN:	Detective Dillmann, were you ever informed by Sam Corey at the time you took the statement that he was represented by an attorney?
DILLMANN:	No, sir, I wasn't.
WHALEN:	Did he ever request an attorney?
DILLMANN:	No, sir. He was cooperating one hundred percent.
DYMOND:	Did you ever advise him that he had a right to have an attorney present?
DILLMANN:	No, sir, I didn't.
DYMOND:	And that anything he said might be used against him?
DILLMANN:	No, sir.
DYMOND:	I submit it.

What Dymond submitted was a motion to declare Corey's San Antonio statement inadmissible as evidence. Possibly, because of the Miranda decision, which entitled a suspect to be informed of his rights, the entire case could be thrown out. I held my breath. All the work, the entire quest to catch the killer, could go to naught if the ruling went against us.

WHALEN:	Your Honor, my argument to the Court would be that Detective Dillmann's testimony, and the questions in this statement, reflect nothing more than a standard statement taken from a potential witness in the case. It's not a question-and-answer-type interrogation of a suspect. And it is perfectly clear, in addition to this, that the statement was given freely and voluntarily. That's the crux of the matter.
BECKER:	It goes to the fact, Mr. Whalen, of whether it becomes an—it stems from an investigatory stage to an accusatory stage. Some of the questions in the statement almost imply accusatory. Do you have any citations to show me

	with regard to the switching from investigatory stage to an accusatory stage?

WHALEN: Not at hand, Your Honor, but if the Court desires some authority, I would request a short recess.

BECKER: Mr. Dymond.

DYMOND: All I could do is cite Miranda, Your Honor.

BECKER: I'm very familiar with Miranda. I'm sure every judge and every lawyer, probably every lay witness is. I'm talking about investigatory to accusatory. You see, the Miranda warnings don't come into play until a person has come under an accusatory stage of the proceedings.

DYMOND: When the investigation focuses on . . .

BECKER: Correct.

WHALEN: Your Honor, I think we have sworn testimony that this was not the case. Specifically on that point, we have no testimony to the contrary.

BECKER: I'm going to take a ten-minute recess. I'd like to see what authority—I'm talking about the accusatory and investigative stage. At what point, and so on. I want to look at the statement in my chambers and go through those questions again.

When court reconvened, San Antonio Detective Bernard Koby temporarily replaced me on the stand. Koby told the court I did not pose as an insurance investigator, no threats were used against Corey, and the preacher was not a suspect in the case, merely someone with a possible link to Giesick's whereabouts. Based on Koby's testimony, Judge Becker ruled Corey's statement admissible.

I came back to the stand and, all told, testified for some four hours. Whalen handed each juror a copy of Corey's statement, and made sure his misstatements didn't go unnoticed. Corey said he'd lied about being in New Orleans at the time of the murder because he didn't want his wife to know he'd been with a prostitute.

But why did he lie about talking with the Albanowskis on the day of the murder? About the nonexistent witnesses to the wedding? About returning to New Orleans three days after the murder to pick up his car?

I testified about recovering the hair from underneath the Monte Carlo, a car we could connect with Corey. I told about Patricia's exhumation, and taking patches of her hair and scalp to the FBI lab. It would be up to Special Agent John Hicks to make the connection between the two samples.

Judge Becker had admitted Corey's statement into evidence, but Dymond kept hammering on the subject during cross-examination. Hadn't I suspected Corey at the time? It seemed I had to find different ways to say no. I believed Dymond was thinking ahead, to the possibility of losing the case, and the statement could be the basis of appeal: he tried to draw an answer from me to prove I'd violated the preacher's rights.

I believe a person has to experience hostile cross-examination from a lawyer of Dymond's ability to appreciate how tiring and nerve-racking it can be. I came off the stand with leaden legs, mind foggy, dizzy, stomach turning flip-flops. But I also had a bracing feeling. The case against Corey continued to go forward as planned.

Criminalist John Palm told how we recovered the hairs from the Monte Carlo.

FBI Special Agent John Hicks testified, "I found that the hairs recovered from the vehicle exhibited the same microscopic characteristics as the hairs submitted as being those of Patricia Albanowski." Thus, we felt we'd produced the murder weapon.

Methodist Hospital night supervisor Dorothy Bryant testified that not only had she examined Patricia after the ambulance brought her in, but, at Giesick's request, telephoned Corey to come to the hospital. And she saw Corey there. This, of course, corroborated a portion of Giesick's testimony, but what seemed to make a larger impression on the jury was Ms. Bryant's description of "the tire mark on the left side" of Patricia's face.

Steve Lamartiniere, a guard at Methodist Hospital, also testified that he saw Corey at the hospital.

Louis Malain of Avis was an important prosecution witness. He identified Corey as being with Giesick when the original rent-a-car was exchanged for the murder vehicle.

Joe Schumacher, Ramada Inn manager, testified that Corey returned to the motel three days after Patricia's death to retrieve clothing Giesick had left behind. Whalen knew Corey would claim that much more time than three days had elapsed.

Josephine Albanowski, conservatively dressed, not wanting to take the stand but knowing it was necessary, told how Corey accepted donations at her daughter's wake. Dymond established that the donations were given freely, not solicited, and let Mrs. Albanowski go. No good could come to the defense from this grieving woman's testimony.

David Merrick, Mutual of Omaha salesman, told of Corey's and Giesick's coming to Dallas' Love Field on January 10, and asking questions about hit-and-run coverage. Corey "prompted" Giesick on what to ask, Merrick said. "Mr. Corey told Mr. Giesick to say just about everything. . . . Mr. Giesick didn't really say that much without his friend's prompting."

After David Merrick, Whalen rested the prosecution's case. Barring defense miracles, I felt Corey would be convicted. We'd supplied the motive: $350,000 in insurance money. The murder weapon: Avis' white-over-maroon Monte Carlo. The means: Corey's presence in New Orleans with Giesick. The Giesicks themselves placed Corey at the wheel of the Monte Carlo.

If Corey's attorney had been court-appointed, I thought his fate likely would already be sealed. But he had Irvin Dymond, the very best in New Orleans, and now Dymond rose from his chair, brimming with confidence, to call Michiko Fukushima to open the defense.

Ms. Fukushima had worked for Corey as a masseuse

and now owned the Tokyo House, but she didn't come into court dressed in hot pants or overly madeup. She looked attractive, intelligent, a young businesswoman on the rise. Ms. Fukushima testified that when in March 1974 she told Giesick about a dispute she had with Sam Corey, Giesick replied: "He's not going to bother you any longer because I'm going to blame him for everything."

"Everything" didn't get specified, but I thought it obvious what Dymond wanted the jury to speculate.

Was this going to be the defense? I wondered. An all-out attack on Giesick? I believed the chance existed to convict without the testimony of either Giesick, but I stood alone in that regard. Perhaps pounding on Giesick did indeed represent the path to acquittal.

Alice Daffron, another attractive masseuse who had worked for Corey, had an even stranger tale to tell. I didn't doubt it was true. I could only regret the day I'd ever heard the name Giesick.

Ms. Daffron testified that Giesick had offered to have her husband killed so she could collect insurance money and share it with Giesick.

Hostility and repugnance toward Giesick became almost tangible emotions in the courtroom. And the worst hadn't been heard yet. Dymond called Carol Wheeler, who had managed the Tokyo House for Sam Corey.

"In telling various stories about Brazil," Carol Wheeler testified, "the country Mr. Giesick said he was from, he told fantastic tales of a slave market that is there, and people just sometimes disappear and turn up on the Brazilian slave market—women primarily. And from the slave market, they're sold and they go to all parts of the world for whatever reason."

"Did Giesick ever mention any particular girl," Dymond asked, "in connection with the slave market?"

"Louise Rambo—Skeeter. She was called Skeeter."

"What did he say?"

"He was plotting to put her on this Brazilian slave

market, and I think he said she would bring twenty-five thousand dollars.''

Next Carol Wheeler talked about a masseuse Giesick ''treated'' in his role as a psychologist: ''Tina Henson was progressively moody rather than progressively better, and I asked Dr. Guilliam what the problem seemed to be. He told me he was having difficulty establishing a good rapport with her, and that he believed through frequent sexual intercourse with him that this would help establish a rapport.''

''Frequent intercourse with whom?'' Dymond asked.

''With Tina Henson.''

''Tina Henson and whom?''

''Dr. Guilliam.''

And, finally, this last shot:

DYMOND: To your knowledge, was Jim Guilliam, or Claudius Giesick, whatever you want to call him, ever barred from the Tokyo House?

WHEELER: Yes.

DYMOND: Who barred him?

WHEELER: I did.

DYMOND: Why?

WHEELER: Because he was making advances toward my daughter, who was fourteen years old at the time.

DYMOND: Did he admit that to you?

WHEELER: Yes, he did.

DYMOND: What did he say?

WHEELER: He said, ''Well, she's an attractive young girl, and she needs to get her sexual experience from someone who knows exactly what he's doing.''

DYMOND: Was he still posing as a psychologist at the time?

WHEELER: Yes.

DYMOND: What did you tell him?

WHEELER: I told him he had thirty seconds to get off my

property before I filed charges against him for child-molesting.

The final witness Dymond called—final, that is, unless he decided to put Corey on the stand—was Sandra Webster, a college student and one-time masseuse. Ms. Webster said that on January 13, 1974, Corey told her he had a bad back, and asked if she would drive him to New Orleans.

If Corey had planned to commit a murder, Dymond wondered aloud to the jury, would Corey invite a masseuse along with him?

The defense attorney, stuffing papers into his briefcase after court adjourned, had done an A-one job of demolishing Giesick. I didn't think, however, that he'd saved Corey.

—17—

THE BIG COURTROOM filled up as soon as the doors opened. The much-awaited day had arrived. If it had been a championship boxing match, the promotional posters might have ballyhooed: Fight to the Finish—Ralph (The Whacker) Whalen versus Sam (The Preacher) Corey. But this confrontation loomed more important than any boxing contest. Corey's life hung in the balance.

A very good preliminary bout threatened to cancel the main event. Paired against each other in the courthouse corridor were Corey's co-counsels, Irvin Dymond and William Miller. They stood toe-to-toe, neither giving an inch, talking loudly, gesticulating, each one convinced that what the other proposed represented madness.

It was a battle of major proportions, and it was not waged in secrecy or behind closed doors. I watched in amazement, this apparent falling-out between Corey's brain trust. Others watched, too. The dispute must have raged unresolved for a considerable time, for now it had spilled into the open just moments before court reconvened. Neither participant in the heated debate seemed to be changing the other's mind.

I knew whose corner I was in: Dymond's. He wanted to put Corey on the stand. He believed that the State's case was a strong one and that his client should have the chance

247

to save his own life. If he could. Only Giesick and Giesick's wife had placed Corey behind the wheel of the murder vehicle. Maybe the defendant could come across to the jury as a concerned, compassionate minister who'd tried to save Patricia's life, only to be betrayed by the treacherous Giesicks.

I had my own reason for wanting Dymond to prevail. I knew Whalen had gambled, holding back two key rebuttal witnesses in case Corey did testify. If Corey stayed off the stand, these witnesses would never testify. The court wouldn't allow it, since the State had rested. But they could be called for rebuttal. Whalen knew what part of Corey's testimony *had* to be, because the preacher had earlier taken the stand under oath at his bond hearing. What he said at that time could now burn him.

William Miller passionately proclaimed that Corey could be committing suicide on the stand. The preacher *looked* evil. No jury member would buy his contention that he had come to New Orleans to save Patricia's life. Far better, Miller thought, to hammer at Giesick in closing arguments. Make the jury forget about Corey and obsess them with Giesick. Corey, Miller believed, needed only one juror so fed up with the self-serving Giesick that he forgot everything else. Dymond, the spellbinder, might very well net that one juror. Or two or three. Better to swim in these waters than to allow Whalen, a shark honing in on blood, to ravage their client.

Dymond prevailed. He was in charge of the trial. Miller's domain encompassed research and investigation. This didn't mean Miller had to present a united front and pretend to agree with his colleague. He made it clear he thought a terrible mistake had been made.

The news that Corey would testify surprised and delighted Whalen. He'd gambled, keeping those rebuttal witnesses off the stand, without really believing he'd win. When he received the news, his face underwent a literal transformation. It became stone-hard. His eyes, cold as ice, seemed to reflect a grim, terrible determination. He wouldn't for an instant take lightly this most important moment of his young career, but that wasn't primary. He loathed what Corey had done, and welcomed the role he'd been handed, that of Patricia's avenging guardian angel.

What follows, in front of a tensed courtroom, is Irvin Dymond's entire examination of Sam Corey:

DYMOND: Mr. Corey, you are Sam Corey, the defend-
           ant in this case, is that correct?
COREY: Yes, sir.
DYMOND: Mr. Corey, did you kill Patricia Giesick?
COREY: No, sir, I did not.
DYMOND: Did you participate in any way in killing her?
COREY: No, sir, I did not.
DYMOND: Did you ever agree with her husband to assist
           him in killing her?
COREY: Never.
DYMOND: I tender the witness.

In short, that was it. I know it caught Whalen off guard to have his nemesis so suddenly handed over to him. I could only speculate, straining to catch every critical word in the case (*my* case, I alone had brought it this far, there would have been no trial if I hadn't pushed and tugged), why Dymond had been the soul of brevity. I could only figure he didn't want to lock Corey into a lot of answers. He'd permit Corey to freewheel it. Maybe the preacher could save his own life. Certainly Corey seemed relaxed and confident enough. He smiled at the jury, and then at Whalen, who intended to torment him and wasn't smiling at all.

WHALEN: Mr. Corey, were you in New Orleans on
           January 16, 1974?
COREY: Yes, sir.
WHALEN: Why were you in New Orleans on January
           sixteenth?
COREY: Because I feared for the girl's life.

WHALEN:	You cared a lot about Patricia Giesick?
COREY:	I didn't know her very well.
WHALEN:	And yet you came all the way to New Orleans to protect her life, is that right?
COREY:	Yes.
WHALEN:	On what day did you arrive in New Orleans?
COREY:	January fourteenth.
WHALEN:	Where did you stay?
COREY:	Well, I checked into two motels.
WHALEN:	Where did you check in first?
COREY:	To a Holiday Inn in Metairie.
WHALEN:	Did you make any phone calls from that motel?
COREY:	I don't recall, sir.
WHALEN:	Did you call Kathy Giesick from that motel?
COREY:	I don't recall.
WHALEN:	Do you recall the Giesicks' phone number?
COREY:	No, sir.
WHALEN:	There has been testimony in this trial that 653-0470 is their number. Do you know if you called the number 653-0470 from that motel?
COREY:	I don't recall, sir. It's been a long time ago.
WHALEN:	I'll show you a document, which I've marked S-50. Does this document read ''Long Distance Telephone Calls'' at the top?
COREY:	Yes, sir.
WHALEN:	And underneath that, does it say, ''Name, Corey''?
COREY:	Yes, sir.
WHALEN:	And underneath that, does it say, ''Number Called, Area Code 512-653-0470''?
COREY:	Yes, sir.
WHALEN:	Is the date 1-14-74?
COREY:	Yes, sir.
WHALEN:	What motel did you stay in after that?
COREY:	I moved to the Quality motel.
WHALEN:	Did you call Kathy Giesick from that number?

COREY: I don't recall.

WHALEN: Did you call 653-0470 from that number?

COREY: I don't recall.

WHALEN: I show you a document marked S-51 and ask you if it bears the words, "Telephone Voucher"?

COREY: Yes, sir.

WHALEN: And above "Guest," does it say "Corey"?

COREY: Yes, sir.

WHALEN: And above "Phone," does it say, 512-653-0470?

COREY: Yes, sir.

WHALEN: Does that refresh your memory any, Mr. Corey? Do you recall now phoning Kathy Giesick from the Holiday Inn or from the Quality Inn?

COREY: No, sir, it does not refresh my memory.

WHALEN: Isn't it a fact, Mr. Corey, that you called Kathy Giesick from both of those motels to check in with her, as prearranged by you and Jim Giesick?

COREY: No, sir.

WHALEN: Do you know a gentleman by the name of Pete Franklin, Mr. Corey?

COREY: Yes, sir.

WHALEN: Who is Pete Franklin?

COREY: He's a reporter from San Antonio.

WHALEN: Didn't you tell Pete Franklin that you admitted to having been with Giesick at the Dallas–Fort Worth airport many times, but that you had "absolutely nothing to do with any insurance"? Did you tell him that?

COREY: I don't recall.

WHALEN: Did you say that you were never with him at any time when he purchased insurance for himself or for his bride, nor were you with Giesick when he inquired about insurance? Did you tell Pete Franklin that?

COREY: I don't know. I don't know if he even asked me that.

WHALEN: I show you a document which I've marked S-52 and ask if you can read the parts underlined from that document?

COREY: It says—these are just sections of sentences. "Corey admitted to having been with Giesick many times at the airport. He absolutely had nothing to do with any insurance," and then it skips over to another paragraph. "Nor was he with Giesick when the latter inquired about insurance, he said."

WHALEN: Did you tell Pete Franklin that?

COREY: I don't recall.

WHALEN: Did you read this article when it came out in the San Antonio newspaper?

COREY: I've read so many articles about this matter—I don't remember. Some I've read and some I haven't.

WHALEN: Mr. Corey, did you write a check to Kathy Guilliam on January 15, 1974?

COREY: No, sir.

WHALEN: For $575.19?

COREY: No, sir.

WHALEN: I show you a document marked S-53, what appears to be a Xerox copy of both sides of a check. Does that refresh your memory at all?

COREY: Well, sir, the Giesicks had forged my signature on bank notes and checks several times, and I don't know whether this is my check.

WHALEN: You don't remember writing that check?

COREY: No, sir.

WHALEN: Who is the check written to?

COREY: I can barely read it. Like I said, they've forged my name on notes and checks.

WHALEN: Does that look like "Kathy Guilliam" to you? "Pay to the order of Kathy Guilliam"?

COREY: I can see "Kath," but I can't make out the last word.

WHALEN: Is it signed by Samuel Corey?

COREY: It bears that name but, as I said, they've forged my name many times before.

WHALEN: And you still do not recall having called Kathy Giesick?

COREY: No, sir.

WHALEN: Now, you go by the title of Reverend Corey, do you not?

COREY: No, sir.

WHALEN: Have you gone by that title before?

COREY: Occasionally.

WHALEN: Are you in fact a minister?

COREY: Yes, sir.

WHALEN: And from where did you receive your title of minister?

COREY: I received my training in one church, and was ordained in another church.

WHALEN: In what church were you ordained?

COREY: I was ordained in the Calvary Grace Christian Church.

WHALEN: Where is that located?

COREY: The home office is—the international superintendent—is in Fort Lauderdale, Florida.

WHALEN: Where are the headquarters of the Calvary Grace Christian Church of San Antonio?

COREY: That was the church I was going to start and never did.

WHALEN: Would you be kind enough to tell us, Mr. Corey, why it was that you became ordained by the Calvary Grace Christian Church?

COREY: I'll be happy to.

WHALEN: Tell us, please.

COREY: I was in the massage business in Texas, and I had several massage parlors throughout the state. Acting on the advice of my attorney at the time, I was fearful that in the upcoming legislature session an ordinance or a state statute would, for all practical purposes, put legitimate massage parlors out of business. After discussing this with my attorney and acting on his advice, we decided to incorporate a church after I was ordained because I already had the qualifications for ordination. We would form a church; and just like the Indians can smoke peyote as a religious rite, I would try to develop massage as one of the religious rites of the church. This was my intention. Whether it was good judgment or not, I was acting on the advice of my attorney. The idea was not to avoid taxes, because we intended to go before the Internal Revenue and get a tax ruling. If they approved it, then we would go ahead. If they didn't approve it, then we wouldn't. That was it—pure and simple.

WHALEN: You were going to become ordained so that you could make massage a religious rite, is that right?

COREY: Yes, sir.

WHALEN: Now, you performed the marriage of Jim Giesick and Patricia Albanowski?

COREY: Yes, sir.

WHALEN: When did you first learn Giesick's name was Giesick and not Guilliam?

COREY: I'm not sure when it was.

WHALEN: You had known it for some time, hadn't you?

COREY: I don't know how long I knew it.

WHALEN: Were you aware of the fact that he was still married to Kathy Giesick at the time you conducted this ceremony?

COREY: No, sir.

WHALEN: Weren't you in fact in the Giesick home with Jim Giesick and Kathy Giesick on January

	second, the date you married Jim Giesick and Patricia Albanowski?
COREY:	No, sir. I don't recall being there.
WHALEN:	You don't recall being there? On January second—the same date they were married?
COREY:	No, sir.
WHALEN:	I'll show you S-15. Was that the statement you gave to Detective Dillmann, Detective Koby, and Walter Dennis?
COREY:	It looks like it.
WHALEN:	Does it bear your signature on each page?
COREY:	Yes, sir.
WHALEN:	Does it bear your signature where it says "Sworn to and subscribed before me"? Would you examine the lower left-hand corner?
COREY:	What's the question?
WHALEN:	Do you see the words, "Sworn to and subscribed before me this seventeenth day of February, 1974"?
COREY:	Yes.
WHALEN:	Is that right beneath your signature?
COREY:	It's right beneath my signature, with the addition that I added to this in my handwriting.
WHALEN:	Which was you could change your mind later if you wanted to, is that right?
COREY:	It says, "With the right to make a change, if I should recall."
WHALEN:	"Something different"?
COREY:	It just says, "If I should recall."
WHALEN:	You see the words "something different" down there?
COREY:	Oh, beneath that—yes.
WHALEN:	You lied in that statement, didn't you?
COREY:	Yes, I did.
WHALEN:	You swore to that statement, didn't you?
COREY:	Yes, I did.
WHALEN:	You later told Detective Koby that the reason you lied in that statement was because you

were with a prostitute in New Orleans, is that correct?

COREY: I told him I was with a young lady.

WHALEN: And you didn't want your wife to find out?

COREY: Yes.

WHALEN: How long have you been in the massage business?

COREY: Since—I don't know—1970, I think.

WHALEN: Several years?

COREY: Yes, sir.

WHALEN: Have you ever known massage parlors to be associated with prostitution?

COREY: They have that reputation.

WHALEN: You arrived in New Orleans on the fourteenth, checked into the Holiday Inn, checked out later and went to the Quality Inn, is that correct?

COREY: I suppose. It sounds about right.

WHALEN: And Giesick was staying at the Ramada Inn, is that correct?

COREY: Yes, sir.

WHALEN: Didn't you, in fact, have a room facing the Giesick room?

COREY: The room the clerk gave me faced the room, yes.

WHALEN: You did have a room facing Giesick's room?

COREY: I didn't pick out the room.

WHALEN: Later on, on the night of the fifteenth, you went with Giesick to the Avis car rental agency at the New Orleans airport and exchanged an automobile, did you not?

COREY: When?

WHALEN: About two in the morning.

COREY: On what day?

WHALEN: The fifteenth.

COREY: Yes, sir. I don't know the time, but I did go.

WHALEN: Did Giesick come get you to go exchange that automobile?

COREY: Yes, sir.

WHALEN: Where were you at the time he came to get you?

COREY: In bed asleep.

WHALEN: You got up at two A.M. to go all the way out to the New Orleans airport?

COREY: He insisted I go with him.

WHALEN: Did you do it as a favor for a friend or because you were afraid of Giesick?

COREY: He asked me to go, and I went.

WHALEN: This is the same man you drove all the way from San Antonio to New Orleans for, is that right?

COREY: I didn't drive here for him.

WHALEN: You drove over here for Trish?

COREY: I feared for the girl's life.

WHALEN: Mr. Corey, do you recall making a previous sworn statement that you didn't care anything about Trish Albanowski?

COREY: I don't know how to answer that, sir.

WHALEN: It's a simple yes or no, Mr. Corey. Do you recall having been in this judge's court, under oath, and saying, ''I didn't care anything for the girl''?

COREY: I didn't know the girl well, but I feared for her life.

WHALEN: Mr. Corey, when you went to the Avis Rent A Car company, did Mr. Giesick try to get you to use your credit card?

COREY: Yes, sir.

WHALEN: You have any way to explain why Mr. Malain of Avis doesn't recall that?

COREY: I can't speak for him. I know what I recall.

WHALEN: Who did most of the talking? You or Giesick?

COREY: Giesick did.

WHALEN: Can you explain why Malain would say you did most of the talking?

COREY: Because Giesick couldn't prove who he said

	he was, and Giesick asked me to vouch for him.
WHALEN:	How long did you suffer under the misbelief that Giesick was actually a consulting psychologist?
COREY:	Right after Detective Dillmann came to San Antonio.
WHALEN:	Isn't it a fact, Mr. Corey, that you knew for a long time—as you and Giesick were setting up insurance schemes—you knew good and well he wasn't a consulting psychologist?
COREY:	No, sir.
WHALEN:	Did you pay him?
COREY:	Yes, sir.
WHALEN:	Regularly?
COREY:	Not regularly, no.
WHALEN:	How often did you pay him?
COREY:	Irregularly.
WHALEN:	Were you at one time an insurance adjuster, Mr. Corey?
COREY:	Yes, sir.
WHALEN:	What did you do on January fifteenth in New Orleans?
COREY:	What did I do?
WHALEN:	Yes. Where were you at let's say about six P.M.?
COREY	I don't know. I don't know where I was at six P.M.
WHALEN:	Did you go to a place called the Magic Touch Massage Parlor?
COREY:	I don't know the time. I did go to that massage parlor. Yes, sir.
WHALEN:	Did you get a massage there?
COREY:	Yes, sir.
WHALEN:	Were you administered a local there?
COREY:	Yes, sir.
WHALEN:	What's a local, Mr. Corey?

COREY: A local is where they, in a massage parlor, where the genitals are massaged.

WHALEN: What did you do after you got your local?

COREY: Finished the massage.

WHALEN: And then what?

COREY: I went back to the motel and took a shower.

WHALEN: Alone?

COREY: Yes, sir.

WHALEN: What after that?

COREY: I went back downtown to meet the young lady who was going to escort me around New Orleans.

WHALEN: You know what her occupation was?

COREY: I didn't ask her.

WHALEN: Do you recall stating previously that she was a hooker?

COREY: Please, sir?

WHALEN: Do you recall having stated earlier that she was a hooker?

COREY: I believe that term was used.

WHALEN: By you, is that correct?

COREY: Yes, sir. I'm very apologetic for using that term.

WHALEN: Was she a hooker, Mr. Corey?

COREY: No, sir.

WHALEN: Oh, she was not?

COREY: Not to my knowledge.

WHALEN: You have any way of explaining why you would refer to this young lady as a hooker when you don't think she's a hooker?

COREY: It's just a term I used.

WHALEN: What did you do with this young lady?

COREY: When?

WHALEN: After you met her the second time.

COREY: We rode around New Orleans. She showed me different interesting things in the city.

WHALEN: What time did you return to your motel?

COREY: I don't know exactly.

WHALEN: You recall having stated previously it was about eleven o'clock?

COREY: I would say around that time, yes, sir.

WHALEN: Were you alone when you returned to your motel?

COREY: No, sir.

WHALEN: Who was with you?

COREY: The young lady.

WHALEN: How long were you with the young lady?

COREY: Through the evening. Through the night into the next day.

WHALEN: Until what time?

COREY: I don't know exactly. The next morning.

WHALEN: When did you next leave the motel?

COREY: I don't know. I think sometime I went out for some crackers and cheese or something. I don't know what time.

WHALEN: Was that shortly after you arrived with the young lady at the motel?

COREY: I don't know how much time elapsed.

WHALEN: Do you recall having said previously that it was shortly thereafter?

COREY: It was after we arrived. I don't know how long it was.

WHALEN: So much as two hours later?

COREY: I don't know.

WHALEN: Do you recall having stated that it was shortly thereafter? Do you remember saying that?

COREY: I don't remember saying it. It was after we arrived.

WHALEN: How long were you gone from the room to get the crackers and cheese?

COREY: Ten minutes.

WHALEN: Ten minutes?

COREY: Or so, yes, sir.

WHALEN: Where did you go?

COREY: To an ice house or convenience store.

WHALEN: Where was it in relation to the motel?

COREY: It was across the street.

WHALEN: Was it directly across the street?

COREY: I don't remember the geographic location.

WHALEN: Mr. Corey, do you often have this much trouble with your memory?

COREY: No, sir. It was a long time ago.

WHALEN: When was the next time you left your room?

COREY: When the nurse called me from the hospital.

WHALEN: About what time was that?

COREY: I didn't check my watch.

WHALEN: Mr. Corey, did you leave your room about two A.M. and return about two-thirty on January 16, 1974?

COREY: I don't believe I did, sir. No.

WHALEN: Did you, Mr. Corey, at about two A.M. go to the night auditor at the Quality Inn and speak with him, and then speak with him again about thirty minutes later?

COREY: I don't recall it. I may have, but I don't recall it.

WHALEN: You may have?

COREY: I may have.

WHALEN: You don't recall doing that?

COREY: No, sir.

WHALEN: Do you recall at about two A.M. going to the night auditor of the Quality Inn motel and asking him for some aspirin? Do you recall doing that?

COREY: No, sir.

WHALEN: Do you recall then leaving there, and returning about thirty minutes later after he had said you could find some up the road at the 7-Eleven? Do you recall coming back and telling him you found some aspirin at the Tastee Donut Shop? Do you recall that, Mr. Corey?

COREY: No, sir.

WHALEN: Do you recall being in your room at about two-fifteen that morning?

COREY: I suppose I was.

WHALEN: So to the best of your recollection, you were in that room with the young lady at that time, is that correct?

COREY: As best I recall, yes, sir.

WHALEN: You weren't in fact out on Michoud Boulevard crushing a young girl's skull with your car, were you, Mr. Corey?

DYMOND: Your Honor, I object to this. There has been no testimony that anybody's skull has been crushed. As a matter of fact, there wasn't even a skull fracture.

BECKER: It's a matter for the jury to determine, Mr. Dymond.

WHALEN: I'll rephrase the question, Your Honor.

DYMOND: Just a moment. To which ruling, I want to note an objection and move for mistrial because of the deliberate inflammatory statement made to the jury by counsel.

BECKER: Denied.

DYMOND: Reserve a bill.

WHALEN: About what time did you get to the hospital, Mr. Corey?

COREY: Shortly after I talked with the nurse.

WHALEN: At what time? Do you have any idea?

COREY: I didn't check the time, sir.

WHALEN: You went straight to the hospital from your motel room?

COREY: Yes, sir.

WHALEN: When was the next time you returned to the motel room?

COREY: Later in the morning.

WHALEN: Was it daybreak?

COREY: I recall that—I don't know the time, but I recall it was dark. It was so foggy there were children, it seems as though there were chil-

	dren going to school. I seem to recall that. I know it was dark.
WHALEN:	You remember saying it was around daylight when you told Mrs. Bryant you were going to leave?
COREY:	I think it was.
WHALEN:	And that's the first time you went back to your motel room, is that right?
COREY:	Yes, sir.
WHALEN:	At that time, Mr. Corey, what did you do with the young lady?
COREY:	I told her what happened and I offered to take her wherever she wanted to go. I took her to a Holiday Inn located on the Interstate. I'm not familiar with the streets. I know it was Chef Boulevard and Interstate 10.
WHALEN:	Where did you go from there?
COREY:	I went back to the hospital.
WHALEN:	How long did you stay at the hospital?
COREY:	Until later in the day, in the morning.
WHALEN:	About eleven A.M.?
COREY:	I believe that's correct.
WHALEN:	Where did you go then?
COREY:	From the hospital, I believe Giesick wanted me to take him back to his car.
WHALEN:	Where did you go next?
COREY:	The complete sequence of events, where we went from one place, one minute to the next, I don't recall. I do recall he asked me to go with him to the funeral home to make arrangements for Patricia's funeral.
WHALEN:	Before the girl was dead?
COREY:	No. This was after she was dead.
WHALEN:	Where were you when you found out she was dead?
COREY:	At this point, I'm not really sure. I've heard a motel clerk say I was at the Ramada Inn. I heard someone else say I was at the Quality

Inn. I heard Giesick say I was at the hospital. At this point I don't really know.

WHALEN: Somehow I didn't expect you would.

DYMOND: Your Honor, I'm going to object to that, and again move for a mistrial. Counsel is not testifying. It's an uncalled-for remark. I'll ask that the Court instruct him to refrain from that practice.

BECKER: The mistrial is denied, Mr. Dymond. I'm going to instruct Mr. Whalen to refrain from making comments, and instruct the jury, ladies and gentlemen, to disregard the last comment by the district attorney.

WHALEN: Mr. Corey, on November 7, 1974, in the Criminal District Court for the Parish of Orleans, Section E, do you recall having made the statement that "Trish didn't mean a great deal to me"?

DYMOND: Your Honor, I object on the grounds that the proper predicate has not been laid.

BECKER: He can answer it. I'll overrule the objection.

COREY: I remember you asking me something to that effect, or somebody asking me something to that effect. Are you asking me that again?

WHALEN: I'm asking you if in response to a question by your attorney, Mr. Dymond, on that date, you said, "You understand Trish didn't mean a great deal to me"?

COREY: I didn't know her well.

WHALEN: Did you say that, Mr. Corey? Do you recall having said that?

COREY: I believe I said something to that effect, yes.

WHALEN: This is the same girl you drove from San Antonio to New Orleans to protect, is that correct?

COREY: I came over here because I feared for Trish's life.

WHALEN: Now, where were you when you got the

phone call which made you fear for Patricia's life?

COREY: I was in San Antonio.

WHALEN: Where was Giesick?

COREY: He said he was calling me from Dallas.

WHALEN: Did you return with Giesick to the hospital when you got the news of Patricia's death?

COREY: I remember—yes, sir. I must have.

WHALEN: Do you remember going into the chapel of that hospital with Giesick, and clapping your hands, and saying, "We made it. It's going to work. She's going to die"?

COREY: No, sir.

WHALEN: Is that your memory failing you again, Mr. Corey?

COREY: No, sir. That never happened.

WHALEN: When was the next time you were in New Orleans after January sixteenth?

COREY: When I came back to get my automobile.

WHALEN: How much later was that?

COREY: It was after Trish's funeral.

WHALEN: Can you approximate how much time had passed?

COREY: No, sir. I really can't. I would say several weeks.

WHALEN: Six or seven weeks perhaps?

COREY: No, I wouldn't say that. I can't say that, sir. I . . .

WHALEN: Would it have been more than three days?

DYMOND: Your Honor, I ask that the witness be permitted to finish his answer.

BECKER: Give the witness an opportunity to complete his answer before asking another question, Mr. Whalen.

WHALEN: Yes, sir. Would it have been more than three days?

COREY: Yes.

WHALEN: Would it be more than two weeks?

COREY: It's possible.

WHALEN: Is it probable?

COREY: I can't answer that.

WHALEN: What did you do when you got back to New Orleans the second time?

COREY: I went to the motel and picked up the car and headed back for San Antonio.

WHALEN: Did you go to the Ramada Inn to pick up Giesick's clothing?

COREY: Giesick asked me to go in and pick up his cleaning, and I went in and the clerk said that it wasn't ready. He said they couldn't find it, is what it was. He told me he was calling the cleaners and I got tired of waiting for it. About thirty minutes elapsed, or I don't know how much time it was, but I got tired and I went on back to the car and told Giesick. He was out in front of the motel. I told him I was tired of waiting for his clothing, and we got in the car and went back to San Antonio.

WHALEN: Mr. Corey, was Giesick a close personal friend of yours? Were you extremely fond of him?

COREY: At one time we were friends.

WHALEN: How about January 14, 1974, were you close personal friends then?

COREY: January fourteenth? Not at that time, no. That was when I came over here.

WHALEN: How about when you returned to New Orleans the second time, were you close personal friends then?

COREY: That's very hard to answer. I had asked—I had tried to get him to stay away from the Tokyo House, but he was very difficult to get to stay away.

WHALEN: You tried to keep him away from your place of business, is that right?

COREY: Yes, sir.

WHALEN: And that's the same man you drove from San Antonio to New Orleans for, drove back to

New Orleans from San Antonio to drive an automobile back, and went all the way back to San Antonio? Is that the same man? The man you barred from your place of business?

COREY: He had requested . . .

WHALEN: I want a yes or no answer, Mr. Corey. Is that the same man?

COREY: Giesick asked me to . . .

WHALEN: Your Honor, would you instruct the witness to answer my question yes or no, and then he's entitled to explain it.

BECKER: Answer the question yes or no and then you'll have an opportunity to explain your answer.

COREY: What is the question, sir?

WHALEN: Are you telling me now—are you telling these ladies and gentlemen of this jury—that a man you barred from your place of business is the same man you drove to New Orleans for, and went to a funeral with, and came back to New Orleans for, flew back to drive an automobile back to San Antonio for? Are those one and the same people?

COREY: Yes.

WHALEN: You may explain, if you desire.

COREY: I went to the funeral because I felt sorry for the girl. I felt sorry for Jim. I did not know it was a murder. The mother of the girl called me, and she told me about the wake and invited me to the wake. I told her I would try to get to the wake, and if I couldn't get to the wake, I would try to make it to the funeral.

WHALEN: Did her mother invite you to wear a Roman collar to the funeral?

COREY: No, sir.

WHALEN: Did her mother invite you to take contributions from people at the funeral to say prayers for her dead daughter?

COREY: No, sir. May I explain that?

BECKER:	Yes, sir.
COREY:	I wore a Roman collar and a blue suit, which was indicative of a Protestant clergyman. Many Protestant clergymen dress this way. I was at a reception. I've never been to a reception after a funeral, but apparently it was the custom in that part of the country to do this, and there was drinking and eating and people came up to me and gave me a couple of bucks, a couple of dollars. They said, "Would you pray for me?" I didn't want to offend them and say no, or refuse their money, and I just accepted it and said, "Yes." I didn't want to hurt their feelings. There wasn't more than seven or eight dollars involved and I certainly didn't solicit any. The people did this on their own.
WHALEN:	Mr. Corey, did you study for several years in the Catholic Church?
COREY:	Yes, sir.
WHALEN:	Are you familiar with the Catholic custom of giving tokens to a priest to say prayers? Is that a custom that's foreign to you, having studied several years in the Catholic Church?
DYMOND:	Your Honor, I'd ask that the witness be permitted to answer one question before one's propounded to him.
BECKER:	All right, sir. Mr. Whalen, ask one question at a time and give the witness a chance to answer your question.
WHALEN:	Yes, sir.
COREY:	Would you repeat the question, sir?
WHALEN:	With your years of experience in the Catholic Church, are you unfamiliar with the Catholic custom of offering money to a priest to say prayers at a funeral?
COREY:	I'm familiar with the custom.

WHALEN: It's not a custom which you'd say is peculiar to New Jersey?

COREY: I didn't say that, sir. I said the reception after a funeral—I'd never been to that before.

WHALEN: Are you ordained in the Catholic faith?

COREY: Yes, sir.

WHALEN: On December 14, 1973, did you co-sign a note for Charles J. Guilliam in the amount of $1,543.13?

COREY: I never co-signed a note for Giesick.

WHALEN: I ask you to examine the document, S-55. Does this appear to be a note?

COREY: It appears to be a note.

WHALEN: To Charles J. Guilliam.

COREY: Yes.

WHALEN: Does it bear your signature?

COREY: It bears the words "Samuel Corey," but that is not my signature.

WHALEN: Whose signature is it?

COREY: I do not know. That's one of the notes he forged my signature on.

WHALEN: You have any idea why Mr. Giesick would feel so at liberty to forge your name?

COREY: No, sir.

WHALEN: When did you become aware of the fact that he had forged your name on that note?

COREY: When the banker asked me about it after he was indicted.

WHALEN: The due date on the note was March fourteenth, wasn't it?

COREY: I never saw the note until this moment, sir.

WHALEN: Is this note marked "Paid, March 5, 1974"?

COREY: Yes, sir.

WHALEN: You have any idea when you and Mr. Giesick were indicted?

COREY: I thought it was in June.

WHALEN: You have any explanation for why it would

	be after the indictment before you found out about this?
COREY:	The banker never asked me about it until he saw me one day after the indictment.
WHALEN:	Were you in financial difficulty in January 1974?
COREY:	It depends on what you call difficulty. I owed people money, but I was living all right.
WHALEN:	Did you owe several people money?
COREY:	Yes, sir.
WHALEN:	Had you in fact been sued by several people to collect on the money you owed them?
COREY:	I was sued, yes. It was a disagreement on the amounts owed.
WHALEN:	I ask you again, Mr. Corey, on January 2, 1974, were you in the Giesick home in the presence of Jim Giesick and Kathy Giesick?
COREY:	January second?
WHALEN:	January 2, 1974, the day you married Jim Giesick to Patricia Albanowski.
COREY:	No.
WHALEN:	I ask you again if on the morning of January 16, 1974, at approximately two A.M., if you went to the night clerk of your motel, asked him for aspirin, and then left the lobby? Did you do that?
COREY:	I don't—on the sixteenth?
WHALEN:	On January sixteenth. About fifteen minutes before Patricia Giesick was killed.
COREY:	I don't recall.
WHALEN:	Did you, about fifteen minutes after Patricia Giesick was killed, go back into that same motel, speak to that same clerk, and tell him you found aspirin at the Tastee Donut Shop down the road?
COREY:	No, sir, I don't recall that.
WHALEN:	I have no further questions.
BECKER:	Mr. Dymond, any further questions?

DYMOND: No further questions, Your Honor.

The defense rested after Corey's testimony. I believed Whalen easily had bested the preacher; bad as it looked for the defendant, it would get worse when the rebuttal witnesses testified. Juries could be totally unpredictable, and one person might still exist so appalled by Giesick he or she couldn't focus on Corey, but I suspected we approached the end of the long road with victory at last in sight.

No one I talked with thought Corey had made a good impression on the witness stand. His friendly professorial demeanor had degenerated into evasiveness under Whalen's determined questioning. Corey's talk about a "local" hadn't sat well with the jurors (regardless that it had little to do with his guilt or innocence), and he had pleaded "I don't recall," a phrase given a bad name by Watergate, far too many times.

Young Patricia Clor, following Corey to the stand, gave the lie to part of his testimony by telling the jury she saw him at the "Guilliam" home on January 2, 1974, the day of Patricia's marriage, with Jim and Kathy Giesick. Then the second star rebuttal witness, Quality Inn night auditor E. J. Swindler, recalled what Corey couldn't, that the preacher had indeed left the motel, saying he needed an aspirin, at about 2:00 A.M. on January 16, the morning of the murder, and returned about 2:30 A.M.

The four days of the trial ended after Swindler's appearance. Whalen ended the State's case; Dymond rested for the defense. Everyone who attended agreed they had witnessed a sensational courtroom drama, packed with remarkable testimony. Now only the closing arguments separated Corey from Judgment Day.

The final arguments lasted until nearly midnight, but no one in the crowded courtroom complained. Both Whalen and Dymond waxed brilliant. I believe they could have spoken for days and still people would have wanted more.

"It's so theatrical," Diane whispered. "Just like TV."

I kept one eye on the attorneys, the other on the Albanowskis. Josephine and Stanley appeared grim, worn out, like soldiers exhausted at the end of a long march. Numerous times I'd told them they didn't have to stay for all of this, but they'd traveled as far as I had, and intended to see whether the justice system served Patricia.

Whalen paced a lot. He'd told the jury at the start of the trial that the case resembled a puzzle, with all the pieces needing to be fitted in. He'd done that, he said. The case was airtight. Whalen seethed with animal energy, a tiger pacing back and forth, reminding the jury of its duty.

Dymond relied on his marvelous, resonant voice. He seemed scarcely to move. Like a great actor, he knew all eyes riveted on him, all ears listened for his every word. He heaped deserved abuse on the Giesicks. He never let up. Maybe he would get that one juror. Certainly he reached back over all the years, all the victories in his spectacular career, to summon up the words and emotion that somehow would save his client from the electric chair. When he sat down there were more than a few people who thought his eloquence might have saved Corey.

By Louisiana law Whalen got the first chance to address the jury in closing arguments, and the last. Whalen had been coldly logical the first time. He'd said he just wanted the jury to understand clearly what had happened, to base its decision on the evidence, not the smoke screen of Giesick that Dymond threw at them. Dymond, said Whalen, wanted the jury to find Corey innocent because Giesick was guilty.

The second time Whalen attacked (that is the right word) Corey with all the venom it is possible for one human being to muster against another. Whalen painted a chilling macabre picture of the preacher cold-bloodedly plotting murder; of Corey crouched behind the wheel of the rented Monte Carlo, waiting for Giesick's flashlight signal; of Corey aiming the car at Patricia; of Corey running her down as she lay helpless in the street; and, lastly, perhaps unforgivably, of Corey ecstatic about what he'd done.

As Whalen neared the finish his voice lowered. He wanted to share something with the jury. "Ladies and gentlemen," he said softly, "my conscience bothers me. It bothers me a great deal." Now he raised his voice, almost to a conversational level. "I made a deal with a murderer, and I'm haunted by it." He paused, then spoke quite loudly. "Yes, my conscience bothers me! But I did what I had to and I accept responsibility!" Finally, Whalen wheeled around, pointed his finger directly at Corey, and his voice rose to a crescendo:

"I made a deal with a sinner to catch the devil!"

Sam Corey still sat at the defense table (he'd only had time for a short talk with a newspaper reporter) when the court clerk announced that the jury had reached a verdict. "Jesus Christ, already?" Corey said.

It took everyone by surprise. Many people who had sat through the entire trial had gone to get an early-morning bite to eat and missed the conclusion. The New Orleans *Times-Picayune* described what happened:

After only 20 minutes of deliberation early Saturday, a jury found Texas preacher and massage parlor operator Samuel Corey guilty of first-degree murder in the hit-and-run slaying of honeymoon bride Patricia Ann Giesick.

Criminal District Court Judge Rudolph F. Becker III asked Corey to rise and face the jury about 1:25 A.M. Saturday to hear their verdict in the case.

With the same nonchalance he maintained throughout the four-day trial, Corey heard minute clerk Michael Roig say, "On this day, April 26, 1975, we, the jury, find Samuel Corey guilty as charged."

Sheriff's deputies immediately took Corey into custody and led him through the back of the court into Parish Prison, where, one deputy said, "A cell has been waiting for him."

One more thing was required of me. I'd intentionally not told the Albanowskis that the jury had a verdict. Now I went to their hotel room and looked from one to the other. "We got him," I said.

——Epilogue——

IN *THE NUN'S PRIEST'S TALE* Geoffrey Chaucer wrote,
"Murder will out," a dubious proposition, but in this case
it happened.

Judge Becker sentenced Sam Corey to die in the electric
chair, but the United States Supreme Court outlawed the
death penalty (later reinstating it), and the preacher now
serves a life term at Louisiana State Penitentiary in Angola. I thought Becker's sentence was the appropriate one,
but didn't allow its being changed to get under my skin. A
cop can drive himself crazy—many do—if he confuses his
function with that of the courts. I'd done my best; I
couldn't do any more. The courts, which ultimately decide
such matters, believed they did their best.

Claudius James Giesick resided in the same institution
as Corey, doing twenty-one years, which turned out to be
eleven. He was released on May 17, 1986. Again, I'd be
driven mad if I concentrated on the injustice of the le-
niency of his sentence, and those of others I know. It's
simply not my job to sentence, and I need to bear that in
mind. The gates had barely slammed shut on the con man,
by the way, when he announced that Corey had been
framed. Giesick said he planted strands of Patricia's hair
on the undercarriage of the rented Monte Carlo, which he
figured I would ultimately discover. However, when he

learned he could receive an extra ten years in prison, the murderer repudiated his frame-up story.

Ralph Whalen decided not to prosecute Kathy Giesick, a decision that elicited howls of outrage from Irvin Dymond. He thought it obvious a deal had been made in exchange for her testimony. Actually, because of the arrangement with Claudius Giesick, the more satisfying route would have been to pursue Kathy. Revenge: make her pay for what her husband didn't have to. But Whalen felt she represented no threat to society. After searching deep into her involvement, he concluded that she had been manipulated into the crime by Giesick, and frightened into it by Corey.

Not long after prosecuting the Corey case, Whalen entered private practice. He has enjoyed some remarkable successes. Irvin Dymond still practices law, but when he retires, The Whacker will rank among the heirs apparent to his former antagonist's reputation as New Orleans' ablest barrister.

My own performance in this difficult murder case brought many of the benefits I'd sought, especially in the area of being accepted by the older detectives. If I was not completely accepted by them, I'd at least made an important first step. Every man in the Homicide Unit took time to shake my hand, pat my back, offer some form of congratulations. As the case drew increasing attention from the press and the police brass, they began following it as if it were their own. I could sense the subtle transition from my being an "outsider" to becoming one who might belong.

My family and I became friends of the Albanowskis. Twice we persuaded them to spend vacations at our home. I am human enough to wish that these people whose lives I touched could somehow be free of their terrible memories.

But what, after all, did the Albanowskis receive, except simple justice in an excruciatingly painful way. Our "great victory" couldn't bring back Patricia. Still, we do what we can, and hope it has some meaning and benefit, and then move on.